Tom Stevenson's

Champagne & Sparkling Wine Guide

4th Edition

D1737294

Tom Stevenson's

Champagne & Sparkling Wine Guide

4th Edition

THE WINE APPRECIATION GUILD

This completely revised edition
first published in the USA in 2002 by
The Wine Apprecaition Guild
America's Leading Wine Book Publisher
360 Swift Avenue
South San Francisco
CA 94080
Phone (800) 231 9463
Fax (650) 866 3513
E-mail info@wineappreciation.com
Website www.wineappreciation.com

First editions published in 1998 by Dorling Kindersley

ISBN 1 891267 41 8

Printed and bound in Italy by Lego Print

Contents

Foreword	6
Sparkling Wine – How it is Made	8
Storing and Serving Sparkling Wine	10
Sparkling Wine Styles	12

This Year's Tastings

How to Read the Tasting Notes and Scores	15
Comparitive Performance Tables	19
A-Z of Tasting Notes	52

Annual Crémant Competition	193
Glossary	198
US Retailers	219
Tasting Note Forms	235
Acknowledgments	238

Foreword

In the Foreword to the first edition of this guide I
mentioned that the Titanic was not launched with a bottle
of Champagne and we all know what happened to her. In
tracking down the truth about a story concerning a Nyetimber
wine called Aurora and a P&O ship of the same name, I was
reminded that the latter was another ship launched without
Champagne. Remember? It was only last year, poor old
Princess Anne was bashing away with a bottle of Champagne
and it just wouldn't break. The Aurora didn't sink, thank
goodness, but after just 18 hours into her maiden voyage she
broke down and had to be towed home. No wonder sailors
are a superstitious lot!

On the subject of Champagne, everyone seems convinced
that its sales have plummeted, but I'm here to tell you that
they haven't. It is just that the champenois are such manic-
depressives that they have become their own worst enemy.
Two editions ago I explained how the Millennium had come
as something of a surprise to the Champagne industry. Prior
to the 2K revelation the champenois had been in one of its
depressed moods. This had started after the economic slump
of the early 1990s, when it was estimated that Champagne
was 250 million bottles overstocked. So it was all gloom and
doom. Then someone mentioned the so-called 'millennium
effect' and a deflated industry was suddenly brimful of
confidence, wondering how much they could sell a quarter of
a billion bottles for. From this manic stage the champenois
sank into deep depression on hearing the news that sales had
dropped from 327 million bottles in 1999 to just 253 million
bottles last year. Then the rumour started circulating that
there had in fact been no millennium effect and so we have
another so-called crisis and yet more despair.

The truth is that Champagne sales in 1996 were an all-time record, the millennium effect was not just a one year blip, but a three year peak (1997, 1998 and 1999), when sales outstripped production. But not stocks, thanks to the 250 million bottle excess. The peak of the peak was, of course, 1999, when almost a one-third of a billion bottles were sold. As soon as it seemed inevitable that sales would drop the following year, the champenois shot themselves in the foot by talking about a 'post-millennium hangover' and then began to doubt whether there had been any millennium-effect. Well of course there had. A massive three-year peak and all they had to ask themselves was what happens after a peak in sales? A drop in sales naturally enough. One is the consequence of the other. If sales did not drop, there would be no peak in the first place. It is illogical to treat one side of the millennium peak as good and the other as bad. Unless, of course, the drop in sales actually went right through the floor, but they dropped back to 253 million bottles, a mere three million short of the pre-millennium all-time record. That's not a hangover, that's not even a mild headache.

Although 1996 saw record sales, prices were still depressed, but the price received for every single bottle leaving the cellars in the 'post-millennium hangover' year 2000 was on average a thumping 33 per cent up. So Champagne is in no crisis. It is the healthiest it has been in more than a decade.

Tom Stevenson

Sparkling Wine – How it is Made

The theory behind sparkling wine is simple. Fermentation converts sugar into alcohol and carbonic gas – if the gas is set free the wine is still, if not, it is sparkling. To capture the gas, the wine undergoes a second fermentation in a sealed container. The gas gushes out in the form of tiny bubbles when the container is opened. According to research carried out by Moët & Chandon there are on average 250 million bubbles in a bottle of sparkling wine. The internal pressure in a bottle of sparkling wine is equivalent to the pressure of a double-decker bus tyre.

The Grapes

Various are used, but Chardonnay and Pinot Noir are best for premium quality sparkling wine – they are relatively neutral, with a good balance of sugar and acidity when ripe.

Cuve Close Method

Most cheap fizz is produced by cuve close (or 'Charmat' or 'tank' method). Both fermentations take place in large vats, then the wine is bottled under pressure. As cuve close is a bulk-production method it attracts low-calibre base wines, but the speed and minimum yeast contact makes it perfect for sweet, aromatic fizz such as Asti.

Méthode Champenoise

The greatest brut-style (dry) sparkling wines are made by méthode champenoise. As in cuve close, the first fermentation takes place en masse, sometimes in oak barriques, but the second takes place in the actual bottle in which the wine is sold. (See table on the opposite page for a list of terms.)

Malolactic Conversion

Most fizz undergoes 'malolactic', a natural process of fermentation that converts hard malic acid into soft lactic acid and adds creaminess to the wine. Of the few producers who prevent the malolactic, Bollinger, Alfred Gratien, Krug and Lanson are the most famous. In the New World the malolactic is often overworked because grapes are picked early, and have higher levels of malic acid.

Blending and the Pris de Mousse

The blending (assemblage) of the base wine is undertaken after the first fermentation. The champenois are the masters of this, and may create a non-vintage cuvée from as many as 70 base wines. Sugar, selected yeasts, yeast

Méthode Champemnoise Terms

In the European Union the term méthode champenoise is reserved for Champagne. However, the terms below are all synonymous with it.

English-Language Countries
Traditional Method

France
Méthode Traditionnelle
Méthode Classique
'Crémant' appellations

Spain
The 'Cava' appellation

Italy
Metodo Classico

Metodo Tradizionale
Talento

Germany
Flaschengärung nach dem Traditionellen
Verfahren
Klassische Flaschengärung
Traditionelle Flaschengärung

South Africa
Cap Classique

nutrients and a clarifying agent are then added to induce the mousse. The second fermentation is often referred to as the prise de mousse, or 'capturing the sparkle', and it can take months to complete. In contract to the first fermentation, which should be relatively fast and warm, the second is slow and cool.

Autolysis

When the second fermentation is complete, the yeast cells undergo an enzymatic breakdown called autolysis, which is epitomized by an acacia-like flowery freshness. Good autolysis adds complexity and ensures finesse.

Remuage and Disgorgement

In méthode champenoise only, the yeast deposit created during the second fermentation is encouraged down the neck of the inverted bottle into a small plastic pot held in place by a crown-cap. Remuage (or riddling), as this is called, takes eight weeks by hand, or eight days by machine. The sediment is removed (disgorged) by immersing the bottle in freezing brine, and ejecting the semi-frozen pot without losing too much wine or gas.

The Dosage

Before corking, the liqueur d'expédition is added. In all cases except extra brut (very dry), this will include some sugar. The younger the wine, the greater the dosage of sugar required.

Storing and Serving Sparkling Wine

Most fizz is best drunk within a year or so. Only a few cuvées are capable of developing truly complex aromas and flavours after disgorgement.

Why Store?

Typically, Chardonnay turns 'toasty' and Pinot Noir 'biscuity', although the reverse in possible and even a whiff of clean sulphur can in time contribute to the toastiness of a wine. Some first-class Chardonnays develop specific, complex aromas such as flowery hazelnuts, creamy brazil nuts and mellow walnuts. The greatest Champagnes can age gracefully for decades, to create rich nuances of macaroons, coconut, cocoa and coffee.

How to Store

Fizz is more sensitive to temperature and light than other wines, but there should be no problem keeping it for a year or two at any fairly constant temperature between 12 and 18°C (40-60°F). Higher temperatures increase the rate of oxidation; erratic temperatures can seriously damage the wine. If you do not have a cellar, keep it in a cool place inside a box. Very long-term storage should be at 9-11°C (48-52°F) in total darkness. There is no reason why bottles should be stored horizontally apart from to save space: the CO_2 in the bottle neck keeps the cork moist and swollen even when upright. Some Champagnes have retained their sparkle for a century under ideal conditions.

Some Champagnes, such as Roederer Cristal, are shipped with a yellow, anti-UV wrapping, which you should leave on while storing. Brown-glass bottles offer better protection against ultra-violet than green-glass, and dead-leaf or dark green is better than light or bright green.

Chilling

Temperature determines the rate at which bubbles in a sparkling wine are released. Bubbly should not be opened at room temperature – the wine will quickly froth up and go flat. Chill it, ideally down to 4.5-7°C (40-45°F), the lower temperature for parties and receptions where the room temperature is likely to rise.

It is okay to chill wine in a refrigerator for a couple of hours, but try not to leave it longer than a day because the cork might stick or shrink. Emergency chilling of a sparkling wine by putting it in the coldest part of a deep-freeze for 15 minutes is fine.

A bucket of ice and water (never just ice, the water is essential for transferring temperatures) is still one of the best and quickest ways to chill a bottle of fizz, but faster still are the gel-filled jackets that are kept in the deep freeze and slip over the bottle for about six minutes. A useful tip when using either ice-buckets or gel-filled jackets is to invert the bottle gently two or three times before opening. This prevents the wine in the neck being significantly warmer than the rest of the bottle, which reduces the chance of the wine gushing like a fountain when the bottle is opened, not to mention ensuring that the first will be as chilled as the last.

Opening

Remember that the secret of success is to try and prevent the cork from actually coming out. Remove the foil to begin, or simply score around the base of the wire cage. Then gently untwist the wire and loosen the bottom of the cage, but don't remove it. Hold the bottle with a cloth if you are a novice, and completely enclose the cork and cage in one hand (the right, if you are right-handed). Holding the base of the bottle with your other hand, twist both ends slowly in opposite directions, backwards and forwards. As soon as you feel pressure forcing the cork out, actually try to push it back in whilst continuing the twisting operation ever more gently until the cork is released from the bottle with a sigh, not a bang.

Pouring

A good tip is to pour only a little into each glass so that by the time you return to the first glass its foam will already have settled. The alternative is to wait ages for each one to settle as you are pouring. Top up each glass to between two-thirds and three-quarters of the vessel – no more. Do not tilt the glass and pour gently down the inside, it is not lager!

Glasses

A flute or a tulip-shaped glass is ideal and almost any vessel other than a coupe will suffice. The wide, shallow coupe is the worst possible choice for sparkling wine because the mousse goes flat far too quickly and the wine's aroma cannot be appreciated. Whatever glass shape used, the finer the rim the better.

Sparkling Wine Styles

Categories of style include basic divisions of sweetness, vintage and non-vintage, grape variety, colour and degree of mousse.

Sweetness

Brut is the classic style of dry sparkling wine, with Extra-Brut and Brut Nature being drier still. These terms are all widely used on an international basis despite their French origin, whereas the progressively sweeter styles of Sec, Extra-Sec, Demi-Sec and Doux are invariably translated, thus Sec becomes Seco in Portugal and Spain, Secco in Italy and Trocken in Germany (see Glossary for more details).

What's in a Vintage?

A Champagne vintage implies that the harvest was exceptional, while for most other fizz 'vintage' is best regarded as a statement of age, not quality. Vintage Champagne must be 100 per cent from the year, but elsewhere it varies (95 per cent in California; 85 in Australia). Store vintage Champagne for 8-10 years from the date of harvest. The term non-vintage (NV) sounds derogatory to many people, but wines from various years can be skillfully blended to create some of the finest cuvées available.

Grape Varieties

Champagne's classic trio of Chardonnay, Pinot Noir and Meunier are generally accepted as the grapes best-suited for a classic brut style of Sparkling wine. The only real resistance to this concept is in Spain where the traditional varieties are Parellada, Macabéo and Xarel.lo while Moscato or Muscat is widely regarded as the finest variety for intensely sweet sparkling wines such as Asti. Australia has made Shiraz the first choice for sparkling red wines, although Cabernet, Merlot and other varieties are used. Riesling is traditional for classic Sekt and readers of this guide will know that this is not necessarily an oxymoron. The list is endless, although most of it is full of duds, such as Prosecco, an Italian grape that makes Parellada characterful by comparison.

Colour

Pure Chardonnay blanc de blancs (white wine made from white grapes) make good brut-style sparkling wines, and the best come from the Côte des Blancs in Champagne. In the New World, blanc de noirs (white wine made from black grapes) can be various shades, but in Champagne the skill is to produce as clear a wine as possible from Pinot Noir or Meunier, and the most famous is Bollinger's Vieilles Vignes Françaises. Champagne rosé can be made by blending white wine with a little red. Sparkling red wines are also available, such as Australian Sparkling Shiraz mentioned above.

Crémant

The crémant style is noted for its soft, creamy mousse. As a term it originated in Champagne, but since the introduction of Crémant AOCs (Alsace, Bordeaux, Bourgogne, Die, Gaillac, Jura, Limoux, Loire and Luxembourg) it has been banned in all other EU appellations, including its region of origin! Few producers outside France have a reputation for a true crémant style. Normal fizz has a pressure of 5-6 atmospheres, while crémant has 3.6, but to be a true crémant, the mousse must unfold slowly, leaving a creamy cordon in the glass. Mumm de Cramant (sic) used to be known as Crémant de Cramant and was the best known crémant in Champagne. Franciacorta uses the term satèn (satin).

Prestige or Deluxe Cuvées

These are cuvées that producers feel best epitomize their house style. The greatest known examples include Dom Pérignon (made by Moët & Chandon), Cristal (by Louis Roederer) and Belle Epoque (by Perrier-Jouët). The entire range of Krug is sold at prestige or deluxe quality prices, which is why it is unfair to compare Krug Grande Cuvée with the brut non-vintage of most other houses. Such wines are produced in tiny quantities, and it is their rarity value that determines the high price. The strictest selection of base wines is the most significant defining factor in any prestige cuvée.

This Year's Tastings

Performance tables and an alphabetical, cross-referenced listing of recommended producers and brands, with notes on over 1,000 individual Champagnes and sparkling wines.

How to Read the Tasting Notes and Scores

How the Wines are Tasted and Judged

Almost all the wines in this guide are recommended by me; less than four per cent of the wines carry a **?** sign, indicating that they are in an unusual developmental stage and cannot be fully judged yet, but there is evidence to suggest they are likely to be good when ready. Most wines were tasted blind (with labels covered) at my own professionally equipped facility, where producers submit samples. Others were tasted at special tastings organised for the purpose of this guide by various trade bodies.

In addition to regular trips to Champagne I travel to different sparkling wine regions each year to carry out in-depth tastings in situ. Champagnes have to score 80 or above to qualify for this guide; other sparkling wines have to score 70 or above.

The Tasting Process

All wines are chilled and tasted against others of a similar style and category (e.g., blanc de blancs, rosé, same vintage, etc.). It is more crucial to taste sparkling wines chilled than it is for any other style of wine. This is because temperature affects the release of carbonic gas, which affects the tactile impression of the mousse and the balance of the wine. Most wines are tasted in my own facility because I do not wish to be influenced by other people's comments. This also allows me to devote as much time as I like to each wine, to search out finesse, rather than size (which is all too obvious and thus the bane of blind tastings). I compare and contrast as many different permutations within a category as possible because the positioning of a wine in a line-up can dramatically influence its perception. Obviously I open the back-up for any faulty wine, but so many faults are not easily discernible. Subliminal cork or TCA taint, for example, can wipe the fruit out of a wine without giving any clue that there is a fault. Only by comparing it with exactly the same wine without such a fault can the problem be recognised. I have therefore devised a system whereby a second chilled sample can be on the table within four minutes. This encourages me to open a second bottle even if I have the slightest doubt. Last, but by no means least, some wines that do not shine in the cold, analytical setting of a blind tasting can hint at their usefulness at the table, so they are lugged home where supper is swamped in a sea of covered-up bottles and a different insight gleaned.

In addition to all the normal negative attributes, sparkling wines are marked down if they posses amylic aromas (peardrops, banana, bubblegum) or if they are dominated by heavy-handed malolactic (buttery, caramel, butterscotch) or new oak because all these characteristics detract from the finesse and vitality of this particular style.

How the Wines are Described

It is harder to describe a wine with a few words than it is to use many, and a quick flick through this and all previous edition of the guide will indicate how dismally I have failed in this respect. When describing the actual wine I try to be specific because it is easier for readers to distinguish between two wines if the fruit in one is, say, strawberries, while the other is, maybe, pineapple. If, however, I describe one as having aromas of strawberries, blackberries, cherries, bitter chocolate, coffee and toast, while another is raspberries, redcurrants, damsons, white chocolate, wholemeal biscuit and toast, it is difficult to imagine what either wine tastes like, let alone what makes one different from the other. Should a wine have any of these characteristics, I will list them, but if they're not there, I won't invent them. Many cuvées simply smell and taste like a very fine Champagne without having the slightest hint of any specific fruit, flower, nut, herb or spice. In truth few wines reveal more than one or two specific aromas or flavours.

As far as colour and mousse are concerned, an absence of comment can be taken to mean that they are at least satisfactory. There is little point distinguishing between various hues of straw colour and if the mousse is of normal strength with smallish bubbles, what point is there in repeating this? Only extremes are worthy of note.

I tend to focus on balance and finesse because although these two inseparable characteristics are notoriously difficult to define, they nevertheless represent why one wine might be preferred to another. I also hark on about the level of acidity and whether it is ripe because this is essential to quality in a sparkling wine. I divide sparkling wine into basic styles, be they light-bodied or full, fruit-driven or complex, striving for elegance or character. And when it is obvious to me, I explain how a wine will develop.

The Guide's 100-Point Scoring System

When tasting for this guide, I try to maintain the same yardstick, whatever the origin or style of the wine, but I taste by category and to be absolutely honest I sometimes worry whether an 85-point rated California fizz is indeed the equivalent of, say, an 85-point rated Champagne tasted two or three weeks apart. Hopefully it is – or at least, more times than not.

However, what confuses the concept of the universal score is that the intrinsic qualities of each style or region must be respected. Some critics believe this dilutes the universal yardstick, but if it does then no one could say that a 90-point Bordeaux is the same quality as a 90-point Burgundy, and that would be sheer poppycock.

What the Scores Tell Us

Thanks to Robert Parker, the American wine critic, the 100-point scale is now globally recognised. Since Parker utilises only half the points (the lowest scoring wine in his system receives 50 points) and the lowest score below is 70, it has been suggested that I mark out of 30! I must therefore make it absolutely clear that I use the entire 100-point scale. When tasting I score many wines between 0 and 70, but since they fail to achieve recommendation they are excluded from this book. It is not that I shy away from revealing who makes dross. My *Christie's World Encyclopedia of Champagne & Sparkling Wine* attempts to provide a comprehensive coverage of the subject, including the bad and the ugly, thus scores as low as 35 can be found. This publication, however, is not meant to provide comprehensive coverage. It is a buyer's guide and I reserve all its space for wines readers should buy.

70
The point at which any sparkling wine other than Champagne becomes interesting as far as I'm concerned.

75
Any sparkling wine other than Champagne that receives this score is not just interesting, but good enough to grace the table of a self-confessed Champagne addict.

80
Because Champagne has such intrinsic advantages over sparkling wines produced in less favourable terroirs, this is the level at which I start to take interest in an inexpensive BOB or secondary brand.

85
The sort of quality that Champagne has to be to warrant inclusion in my cellar. If a non-Champagne sparkling wine scores this high, it is of exceptional quality indeed.

90
A top quality Champagne, probably vintage or prestige cuvée. Any wine outside of Champagne scoring 90 points or more can be considered as something truly special. A 90-point wine, Champagne or otherwise, deserves a hefty premium over the competition and will probably repay 3-5 years additional cellarage to reveal its true potential.

95
The greatest Champagnes. Rare even from the top houses. A very special and memorable experience. Most could be left forgotten in a cellar for 10 years without any worry whatsoever.

100
Perfection – impossible!

Notes

The scores for the same wine can fluctuate from year to year because different disgorgements produce wines of a different potential. This also applies to the when to drink time-scales. Furthermore, scores can vary because although I take into account both actual and potential quality, the emphasis in any annual guide must be on the former rather than the latter. When unexpected factors come into play, causing a wine to show less well than predicted in an earlier edition, I give the wine a **?** symbol and try to explain what has happened.

Key

99
Overall score
?
Overall score impossible to judge yet

Ready to drink now until the year indicated

Preferably store until the years indicated

Price Bands

It is impossible to indicate exact prices for different outlets in numerous markets for an international publication, thus the following price bands per 75cl bottle are:

£
Up to £9.99
££
£10-£19.99
£££
£20-£34.99
££££
£35 and above

Please note that these price bands are based on the recommended retail price in the producing country.

Prices in Local Currencies

Where the exact (albeit recommended) retail price in the producing country is available, this is provided. Because of numerous variables, such as local tax and duty, volume shipped and retailer mark-ups, this will create anomalies whereby a cheaper wine becomes disproportionately more expensive in certain countries.

Comparitive Performance Tables

Almost all the wines found in the alphabetical listing are grouped here according to their various categories. This enables readers to zero in on the best quality and value cuvées within a particular country, region, style or vintage. Full tasting notes and when to drink information can be found in the alphabetical listing.

The wines are listed in descending order of score and strictly alphabetical (including first names and initials) within each score, except for the listing by French Francs, which is by price.

Note
Wines not included in the following performance tables include (i) those with a **?** symbol; (ii) where too few wines qualified for a specific category; and (iii) wines that do not fit naturally into any grouping.

Remember!
85 Points
'The sort of quality Champagne has to be
to warrant inclusion in my cellar'
Tom Stevenson
Don't restrict your choice to 90 point wines – I don't!

Champagne

The world's greatest sparkling wine comes first. If and when any other area produces a greater volume of higher quality sparkling wine, I will happily place that first and Champagne second.

Champagne, Brut Non-vintage & Multi-vintage

In the last two editions I restricted this category to basic brut non-vintage, weeding out not just deluxe and special cuvées, but also any non-vintage cuvées that sold at a premium over the same producers regular non-vintage. However, such division and classification was not clear-cut. For example, no one would argue the fact that Moët & Chandon Brut Impérial is that producer's house non-vintage, yet it sell for a premium over Moët & Chandon White Star, a Champagne that Moët has not seen fit to show to me once in a quarter of a century! In fact, I have never seen it at a trade tasting or wine fair in the UK. The only times I have ever tasted it have been when travelling in the USA, where most of it is sold, I suspect. If I had applied my own criteria strictly, Brut Impérial would not have appeared under this section in previous editions and not to include the world's largest-selling brut non-vintage would have been ridiculous. I have decided, therefore, to encompass every recommended Champagne that does not carry a single vintage, whether it is absolute entry-level or a deluxe 'multi-vintage' cuvée.

A Brut style must have between 0 and 15 grams per litre of residual sugar (added as the dosage after disgorgement), although most Champagnes at the lower-end of this scale will be sold as an Extra-Brut or a Brut Nature. The sugar should not be noticeable, even at the top end of the range, if properly balanced by ripe acidity. A true Brut should thus taste dry, but this does not mean austere, as young cuvées should possess fruit, while mature ones will have a mellowed richness.

95	££££	Grand Siècle NV La Cuvée, Brut
95	££££	Krug Grande Cuvée NV Brut
93	££££	Jacquesson & Fils NV Mémoire du XX ème Siècle, Brut
91	££	Charles Heidsieck NV Brut Réserve, Mis en Cave en 1996
90	££	Pierre Paillard NV Bouzy Grand Cru Brut
90	££	Vilmart & Cie NV Grand Cellier, Brut Premier Cru
90	££	Charles Heidsieck NV Brut Réserve, Mis en Cave en 1997
90	£££	Jacquart NV Brut de Nominée
90	£££	Bollinger NV Special Cuvée, Brut (*magnum*)
90	£££	Gosset NV Grande Réserve Brut (*magnum*)
90	££££	Moët & Chandon Les Champs de Romont NV Sillery Grand Cru
89	££	De Saint Gall NV Brut Sélection
89	££	Charles Heidsieck NV Brut Réserve, Mis en Cave en 1995
88	££	Benoit Lahaye NV Brut
88	££	Louis de Sacy NV Brut Tradition
88	£	Marguet-Bonnerave NV Brut Réserve, Grand Cru
88	£	H. Blin & Co NV Brut Tradition
88	£	Paul Bara NV Bouzy Grand Cru Brut
88	££	Duval-Leroy NV Fleur de Champagne, Brut Premier Cru
88	££	Vilmart & Cie NV Cuvée Cellier, Brut
88	££	Brice NV Aÿ Grand Cru Brut
88	££	Billecart-Salmon NV Brut Réserve
88	££	Deutz NV Brut Classic
88	££	Perrier-Jouët NV Grand Brut
87	££	Bernard Brémont NV Brut
87	££	Eugène Mercier NV Cuvée du Fondateur, Brut
87	£	Marguet-Bonnerave NV Brut Tradition
87	£	Pierre Moncuit NV Brut Réserve
87	££	Marguet-Bonnerave NV Anciens Vintages 1995-1996, Brut Grand Cru
87	££	Piper-Heidsieck NV Brut
87	££	Bruno Paillard NV Brut Première Cuvée
87	££	Brice NV Bouzy Grand Cru Brut
87	££	Mumm Grand Cru NV Brut
87	££	Delbeck NV Bouzy, Brut Grand Cru
87	££	Laurent-Perrier NV Brut L.P.
87	££	Pommery NV Brut Apanage
87	£££	Philipponnat NV Royale Réserve, Brut
87	£££	Canard-Duchêne NV Charles VII Grande Cuvée, Brut
87	£££	Piper-Heidsieck NV Cuvée Spéciale Jean-Paul Gaultier, Brut (magnum)
86	££	Tsarine NV Tête de Cuvée Brut, Chanoine
86	££	Jean-Louis Malard NV Pinot Noir & Chardonnay Brut

86	££	R. Renaudin NV Brut Réserve
86	££	Eric Rodez NV Cuvée des Grands Vintages, Brut Grand Cru
86	£	G. Fluteau NV Brut Carte Blanche
86	££	Henriot NV Brut Souverain
86	££	Moët & Chandon NV Brut Premier Cru
86	££	Alfred Gratien NV Brut
86	£££	R de Ruinart NV Brut
85	££	Baron Albert NV Brut Tradition, Cuvée de l'An 2000
85	£££	Bricout NV Cuvée Arthur Bricout, Brut Grand Cru
85	££	Guy Cadel NV Carte Blanche
85	££	R.C. Lemaire NV Sélect Réserve, Brut
85	££	Eric Rodez NV Cuvée des Crayères, Brut Grand Cru
85	££	Georges Vesselle NV Bouzy Grand Cru Brut
85	£	Henri Mandois NV Cuvée de Réserve, Brut
85	£	Michel Boilleau NV Brut Réserve
85	£	Charles Collin NV Brut
85	£	Henri Goutorbe NV Cuvée Tradition, Brut
85	£	Guy Larmandier NV Brut Premier Cru
85	£	François Secondé NV Brut Grand Cru
85	££	Georges Gardet NV Brut Spécial
85	£	Charles Clément NV Gustave Belon Brut
85	£	Gaston Chiquet NV Tradition, Brut Premier Cru
85	££	Boizel NV Brut Réserve
85	££	Princesse des Thunes NV Cuvée Prestige Brut, Grand Cru
85	££	Joseph Perrier NV Cuvée Royale Brut
85	££	Leclerc Briant NV Cuvée de Réserve Brut
85	££	Gosset NV Excellence Brut (*magnum*)
85	££	Delbeck NV Aÿ Grand Cru Brut
85	££	Pol Roger NV Brut White Foil
85	££	Besserat de Bellefon NV Cuvée des Moines, Brut
85	££	Mumm Cordon Rouge NV Brut
85	££	Pannier NV Cuvée Louis Eugène, Brut
85	££	Tarlant NV Cuvée Louis, Brut
85	££	Veuve Clicquot Ponsardin NV Brut
85	££	Bollinger NV Special Cuvée, Brut
85	££	Louis Roederer NV Brut Premier (*magnum*)
85	££££	Moët & Chandon Les Vignes de Saran NV Chouilly Grand Cru
85	££££	Moët & Chandon Les Sarments d'Aÿ NV Aÿ Grand Cru
84	££	Beaumet NV Cuvée Brut
84	££	Chanoine NV Grande Réserve Brut
84	££	Daniel Dumont NV Grande Réserve Brut
84	££	René James Lallier NV Grande Réserve Brut
84	££	R.C. Lemaire NV Cuvée Trianon, Brut Premier Cru
84	££	Mercier NV Brut
84	££	Cristian Senez NV Brut
84	£	Charles Clément NV Tradition Brut
84	£	Clerambault NV Cuvée Tradition, Brut
84	£	Vilmart & Cie NV Grande Réserve, Brut Premier Cru
84	£	Moutard NV Brut Grande Cuvée
84	£	G.H. Martel & Co. NV Brut Prestige
84	£	Louis de Sacy NV Brut Grand Cru
84	££	Edouard Brun & Cie NV Réserve 1er Cru, Brut

84	££	Canard-Duchêne NV Brut
84	££	Veuve A. Devaux NV Grande Réserve, Brut
84	££	Drappier NV Carte-d'Or Brut
84	££	Roger Pouillon & Fils, 50 ème Anniversaire NV Fleur de Mareuil
84	££	Ayala NV Brut
84	££	Besserat de Bellefon NV Brut Grande Tradition
84	££	Moët & Chandon NV Nectar Impérial
84	££	Delbeck NV Cramant Grand Cru Brut
84	££	Taittinger NV Brut Réserve
84	££	Canard-Duchêne NV Brut (*magnum*)
83	££	Alexandre Bonnet NV Cuvée Prestige Brut
83	£	A. Margaine NV Brut Premier Cru
83	£	Vollereaux NV Brut
83	£	Charles Collin NV Tradition Brut
83	£	Jean Moutardier NV Carte d'Or Brut
83	£	Jean Moutardier NV Carte d'Or Brut
83	£	Baron Albert NV Brut Carte d'Or
83	£	Albert Le Brun NV Vieille France, Brut
83	£	Marie-Noelle Ledru NV Brut Grand Cru
83	££	G. Tribaut NV Grande Cuvée Spéciale, Brut
83	££	Duval-Leroy NV Fleur de Champagne Brut
83	££	Heidsieck Monopole NV Blue Top Brut
83	££	Gauthier NV Grande Réserve Brut
83	££	Alain Thienot NV Brut
83	££	Pommery NV Brut Royal
82	££	G. de Barfontarc NV Extra Quality Brut
82	££	Bricout NV Cuvée Prestige, Brut Premier Cru
82	££	Philippe Gonet NV Brut
82	£	Jean-Paul Suss NV Brut Réserve
82	£	Michel Boilleau NV Cuvée Prestige, Brut
82	££	Moutard NV Brut Réserve
82	£	Clerambault NV Cuvée Carte Noire, Brut
82	££	de Castellane NV Croix Rouge Brut
82	££	Jacquart NV Brut Mosaïque
81	££	Bricout NV Cuvée Réserve Brut
81	££	de Venoge NV Brut Sélect, Cordon Bleu
81	££	Moët & Chandon NV Brut Impérial
80	££	Daniel Dumont NV Grande Réserve Brut
80	££	De Sousa NV Brut Réserve
80	£	Jean Velut NV Brut

Brut Nature & Extra-Brut

Although I am not a great fan of non-dosage Champagnes, this has less to do with the style than its quality. Such wines do not improve with age because sugar is required for a Champagne to age gracefully after disgorgement (see Reaction Maillard in the Glossary). The older a Champagne is before it is disgorged, the less dosage required because it will have a more mellowed taste, but no matter how old or great the Champagne is, without a certain amount of sugar it will turn coarse and oxidative. Sugar brings finesse and enables further ageing.

97	ⓔⓔⓔⓔ	Bollinger 1979 R.D. Extra Brut
95	ⓔⓔⓔⓔ	Bollinger 1985 R.D. Extra Brut
92	ⓔⓔⓔⓔ	Bollinger 1982 R.D. Extra Brut
90	ⓔⓔ	André et Michel Drappier NV Brut Nature, Pinot Noir Zero Dosage
89	ⓔⓔⓔⓔ	Bollinger 1988 R.D. Extra Brut
88	ⓔⓔ	Pierre Gimonnet & Fils NV Cuvée Oenophile, Extra-Brut
88	ⓔⓔ	Duval-Leroy 1995 Fleur de Champagne, Extra Brut Millésimé
87	ⓔⓔ	Roger Pouillon et Fils 1995 Le Millésime, Extra Brut Chardonnay
87	ⓔⓔ	Jacques Selosse NV Extra Brut, Grand Cru Blanc de Blancs

Champagne Sec & Extra-Sec

Sec (or Dry) is rarely seen these days. It can contain anything between 17 and 35 grams per litre of residual sugar, thus ranging between barely sweeter than a Brut and as sweet as a Demi-Sec. Extra-Sec is far more commonly encountered, although only one tasted this year was worthy of recommendation. This style actually overlaps Brut and the dry end of Sec, with between 12 and 20 grams per litre of sugar. These Champagnes can be very useful at the table where savoury dishes contain a certain sweetness or fruitiness.

87	ⓔⓔ	Louis Roederer NV Rich Sec
82	ⓔ	Vollereaux NV Extra Dry

Champagne Demi-Sec

For many years this sweet style, which must have between 35 and 50 grams of residual sugar, has been debased by the vast majority of Champagne producers who have pandered to an unsophisticated sector of French supermarket customers who like to drink sweet. By this I do not mean that sweetness in Champagne or indeed any wine is debasing or that to enjoy sweetness is a sign of poor taste, but there are vast numbers who can only enjoy sweet drinks and cannot taste beyond that sweetness, thus Champagne producers have been able to hide their inferior wines behind a mask of sugar. However, we are gradually seeing a rise in the number of high quality demi-sec produced.

87	ⓔⓔ	Mumm Cordon Vert NV Demi-Sec
85	ⓔⓔ	de Venoge NV Demi-Sec, Cordon Bleu
85	ⓔⓔ	Louis de Sacy 1985 Cuvée Tentation, Demi-Sec
85	ⓔⓔ	Veuve Clicquot Ponsardin NV Demi-Sec
85	ⓔⓔⓔ	Veuve Clicquot Ponsardin 1995 Rich Réserve
83	ⓔⓔ	Jacquart NV Demi-Sec

Vintage Brut Champagne: 1998 & 1997

*First impressions can be misleading, but they do to confirm my feelings
at vin clair stage. Neither year was a great vintage, but like 1992 and 1993
I suspect that we will see a large number of very good Champagnes and not
a few truly excellent one. That is because they were large harvests and with
strict selection it was easy to blend wines well above the average quality.
Furthermore, if we see as many producers declaring these two vintages as we
did 1992 and 1993, it is easier for pundits to find the wines that stick out in
terms of pure quality. In terms of fruit, structure and acidity 1998 seems to
mirror 1993 while 1997 is similar to 1992. In theory the 1997s have a slight
edge over the 1998s, just as the 1992s had over the 1993s, yet it was a close
call and quite possibly the 1993s will eventually be seen to have triumphed,
so who knows? Especially as the earliest that the 1998s can be commercially
disgorged is January 2002 and we won't see many examples of this vintage
on the shelf until the second quarter of 2003. The 1998 here is, of course, a
preview sample.*

87	££	Mumm Cordon Rouge 1998 Brut Millésime
87	££	Mumm Cordon Rouge 1997 Brut Millésime
85	£	Gallimard Père & Fils 1997 Cuvée Prestige, Brut Millésime

Vintage Brut Champagne: 1996

*The problem with announcing that any vintage is special is that it will be a
long time before the first wines hit the market, thus anticipation inevitably
builds up, yet the first Champagnes to be released of any vintage are unlikely
to be the best, consequently hopes are often dashed. It happened with the 1990s,
but look how great those turned out to be (and some like Krug are not expected
to be launched for a year or more). We are now only just beginning to see the
start of the first wave of 1996s. There is some dross, as there always will be,
whatever the vintage, but after they have been eliminated we are left with some
exceptionally fine offerings for such an early juncture in the campaign. I am
more convinced than ever that 1996 could well be greater than 1990.*

98	£££	Vilmart & Cie 1996 Coeur de Cuvée, Brut Premiers Crus
98	£££	Vilmart & Cie 1996 Coeur de Cuvée, Brut Premiers Crus
97	£££	Pol Roger 1996 Brut
97	£££	Gosset 1996 Grand Millésime Brut
91	£	Henri Mandois 1996 Cuvée Victor Mandois, Brut
90	££	Cuvée Charles Gardet 1996 Brut
90	£££	Mailly Grand Cru 1996 La Terre, Brut
90	£££	Pommery 1996 Brut Millésimé, B42
89	£	Henri Mandois 1996 Millésimé, Brut Premier Cru
89	££	Mumm Cordon Rouge 1996 Brut Millésime
88	£££	Perrier-Jouët 1996 Grand Brut
88	£	J. Charpentier 1996 Brut Millésime
87	££	Joseph Loriot-Pagel 1996 Brut Cuvée de Réserve
87	££	Henri Goutorbe 1996 Brut Grand Cru
87	£££	Delbeck 1996 Cuvée Origines, Brut (*magnum*)

85	©©	G.H. Martel & Co. 1996 Cuvée Victoire, Brut
84	©©	Philippe Brugnon 1996 Brut
84	©©	Paul Goerg 1996 Millésimé, Brut Premier Cru
84	©©	Marie-Noelle Ledru 1996 Brut Millésime Grand Cru
84	©©	Egérie de Pannier 1996 Brut
84	©©©	Taittinger 1996 Brut Millésimé

Vintage Brut Champagne: 1995

The extra maturity of the 1993s and 1992s made the best Champagnes from those years seem better than the 1995s last year, but we are now into the full swing of this vintage and it is blossoming beautifully. Not only is this vintage showing more class in general than either 1993 or 1992, it is turning out to be even better than 1995 was expected to be, and there are a number of top-notch 1995s still to come.

97	©©©©	Bollinger 1995 Grande Année, Brut
93	©©©©	Gosset Celebris 1995 Brut
92	©©©©	Louis Roederer 1995 Cristal Brut
91	©	Goutorbe 1995 Brut Grand Cru
91	©©©	Pol Roger 1995 Brut
91	©©©	Pierre Gimonnet 1995 Les Cuvées de l'An 2000, Brut (*magnum*)
90	©©	Ployez-Jacquemart 1995 Brut Vintage
90	©©©	Taittinger 1995 Brut Millésimé
90	©©©	Billecart-Salmon 1995 Cuvée Nicolas François Billecart, Brut
90	©©©©	Deutz 1995 Cuvée William Deutz, Brut
90	©©©	Perrier-Jouët 1995 Belle Epoque Brut
89	©©©	Nicolas Feuillatte 1995 Verzy
89	©©	Drappier 1995 Grande Sendrée, Brut
89	©©©	Deutz 1995 Brut
89	©©©	R de Ruinart 1995 Brut
89	©©©	Louis Roederer 1995 Brut Vintage
89	©©©	Alain Thienot 1995 Grande Cuvée, Brut
89	©©©	Delbeck 1995 Cuvée Origines, Brut (*magnum*)
88	©©	de Venoge 1995 Brut Millésimé
88	©©	Alain Thienot 1995 Brut Millésime
88	©©	Lanson Gold Label 1995 Brut
88	©©	Moët & Chandon 1995 Brut Impérial
88	©©	Egérie de Pannier 1995 Brut
88	©©©	Bruno Paillard 1995 Brut Millésime
88	©©©	Pommery 1995 Brut Grand Cru
87	©©©	Tsarine 1995 Brut Millésime, Chanoine
87	©©©	Nicolas Feuillatte 1995 Mesnil
87	©©	Maurice Vesselle 1995 Brut Millésime, Grand Cru
87	©©	Cuvée Charles Gardet 1995 Brut
87	©©	Joseph Perrier 1995 Cuvée Royale Brut
87	©©©	Veuve Clicquot Ponsardin 1995 Brut Vintage Réserve
86	©©©	Nicolas Feuillatte 1995 Cramant
86	©©	H. Blin & Co 1995 Brut
86	©©	Duval-Leroy 1995 Fleur de Champagne, Millésimé Brut
86	©©	Henriot 1995 Brut Millésimé

85	££	Beaumet 1995 Cuvée Brut
85	£	Demoiselle 1995 Grande Cuvée Brut
85	££	Nostalgie 1995 Brut
85	££	de Castellane 1995 Croix Rouge Brut Millésimé
84	££	Guy Charbaut 1995 Brut
84	££	Daniel Dumont 1995 Brut Réserve Millésime, Premier Cru
84	£££	Nicolas Feuillatte 1995 Chouilly
84	££	Mercier 1995 Vendange Brut
84	£££	Piper-Heidsieck 1995 Brut
84	£	Jean Velut 1995 Cuvée Millésimée, Brut
84	£	Beaumont des Crayères 1995 Fleur de Prestige, Brut
84	££	Tarlant 1995 Brut
84	££	Massé 1995 Brut
82	££	Guy Cadel 1995 Brut
82	££	Heidsieck Monopole 1995 Gold Top Brut
80	££	Besserat de Bellefon 1995 Brut Grande Tradition

Vintage Brut Champagne: 1994

The worst of the lesser vintages between the great 1990s and the excellent 1995s, all four of which were spoiled by rain at harvest time. Nothing this year to challenge Louis Roederer Cristal (92 points) from the last edition.

85	££	La Préférence de Baron Albert 1994 Brut Millésime
82	£££	Louis Roederer 1994 Brut Vintage

Vintage Brut Champagne: 1993

On paper the ripeness and acidity levels achieved during this vintage are less favourable than those of 1992. Tasted blind two years apart Dom Pérignon edges out Louis Roederer Cristal by just one point. I'll have to do a head-to-head at some time!

96	££££	Cuvée Dom Pérignon Brut 1993 Moët & Chandon
90	£££	Vilmart & Cie 1993 Coeur de Cuvée, Brut Premier Crus
90	££££	Pol Roger 1993 Cuvée Sir Winston Churchill Brut
89	£££	Gosset 1993 Grand Millésime Brut
88	£££	Laurent-Perrier 1993 Brut Vintage
88	£££	Pol Roger 1993 Brut
87	£££	Philipponnat 1993 Réserve Millésimée, Brut
87	££££	de Venoge 1993 Grand Vin des Princes Brut
86	££	Gauthier 1993 Brut Millésime
85	££	R. Blin et Fils 1993 Brut Millésime
84	£	Jean Moutardier 1993 Brut Millésime

Vintage Brut Champagne: 1992

Theoretically the only vintage quality year between 1990 and 1995, and although it has provided some excellent Champagnes, 1993 has turned out to be superior.

89	©©©©	Cuvée Dom Pérignon Brut 1992 Moët & Chandon
88	©©©	Pommery 1992 Brut Grand Cru
88	©©©©	Bollinger 1992 Grande Année, Brut
86	©©	Mailly 1992 Deux Mille
85	©©©©	Nicolas Feuillatte 1992 Cuvée Palmes d'Or, Brut (*magnum*)
84	©©	Bricout 1992 Cuvée Millésime Brut
84	©©	Nicolas Feuillatte 1992 Brut Millésimé, Premier Cru
84	©©©	Nicolas Feuillatte 1992 Cuvée Palmes d'Or, Brut

Vintage Brut Champagne: 1991

Although less houses declared this vintage and the ripeness-acidity levels were the less impressive than either 1992 or 1993, some producers evidently got it right. However, Vilmart Coeur de Cuvée in magnum stood head and shoulders above the rest two years ago and has jumped two percentile points in the meantime.

95	©©©	Vilmart & Cie 1991 Coeur de Cuvée, Brut (*magnum*)
87	©©©	Boizel 1991 Joyau de France, Brut
84	©©©	Philipponnat 1991 Réserve Spéciale Brut
84	©©©	Canard-Duchêne 1991 Brut
83	©©©	Alfred Gratien 1991 Brut

Vintage Brut Champagne: 1990

This is not only a true vintage, it is one of the 18 greatest Champagne vintages of the century. It is hard to believe for those who remember the 1976 Champagnes, but the grapes were riper in 1990 than they were in that drought year. What makes 1990 special, however, is that its grapes also possessed surprisingly high the acidity levels, with a much greater proportion of ripe tartaric to unripe malic than any other vintage on record. Sir Winston has been knocked off pole position by Krug (99 points), even though it will not be launched for a year or so and Clos des Goisses joins (from the previous two editions) Billecart-Salmon Grande Cuvée at 96 points.

99	©©©©	Krug Vintage 1990 Brut
98	©©©©	Pol Roger 1990 Cuvée Sir Winston Churchill Brut
96	©©©©	Philipponnat 1990 Clos des Goisses, Brut
92	©©©	L. d'Harbonville 1990 Brut
91	©©©©	Femme de Champagne 1990 Brut Millésime
90	©©©	Pierre Gimonnet 1990 Les Cuvées de l'An 2000, Brut (*magnum*)
88	©©	Chanoine 1990 Millésime Brut

88	€€	Henriot 1990 Brut Millésime
88	€€€	Boizel 1990 Cuvée Sous Bois, Brut
87	€€€	Duval-Leroy 1990 Cuvée des Roys
86	€€	Bricout 1990 Brut Réserve
86	€€	Delbeck 1990 Brut Vintage
85	€€€€	Bruno Paillard 1990 N.P.U., Nec Plus Ultra, Brut

Vintage Brut Champagne: 1989

The middle year of the great trio of exceptional successive vintages, 1989 was marked by the Pinot Noir, which had a physiological problem, causing coloration in some of the cheaper, earlier-released Champagnes. Also, acidity was very low and pH high for such a hyped-up vintage (only 1999 has had worse readings in the last 20 years), consequently some Champagnes were too heavy and oxidative. Krug defied these vintage characteristics to produce an extraordinarily pale Champagne with acidity that is more reminiscent of 1988 than 1989. Very few truly great 1989s are commercially available.

96	€€€€	Krug Vintage 1989 Brut
90	€€€€	Pommery 1989 Louise, Brut
89	€€€€	Noble Cuvée de Lanson 1989 Brut

Vintage Brut Champagne: 1988

Although this vintage comes second to the 1990 out of the trio of three successive great Champagne years, the best 1988s will probably last as long as the best 1990s. I have just one six-bottle case left of Pol Roger 1988 (was 91 points three editions ago, but closer to 95 now) and I'm not sure how long I can keep my hands off it!

97	€€€€	Krug Vintage 1988 Brut
89	€€€€	Jacquesson & Fils 1988 Grand Vin Signature
89	€€€€	Henriot 1988 Cuvée des Enchanteleurs, Brut
88	€€€	Mailly Grand Cru 1988 Cuvée Les Echansons, Brut
85	€€€	Divine 1988 Brut

Vintage Brut Champagne: 1985 and older

As part of the ongoing Millennium celebrations, a number of houses have decided to release old vintages from their library collection (Dom Pérignon did so too late for inclusion in this year's Guide). There is, however, huge variations in quality, which resulted in relatively few of these wines surviving my tasting. The champenois are, after all, French and it must be remembered that the French generally prefer their Champagnes young, thus it is not uncommon to find that the champenois are the last to understand the qualities that make a mature Champagne great. Often they think that because a Champagne is old a certain maderised or oxidised character is acceptable, but it's not, of course. In addition to complexity and finesse, the greatest mature Champagnes are those that remain the freshest and youngest for the longest period of time. It's that simple.

Vintage Brut Champagne: 1985 and older

Only buy older vintages of Champagne that have come direct from the producer's cellars into a winemerchant's own cellars that you now to be good. Preferably buy direct from the producer on a visit. Only buy mature Champagne at auction if the provenance adheres to the above or you have tasted the an example from exactly the same lot.

98 ££££ Krug Collection 1981 Brut
98 ££££ Krug Collection 1979 Brut
98 ££££ Cuvée Dom Pérignon Brut 1964 Moët & Chandon
97 ££££ Krug Collection 1953 Brut
95 ££££ Cuvée Dom Pérignon Brut 1985 Moët & Chandon
92 ££££ Krug Collection 1982 Brut
91 ££££ Cuvée Dom Pérignon Brut 1973 Moët & Chandon

Champagne Blanc de Blancs, Non-vintage

Without doubt blanc de blancs are more expressive from a single vintage, but non-vintage cuvées can offer superb value and, contrary to popular belief, a great many are made.

89 ££ Gaston Chiquet NV Blanc de Blancs d'Aÿ, Brut Grand Cru
89 £££ Billecart-Salmon NV Blanc de Blancs Brut Réserve
88 ££ Eric Rodez NV Blanc de Blancs, Brut Grand Cru
88 £ Guy Larmandier NV Blanc de Blancs, Brut Grand Cru
88 ££ R.&L. Legras NV Blanc de Blancs Brut
88 ££ Brice NV Cramant Grand Cru Brut
87 ££ Vazart-Coquart NV Brut Réserve
87 ££ Henriot NV Blanc de Blancs Brut
87 ££ Delamotte NV Blanc de Blancs Brut
87 ££ Mumm de Cramant NV Chardonnay, Brut Grand Cru
86 ££ Joseph Loriot-Pagel NV Brut Blanc de Blancs
86 £ Vollereaux NV Blanc de Blancs Brut
86 ££ Drappier NV Cuvée Signature, Blanc de Blancs Brut
85 ££ René James Lallier NV Blanc de Blancs, Brut
85 £ Henri Mandois NV Chardonnay, Brut Premier Cru
85 £ Agrapart & Fils NV Brut Blanc de Blancs Grand Cru
85 £ Pierre Gimonnet & Fils NV Blanc de Blancs Brut, Cuis 1er Cru
85 ££ de Castellane NV Chardonnay Blanc de Blancs, Brut
85 ££ Joseph Perrier NV Cuvée Royale, Blanc de Blancs Brut
85 ££ Bruno Paillard NV Chardonnay Réserve Privée, Brut
85 ££ Pommery NV Summertime, Blanc de Blancs Brut
84 £ Pierre Jamain NV Cuvée Caroline, Brut
84 £ Paul Goerg NV Blanc de Blancs, Brut Premier Cru
84 ££ Waris-Larmandier NV Collection, Brut Blanc de Blancs Grand Cru
84 ££ Boizel NV Chardonnay Brut Blanc de Blancs
83 £ Waris-Larmandier NV Tradition, Brut Blanc de Blancs Grand Cru

83   ⓔ   Jean Milan NV Brut Spécial, Blanc de Blancs, Grand Cru
83   ⓔ   Guy Charlemagne NV Réserve Brut, Grand Cru Blanc de Blancs

Champagne Blanc de Blancs: 1997

There are so few 1997s available at the time of writing that it is impossible to generalise about blanc de blancs from this vintage.

87   ⓔ   G. Fluteau 1997 Cuvée Prestige, Blanc de Blancs Brut
86   ⓔⓔ   Pierre Gimonnet & Fils 1997 Gastronome, Blanc de Blancs Brut, 1er Cru

Champagne Blanc de Blancs: 1996

This is shaping up to being a great blanc de blanc vintage, even though the 1996s blended from both Chardonnay and Pinot are definitely superior.

93   ⓔⓔⓔ   Pol Roger 1996 Brut Chardonnay
90   ⓔⓔ   R.C. Lemaire 1996 Chardonnay, Millésime Premier Cru Brut
90   ⓔⓔ   Bonnaire 1996 Grand Cru Blanc de Blanc
88   ⓔⓔ   André Robert Père & Fils 1996 Le Mesnil Blanc de Blancs Grand Cru
88   ⓔⓔ   Pierre Gimonnet & Fils 1996 Gastronome, Blanc de Blancs Brut, 1er Cru
88   ⓔⓔ   Guy Charlemagne 1996 Mesnillésime, Brut Grand Cru Blanc de Blancs
88   ⓔⓔ   Jacquart 1996 Blanc de Blancs, Brut Mosaïque
87   ⓔ   Pierre Jamain 1996 Brut Millésime
87   ⓔⓔ   Pierre Gimonnet & Fils 1996 Premier Cru-Chardonnay, Brut
87   ⓔⓔ   Guy Larmandier, Cramant 1996 Blanc de Blancs Cuvée Prestige
86   ⓔⓔ   Ployez-Jacquemart 1996 Brut Vintage, Blanc de Blancs
85   ⓔⓔ   François Secondé 1996 Blanc de Blancs, Brut Millésime Grand Cru
85   ⓔⓔ   Duval-Leroy 1996 Fleur de Champagne, Blanc de Chardonnay Brut
85   ⓔⓔ   Ayala 1996 Brut Blanc de Blancs

Champagne Blanc de Blancs: 1995

The divide between the good and the very best is much more stark for blanc de blancs in 1995 than it is for classic blends.

95   ⓔⓔⓔⓔ Taittinger Comtes de Champagne 1995 Blanc de Blancs Brut
91   ⓔⓔⓔⓔ Amour de Deutz 1995 Blanc de Blancs, Brut
90   ⓔⓔⓔ   Pol Roger 1995 Brut Chardonnay
88   ⓔⓔ   Pierre Gimonnet & Fils 1995 Fleuron, Blanc de Blancs Brut, 1er Cru
88   ⓔⓔ   Duval-Leroy 1995 Fleur de Champagne, Blanc de Chardonnay Brut
87   ⓔⓔⓔ   Jacquesson & Fils 1995 Blanc de Blancs, Brut Grand Cru
85   ⓔⓔ   A. Margaine 1995 Special Cuvée Club, Blanc de Blancs
85   ⓔⓔ   Nicolas Feuillatte 1995 Blanc de Blancs Millésime, Brut Premier Cru
85   ⓔⓔⓔ   Deutz 1995 Blanc de Blancs, Brut
85   ⓔⓔⓔ   Louis Roederer 1995 Blanc de Blancs Brut
84   ⓔⓔ   Th. Blondel 1995 Vieux Millésime, Chardonnay Brut Premier Cru
84   ⓔⓔ   Pierre Moncuit 1995 Blanc de Blancs
83   ⓔⓔ   Terres de Noël An 2000 Brut Sélection 1995 Grand Cru, Milan

Champagne Blanc de Blancs: 1994 and older

Deluxe cuvées and the best vintages obviously rule. Don't forget Taittinger
Comtes de Champagne 1994 from the last edition (89 points) if you come
across it.

97	££££	Krug Clos du Mesnil 1988 Brut Blanc de Blancs Brut
95	££££	Krug Clos du Mesnil 1988 Brut Blanc de Blancs Brut
93	££££	Dom Ruinart 1990 Blanc de Blancs
92	££££	Salon 1990 Blanc de Blancs Brut
90	££££	Dom Ruinart 1993 Blanc de Blancs
89	££	Palmer 1991 Blanc de Blancs Brut
87	££££	Blanc de Blancs de Lanson 1994 Brut

Champagne Blanc de Noirs, Vintage & Non-vintage

The idea that a blanc de noirs is a big, rich, meaty Champagne came about
because Bollinger set the yardstick with its Vielles Vignes Français. That,
however, is made from overripe grapes grown on ungrafted vines, thus its size
is an anomaly. Needless to say that it usually blasts all opposition for six, but
having rocketed in price from a modest]130 to a mere]200 a bottle, it would
be a crime if it didn't. Some blanc de noirs can have such finesse that it is
hard to imagine that they do not contain a substantial amount of
Chardonnay. Serge Mathieu Blanc de Noirs from the Aube comes to mind.
There is also the notion that these wines are pure Pinot Noir, whereas many
blanc de noirs are blends of both Pinot Noir and Meunier. The following
recommendations are all classic blanc de blancs in that they contain only
black grapes and the aim has been to produce as colourless a wine as possible
from these black-skinned grapes. They are not New World blanc de noirs,
which often contain a small percentage of white grapes and vary in colour
from copper-tinged to full rosé.

98	££££	Bollinger 1992 Vieilles Vignes Françaises, Blanc de Noirs Brut
88	££	Mailly Grand Cru NV Blanc de Noirs, Brut
87	£	Michel Arnould & Fils NV Brut Grand Cru
87	£	André Clouet NV Grande Réserve Brut
86	££	Alexandre Bonnet NV Blanc de Noirs, Brut
85	££	Marie-Noelle Ledru NV Cuvée du Goulté, Brut Grand Cru
84	££	Pommery NV Wintertime, Blanc de Noirs Brut

Champagne Rosé, Vintage & Non-vintage

Almost every producer in Champagne has a non-vintage rosé in its range. The
quality used to be extremely variable, but more producers are taking this style
seriously.

90	£	François Secondé NV Brut Rosé, Grand Cru
89	£££	Gosset NV Grand Rosé Brut
88	£	Pierre Jamain NV Brut Rosé

88	ⓔ	G. Tribaut NV Brut Rosé
88	ⓔⓔ	Moët & Chandon NV Brut Rosé
88	ⓔⓔ	Pommery NV Brut Rosé
87	ⓔ	Henri Mandois NV Brut Rosé, Premier Cru
87	ⓔⓔ	Jacquart NV Brut Mosaïque Rosé
87	ⓔⓔ	Bruno Paillard NV Rosé Brut Première Cuvée
87	ⓔⓔⓔ	Laurent-Perrier NV Cuvée Rosé Brut
86	ⓔⓔⓔ	Philipponnat NV Réserve Rosé Brut
86	ⓔ	Georges Gardet NV Brut Rosé
86	ⓔⓔ	Pannier NV Cuvée Louis Eugène, Rosé Brut
86	ⓔⓔⓔ	Canard-Duchêne NV Charles VII Grande Cuvée, Rosé Brut
85	ⓔⓔ	Bricout NV Cuvée Rosé, Brut
85	ⓔⓔ	Tsarine NV Rosé Brut, Chanoine
85	ⓔⓔ	René James Lallier NV Brut Rosé
85	ⓔⓔ	Pannier NV Brut Rosé
85	ⓔⓔ	de Castellane NV Croix Rouge Brut Rosé
85	ⓔⓔ	Joseph Perrier NV Cuvée Royale Brut Rosé
85	ⓔⓔⓔⓔ	Krug Rosé NV Brut
84	ⓔⓔ	Alexandre Bonnet NV Brut Rosé
84	ⓔ	Jean Moutardier NV Rosé Brut
84	ⓔ	Th. Blondel NV Brut Rosé, Premier Cru
84	ⓔ	Paul Déthune NV Brut Rosé, Grand Cru
84	ⓔⓔ	Louis de Sacy NV Brut Rosé, Grand Cru
84	ⓔⓔ	Duval-Leroy NV Fleur de Champagne, Rosé de Saignée Brut
83	ⓔⓔ	Pierre Mignon NV Brut Rosé
83	ⓔⓔ	de Venoge NV Brut Rosé
83	ⓔⓔ	Boizel NV Rosé Brut
82	ⓔ	Marguet-Bonnerave NV Rosé Grand Cru, Brut

Champagne Rosé: 1996

Most of the region's winemakers claim that Champagne rosé should be consumed when it is young and fresh. If so, why make a vintage? Surely vintage infers a wine that should be aged? Those that do improve with age – often unintentionally – are rare, but if any vintage can produce such anomalies, it must be this one.

94	ⓔⓔⓔ	Pol Roger 1996 Brut Rosé
92	ⓔⓔⓔⓔ	Taittinger Comtes de Champagne 1996 Rosé Brut
85	ⓔⓔ	Alain Thienot 1996 Brut Rosé
85	ⓔⓔⓔ	Deutz 1996 Brut Rosé

Champagne Rosé: 1995

The best wines are slowly taking on a sublime fruitiness achieved by the top 1990 Champagne rosés.

93	ⓔⓔⓔⓔ	Louis Roederer 1995 Cristal Brut Rosé
91	ⓔⓔⓔ	Pol Roger 1995 Brut Rosé
91	ⓔⓔⓔⓔ	Bollinger 1995 Grande Année Rosé, Brut

90	ⓔⓔⓔⓔ	Billecart-Salmon 1995 Cuvée Elisabeth Salmon, Brut Rosé
90	ⓔⓔⓔⓔ	Taittinger Comtes de Champagne 1995 Rosé Brut
89	ⓔⓔⓔⓔ	Perrier-Jouët 1995 Belle Epoque Rosé Brut
86	ⓔⓔⓔ	Moët & Chandon 1995 Brut Impérial Rosé
85	ⓔⓔ	Tarlant 1995 Rosé, Brut Prestige
85	ⓔⓔⓔ	Veuve Clicquot Ponsardin 1995 Rosé Réserve, Brut
84	ⓔ	Beaumont des Crayères 1995 Fleur de Rosé, Brut

Champagne Rosé: 1993 and older

Who would believe that a 10 year old and 20 year old rosé would be topping the charts with an awesome score of 96 points? Certainly not a number of chefs de caves in the region who still cannot take this style seriously. Well, I challenge them to call at 'the most famous address in France' (as Winston Churchill used to say) and try the wines for themselves.

96	ⓔⓔⓔⓔ	Pol Roger 1990 Brut Rosé
96	ⓔⓔⓔⓔ	Pol Roger 1982 Brut Rosé
92	ⓔⓔⓔⓔ	Veuve Clicquot Ponsardin 1990 La Grande Dame Rosé, Brut
92	ⓔⓔⓔⓔ	Pol Roger 1988 Brut Rosé
91	ⓔⓔⓔⓔ	Cuvée Dom Pérignon Rosé Brut 1990 Moët & Chandon
91	ⓔⓔⓔⓔ	Pommery 1992 Louise Rosé, Brut
89	ⓔⓔⓔⓔ	Grand Siècle 1990 Alexandre Rosé, Brut
90	ⓔⓔⓔⓔ	Dom Ruinart 1988 Rosé
87	ⓔⓔⓔ	Pol Roger 1993 Brut Rosé

Other French Sparkling Wines

After last year's record performance by Crémant d'Alsace, I visited the region to taste in even greater depth. Naturally enough, having tasted far more samples of this appellation, it again came out on top.

Remember!

75 Points
'Any sparkling wine other than Champagne that receives this score is not just interesting, but good enough to grace the table of a self-confessed Champagne addict.'
Tom Stevenson
Don't restrict your choice to 90 point wines – I don't!

Alsace, Extra-Brut

It takes a lot to get me to recommend an Extra-Brut. The Blanck is exceptional within its category.

75	ⓔ	Domaine Paul Blanck 1999 Crémant d'Alsace, Extra Brut
70	ⓔ	Domaine Meyer Fonné 1999 Crémant d'Alsace, Brut Extra
70	ⓔ	Klein 1997 Extra Brut Blanc de Blancs, Crémant d'Alsace
70	ⓔ	Klein 1996 Extra Brut Blanc de Blancs, Crémant d'Alsace

Alsace, all other styles

There are a lot of very good sparkling wines being produced in Alsace, but nothing so far that can be compared (in terms of quality, not style) with a very good Champagne. With over 500 producers churning out twice the volume of Saumur there is more than enough critical mass to create the competition necessary for taking these wines onto the next level of quality, so why hasn't it happened? Because less than half-a-dozen producers compete with each other outside of Alsace itself and only two – Dopff Au Moulin and Wolfberger – have any international standing. When we see the smaller producers asserting themselves on the international scene, Crémant d'Alsace will start to come of age and the quality should improve across the board. However, the growers of this region are light-years behind the growers of Champagne, who are themselves light-years behind their Burgundian counterparts in establishing any sort of international reputation, and I cannot see the grower of Alsace discovering a warp-drive in the near future for their varietal wines, let alone their Crémant d'Alsace.

80	ⓔⓔ	Kuentz Bas 1991 Chardonnay Brut, Crémant d'Alsace
80	ⓔ	Domaine Joseph Scharsch 1998 Cuvée Prestige, Crémant d'Alsace
80	ⓔⓔⓔ	Kuentz Bas 1991 Chardonnay Brut RD, Crémant d'Alsace (*magnum*)
79	ⓔ	Willm 1998 Blanc de Noirs, Crémant d'Alsace
79	ⓔ	Wolfberger 1999 Chardonnay, Crémant d'Alsace

78	ⓔ	Domaine Schlegel Boeglin 1998 Crémant d'Alsace Brut
78	ⓔ	Christian Dock 1999 Crémant d'Alsace Brut
78	ⓔ	Bernard Bohn 1995 Rosé, Crémant d'Alsace
78	ⓔ	Heim NV Imperial, Crémant d'Alsace
78	ⓔ	Pierre Sparr 1999 Brut Réserve, Crémant d'Alsace
77	ⓔ	Christian Dock 1998 Crémant d'Alsace Brut
77	ⓔ	François Runner et Fils 1999 Runner, Crémant d'Alsace
77	ⓔ	Domaine Wantz 1999 Crémant d'Alsace Brut
77	ⓔ	Pierre Paul Zink 1998 Crémant d'Alsace Brut
77	ⓔ	Jean Becker 1999 B de Becker, Crémant d'Alsace
77	ⓔ	Crémant d'Alsace 1997 Hartenberg Tokay Pinot Gris Brut
76	ⓔ	Cave Vinicole de Turckheim 1999 Mayerling Brut, Crémant d'Alsace
76	ⓔ	Frey Sohler 1999 Blanc de Blancs, Crémant d'Alsace
76	ⓔ	Lucien Albrecht NV Crémant d'Alsace Brut
76	ⓔ	Crémant d'Alsace 1999 Hartenberg, Blanc de Blancs Brut
76	ⓔ	Paul Ginglinger 1998 Crémant d'Alsace Brut
76	ⓔ	Domaine Daniel Ruff 1999 Blanc de Noirs, Crémant d'Alsace
76	ⓔ	La Cave de Sigolsheim 1995 Brut Rosé, Crémant d'Alsace
76	ⓔ	Domaine Léon Boesch 1996 Cuvée Réservée, Crémant d'Alsace
75	ⓔ	Cave Vinicole de Beblenheim NV Heimberger, Crémant d'Alsace
75	ⓔ	Cave Vinicole de Beblenheim NV Baron de Hoen, Crémant d'Alsace
75	ⓔ	Cave du Roi Dagobert 1998 St. Eloi Rosé, Crémant d'Alsace
75	ⓔ	Clément Weck 1999 Crémant d'Alsace Brut
75	ⓔ	Hubert Metz 1997 Réserve de la Dome, Crémant d'Alsace
75	ⓔ	Domaine du Bollenberg 1999 Eugène, Crémant d'Alsace
75	ⓔ	Domaine Einhart du Westerberg 1998 Einhart, Crémant d'Alsace
75	ⓔ	Henri Schoenheitz 1998 Crémant d'Alsace Brut
75	ⓔ	Spitz 1997 Brut Blanc de Noirs, Crémant d'Alsace
75	ⓔ	Cave Vinicole de Ribeauvillé 1998 Giersberger Cuvée Prestige
75	ⓔ	Domaine Gruss 1998 Brut Prestige, Crémant d'Alsace
75	ⓔ	Bernard Schwach 1999 Brut Réserve, Crémant d'Alsace
75	ⓔ	Domaine Barmes Buecher 1998 Crémant d'Alsace Brut
75	ⓔ	Wolfberger 1997 Prestige Cuvée An 2000, Crémant d'Alsace Brut
75	ⓔ	René Muré 1997 Crémant d'Alsace Brut
74	ⓔ	Cave Vinicole de Beblenheim 1998 Blanc de Noirs Heimberger
74	ⓔ	Cave Vinicole de Ribeauvillé 1998 Giersberger Brut, Crémant d'Alsace
74	ⓔ	Domaine Stentz Buecher 1998 Crémant d'Alsace Brut
74	ⓔ	Cave Vinicole de Cléebourg NV Clérotstein, Crémant d'Alsace
74	ⓔ	Schaeffer Woerly 1998 Crémant d'Alsace Brut
74	ⓔ	Gilbert Ruhlmann 1997 Cuvée Prestige, Crémant d'Alsace
74	ⓔ	Willm NV Crémant d'Alsace Brut
74	ⓔ	Pierre Paul Zink 1999 Crémant d'Alsace Brut
74	ⓔ	Cattin 1999 Crémant d'Alsace Brut
74	ⓔ	Haegelin 1996 Chardonnay, Crémant d'Alsace
74	ⓔ	Victor Hertz 1995 Rosé d'Alsace, Crémant d'Alsace
74	ⓔ	Edmond Rentz 1999 Crémant d'Alsace, Brut Prestige
74	ⓔ	Louis Sipp 1999 Crémant d'Alsace Brut
74	ⓔ	Domaine Albert Mann 1998 Baron de Castex Brut, Crémant d'Alsace
74	ⓔ	Pierre Sparr 1995 Brut Dynastie, Crémant d'Alsace
74	ⓔ	Pierre Sparr 1995 Glorius 2000, Crémant d'Alsace
74	ⓔ	Willm 1997 Prestige Cuvée Emile Willm, Crémant d'Alsace
73	ⓔ	Cave Vinicole d'Orschwiller 1998 Moenchberner, Crémant d'Alsace

73	ⓔ	Wunsch Mann 1998 Crémant d'Alsace Brut
73	ⓔ	Antoine Stoffel 1998 Crémant d'Alsace Brut
73	ⓔ	Maison Zoeller 1998 Crémant d'Alsace Brut
73	ⓔ	Pierre Hutt NV Crémant d'Alsace Brut
73	ⓔ	Domaine Valentin Zusslin NV Saint Valentin, Crémant d'Alsace
73	ⓔ	Dopff & Irion 1998 Crémant d'Alsace Brut
73	ⓔ	Dopff au Moulin NV Cuvée Julien, Crémant d'Alsace
73	ⓔ	Wolfberger 1999 Riesling, Crémant d'Alsace
73	ⓔ	Dopff au Moulin NV Rosé, Crémant d'Alsace
73	ⓔ	René Muré NV Crémant d'Alsace Brut
73	ⓔ	Domaine Léon Boesch 1998 Cuvée Réservée, Crémant d'Alsace
73	ⓔⓔ	Bernard Bohn 1992 Crémant d'Alsace Brut (*magnum*)
72	ⓔ	Baur 1998 Blanc de Noirs, Crémant d'Alsace
72	ⓔ	Paul Buecher 1999 Prestige Rosé, Crémant d'Alsace
72	ⓔ	Baumann Zirgel 1999 Crémant d'Alsace Brut
72	ⓔ	Bestheim 1998 Madame Sans Gene, Crémant d'Alsace
72	ⓔ	Frey Sohler 1998 Riesling, Crémant d'Alsace
72	ⓔ	Victor Hertz 1996 Crémant d'Alsace Brut
70	ⓔ	Gustave Lorentz 1999 Crémant d'Alsace Brut
70	ⓔ	Cave Vinicole d'Ingersheim NV Crémant d'Alsace Brut
70	ⓔ	Metz Laugel 1998 Riesling, Crémant d'Alsace
70	ⓔ	Cave Vinicole d'Ingersheim NV Brut Prestige, Crémant d'Alsace
70	ⓔ	Bestheim NV Crémant d'Alsace Brut
70	ⓔ	Cave Vinicole de Hunawihr NV Calixte Brut, Crémant d'Alsace
70	ⓔ	Domaine Bruno Sorg 1998 Crémant d'Alsace Brut
70	ⓔ	Wolfberger 1999 Crémant d'Alsace Brut
70	ⓔ	André Wantz 1996 Crémant d'Alsace Brut
70	ⓔ	David Ermel 1998 Brut David Ermel, Crémant d'Alsace
70	ⓔ	Willy Gisselbrecht 1999 Blanc de Noirs, Crémant d'Alsace
70	ⓔ	Spitz 1998 Brut Blanc de Noirs, Crémant d'Alsace
70	ⓔ	Stentz Buecher 1997 Chardonnay, Crémant d'Alsace
70	ⓔ	Vignoble Klur 1999 Klur Clement, Crémant d'Alsace
70	ⓔ	Robert Klingenfus NV Crémant d'Alsace Brut
70	ⓔ	Domaine Sipp Mack 1998 Crémant d'Alsace Brut
70	ⓔ	Cave Vinicole d'Orschwiller 1998 Chardonnay, Crémant d'Alsace
70	ⓔ	Cave Vinicole de Ribeauvillé 1998 Cuvée l'Offensee,
70	ⓔ	Domaine Schlegel Boeglin 1996 Réserve de la Vallée Noble
70	ⓔ	Kuentz Bas NV Tradition, Crémant d'Alsace

Gaillac

A dismal performance by Gaillac yielded just two recommendations.

75	ⓔ	Robert Plageoles NV Mauzac Nature, Gaillac
73	ⓔ	Cave de Labastide de Lévis NV Gaillac Brut

Limoux

As I said last year 'I'm seeing less exciting Limoux, whether Blanquette or Crémant, as each year goes by', although no one bothered to submit its finest and most interesting wine, the succulently sweet Méthode Ancestrale.

80	£	Cuvée Maistre Antoine NV Blanquette de Limoux Brut
79	£	Domaine de l'Aigle NV Jean-Louis Denois, Brut Tradition
73	£	Jean Louis Denois NV Blanc de Blancs Chardonnay Brut

Loire, all styles

If not for the Tresor, the Crémant de Loire from the Saumur cooperative would have topped this list, which would have been embarrassing for a leading Saumur producer. It is not that this cooperative happens to have better vineyards outside Saumur, just that the regulations for Crémant de Loire are more user-friendly for those winemakers who try to make a classic quality sparkling wine. As for the Tresor, it is one of the most helter-skelter wines on the market, but this year's performance not only means that it is as good as one of the very best Champagnes in its own right, it is one percentile point short of the deluxe cuvée quality. We all know that the Loire can do it. It is arguably equal to Chablis in its potential to rival Champagne, yet both regions consistently produce more dross than quality. If the winemakers responsible for Pirie, Croser, Roederer Estate, Iron Horse and Domaine Carneros La Rêve were given vineyards here, overnight the Loire would become the hottest place for sparkling wine. Come on guys, do you really need foreigners to show you the way? The main obstruction is, as we all know, that this region (and Chablis) are famous for other still styles of wine. Whoever is brave enough to use first quality grapes from the very best vineyards for sparkling wine will become one of the world's most legendary winemakers. Anyone up for it, or are you all prepared to let an Aussie or a Yank steal the limelight?

89	£	Bouvet Ladubay NV Tresor, Brut Saumur
75	£	CV de Saumur, Crémant de Loire NV Cuvée de la Chevalerie, Brut
75	£	Ackerman Laurance NV Cuvée Excellence, Saumur Brut
74	£	CV de Saumur, Crémant de Loire 1998 Les Médaillés, Brut
74	£	Ackerman Laurance NV Saumur 1811, Brut
74	£	Ackerman Laurance NV 1811 Vouvray Brut
74	£	Ackerman Laurance NV Cuvée Excellence, Crémant de Loire Brut
74	£	Langlois NV Crémant de Loire, Brut Rosé
72	£	Montvermeil NV Crémant de Loire, Brut
72	£	Ackerman NV Cuvée Privée, Crémant de Loire Brut
72	£	Château de Montgueret 1997 Tête de Cuvée, Saumur Brut
72	£	Langlois NV Crémant de Loire, Brut
72	£	Bouvet 1998 Saphir Brut Vintage, Saumur
71	£	Ackerman 1996 Cuvée Jean-Baptiste, Saumur Brut
70	£	Ackerman Laurance NV Privilège Brut, Crémant de Loire
75	££	Zéro par Bouvet-Ladubay 1998 Extra Brut, Saumur
78	£	CV de Saumur, NV Cuvée de la Chevalier, Cabernet Demi-Sec

Australia: Vintage & Non-vintage

As can be gleaned from the results below, the presence of a vintage on an Australian fizz usually represents a step up in terms of quality, although any variation in the different years is more likely to be attributed more to learning curves than climatic conditions.

Remember!

75 Points
'Any sparkling wine other than Champagne that receives this score is not just interesting, but good enough to grace the table of a self-confessed Champagne addict.'
Tom Stevenson
Don't restrict your choice to 90 point wines – I don't!

91	££	Pirie 1996 Pipers Brook
89	££	Pirie 1997 Pipers Brook
88	££	Croser 1998 Petaluma
86	££	Croser 1991 Petaluma
85	££	Chandon Australia 1997 Vintage Blanc de Blancs
84	££	Green Point by Chandon 1997 Vintage Brut
83	££	Green Point by Chandon 1997 Vintage Brut Rosé
80	£	Chandon NV Brut
80	££	Blue Pyrenees NV Midnight Cuvée Chardonnay
80	££	Yellowglen 1997 Brut Pinot Noir Chardonnay Pinot Meunier
80	££	Penley 1994 Coonawarra Pinot Noir Chardonnay
79	££	Glaetzer 1996 Barossa Valley Sparkling Pinot Noir
79	£	Omni NV
79	£	Jacob's Creek Chardonnay Pinot Noir NV Special Cuvée, Selected Reserve
78	££	White Quartz 1997 Organic Sparkling Pinot Noir Chardonnay
78	£	Hardys NV R&R Classic Cuvée
78	££	Wirra Wirra 1997 The Cousins, Pinot Noir Chardonnay
77	£	Strathbogie Ranges 1997 Sparkling Chardonnay Pinot Noir
77	£	Yellowglen NV Brut Pinot Noir Chardonnay
77	£	Sir James 1995 Vintage
76	£	Barramundi Sparkling NV
76	£	Yellowglen NV Pinot Noir Chardonnay Grande Cuvée
76	£	Banrock Station NV Sparkling Chardonnay
75	£	Seaview 1996 Chardonnay Blanc de Blancs, Vintage Research Brut
74	£	Flirt NV Fizz
74	£	Sir James Brut de Brut NV Pinot Noir Chardonnay
74	£	Brown Brothers NV Pinot Noir & Chardonnay Sparkling, King Valley
74	£	Jansz of Tasmania NV
74	£	Blue Pyrenees Reserve Brut NV Chardonnay Pinot Noir Pinot Meunier
73	£	Sir James Cuvée Brut NV Pinot Noir Chardonnay
72	£	Hardys Stamp of Australia NV Sparkling Chardonnay Pinot Noir
72	£	Cranswick NV Pinot Chardonnay
70	£	Sacred Hill NV Brut Cuvée SEA

Australian: sparkling red

This is very much Australia's own style of sparkling wine. Most wines in this category are sparkling Shiraz, but you can get fizzed up versions of Cabernet, Merlot and various blends. The appearance of Pinot Noir is a rarity, especially in its pure form, which is odd since the first Australian red fizz was a 'Sparkling Burgundy' back in 1881. The wines today are generally on the sweet side, very deep in colour and fall into one of two categories: cedary-oaky or fruit-driven. The sight of anything this colour with bubbles can give those brought up on Champagne a shock and this is only made worse by the big smack of tannin encountered in those sparkling red wines of the cedary-oaky style. Champagne drinkers who refuse to consider anything other than the genuine article will be brought within a mile of these wines, but those who are positively interested in the development of sparkling wines beyond the confines of northern France should at least try to understand Australian sparkling red wine. Although the bulk of Aussie red fizz is seen as nothing more (or anything less) than barbecue fodder, there is something of a cult-following for the very best wines.

90	££	Charles Melton NV Barossa Valley Sparkling Red
87	£	Nero NV Sparkling Shiraz
85	£	Chandon Australia NV Sparkling Red, Pinot Noir/Shiraz
85	££	Balnaves of Coonawarra 1999 Sparkling Cabernet
85	££	The Black Queen 1996 Sparkling Shiraz
85	££	Joseph NV Sparkling Red
84	££	Andrew Harris 1997 Double Vision Mudgee Sparkling Shiraz
80	£	Haselgrove NV McLaren Vale Garnet SG-7
80	£	Miranda 1994 Sparkling Shiraz, Barossa Old Vine Reserve
80	£	Omni NV Red
80	££	Leasingham Classic Clare 1994 Sparkling Shiraz
80	£££	Glaetzer NV Barossa Valley Sparkling Shiraz
78	££	McLarens on the Lake NV Sparkling Red Shiraz
77	££	Willows Vineyard, The Doctor NV Sparkling Red, Shiraz/Pinot Noir
75	££	Tatachilla NV Sparkling Malbec

England

England's climate is every bit as variable as Champagne's and the White Cliffs of Dover are part of the same chalk basin that extends under Channel and Paris to emerge in the famous region itself as the Côte des Blancs, so it is little wonder that sparkling wine is England's great wine hope. Furthermore, the English deliberately put the bubbles into wine long before the French did. This was documented by Christopher Merret in 1662, six years before Dom Pérignon set foot in Hautvillers (this document is reproduced in my Christie's World Encyclopedia of Champagne & Sparkling Wine)*, consequently sparkling Champagne was famous enough for English dramatists to wax lyrical about it in 1676 (*The Man of Mode*, Sir George Etherege), 43 years before the French claim to have invented it!*

Remember!

75 Points
'Any sparkling wine other than Champagne that receives this score is not just interesting, but good enough to grace the table of a self-confessed Champagne addict.'
Tom Stevenson
Don't restrict your choice to 90 point wines – I don't!

89	££	Nyetimber 1994 Aurora Cuvée, Chardonnay, Brut (*magnum*)
88	££	Nyetimber 1994 Première Cuvée, Chardonnay Blanc de Blancs, Brut
87	££	Nyetimber 1994 Classic Cuvée, Brut
86	££	Davenport 1999 Brut Reserve
86	££	Bloomsbury 1997 Cuvée Merret, Brut
85	££	Fitzrovia 1998 Cuvée Merret, Brut
85	££	Cavendish 1998 Cuvée Merret
84	££	South Ridge 1998 Cuvée Merret, Brut
80	£	Bruisyard NV Millennium
80	££	Bearsted NV Brut
78	££	Breaky Bottom, Millennium Cuvée Maman Mercier 1996 Brut
76	£	Chapel Down 1995 Epoch Vintage Brut
75	£	Bardfield 1998 Extra-Brut
75	££	Camel Valley 1999 Cornwall Brut
73	£	Chapel Down NV Epoch, Brut
73	£	The English Wine Centre 1996 House Bubbly, Brut RD 2000
72	£	Southern Shore NV Brut
72	£	Davenport 1998 Brut
70	££	Danebury 1995 Cossack, Brut
70	£	Hale Valley 1998 Brut

Germany

*Sekt has historically appealed to Germans and few others. Production is
enormous, more than twice that of Champagne, but most of this is blended
from the dregs of several countries and very little is exported. Until 1986
Deutscher Sekt was a oxymoron, but now has to be the exclusive product of
German wine. Smaller producers have always existed, but the quality of their
wines was little better than that of the biggest bottlers until recently.*

Remember!

75 Points
'Any sparkling wine other than Champagne that receives this score
is not just interesting, but good enough to grace the table of a
self-confessed Champagne addict.'
Tom Stevenson
Don't restrict your choice to 90 point wines – I don't!

Classic Riesling Sekt

*Riesling makes a classic Sekt, but not a classic sparkling wine. Its terpene-
laden character overwhelms the subtle influence of autolysis, thus no
sparkling wine made from this variety will ever achieve classic bottle-
fermented aromas. What it will achieve, however, is what any good still
Riesling can accomplish and that is a classic Riesling bottle-aroma. Call it
petrolly or what you like, but this usually takes a few years after
disgorgement, hence a certain maturity is required. A Champagne-lover who
is also a Riesling-lover should enjoy a mature Riesling Sekt, but only if all
preconceived notions of what a sparkling wine should be are put to one side.*

Riesling Sekt Extra-Brut

*Often less austere than their Champagne counterparts, although subject to
the same 0-6 grams per litre of residual sugar.*

80	££	Prinz von Hessen 1997 Extra Brut
75	£	Hans Lang 1997 Johann Maximilian Extra Brut
72	£	Baron zu Knyphausen 1993 Herrlichkeit Knyphausen
70	£	Winzerverein Deidesheim 1998 Deidesheimer Paradiesgarten Extra Brut

Riesling Sekt Brut

*By far the most successful style, the Reichsrat von Buhl 1999 Forster Pechstein
being equivalent in pure quality terms to a very good Champagne.*

85	££	Reichsrat von Buhl 1999 Forster Pechstein Riesling Brut (*magnum*)
80	£	Markus Fries 1997 Noviander Klosterberg Brut

78	ⓔ	Studert Prüm Maximinhof 1998 Maximiner Cabinet Brut
78	ⓔ	Selbach-Oster 1997 Zeltinger Himmelreich Brut
75	ⓔ	Carl Adelseck 1990 Juwel Brut
75	ⓔ	St. Urbans-Hof 1998 Brut
75	ⓔ	Rainer Eymann 1998 Riesling Sekt Brut
75	ⓔ	Prinz zu Salm Dalberg'sches Weingut 1998 Rheingraf Riesling Sekt Brut
75	ⓔ	St. Laurentius Sektgut 1998 Riesling Brut
75	ⓔ	Hessische Staatsweingüter Kloster Eberbach 1998 Rauenthaler Baiken Brut
74	ⓔ	Freunde von Reinhartshausen NV Hattenheimer Deutelsberg Brut
74	ⓔ	Schales 1991 Riesling Sekt Brut
74	ⓔ	Schubert'sche 1998 Maximin Grünhäuser Riesling Sekt Brut
72	ⓔ	Albert Kallfelz 1999 Kallfelz Riesling Sekt Brut
72	ⓔ	Freiherr von Schleinitz 1999 Riesling Sekt Brut
72	ⓔ	Reichsrat von Buhl 1999 Riesling Brut
72	ⓔ	Sybille Kuntz 1999 Riesling Sekt Brut
72	ⓔ	Fürstlich Castell'sches Domänenamt NV Schloss Castell Brut
71	ⓔ	Heinrich Schmitges 1999 Riesling Sekt Brut
70	ⓔ	C. Rumpel & Cie. 1998 Trabener Gaispfad Brut
70	ⓔ	Max Ferd. Richter 1998 Mulheimer Sonnenlay Brut
70	ⓔ	Heim'sche Privat-Sektkellerei 1999 Martin Heim Brut
70	ⓔ	Saar-Mosel-Winzersekt 1999 Mosel Riesling Sekt Brut
70	ⓔ	Durbacher Wg. 1998 Durbacher Plauelrain Riesling Brut
70	ⓔ	Dr. Pauly Bergweiler 1995 Zeltinger Himmelreich Brut

Riesling Sekt Trocken & Extra-Troken

Technically the same as Sec and Extra Sec, thus the former will have between 17 and 35 grams per litre of residual sugar, while the latter may have between 12 and 20.

77	ⓔ	Carl Adelseck 1998 Juwel Trocken
74	ⓔ	Paul Anheuser 1996 Nahe Riesling Sekt Trocken
74	ⓔ	Schmitt-Peitz 1999 Wallhäuser Pfarrgarten Trocken
73	ⓔ	Tauberfränkische Wg. Beckstein 1998 Becksteiner Kirchberg
71	ⓔ	Schmitges 1999 Riesling Sekt Trocken
70	ⓔ	des Hauses Württemberg 1998 Maulbronner Eilfingerberg Riesling
70	ⓔ	Joseph Deppisch 1998 Franken Riesling Extra Trocken

Other Sekt styles

Regardless of actual quality, most of these wines will be more classic in style as far as most experienced sparkling wine are concerned. Spätburgunder is the most successful variety.

Extra-Brut

80	ⓔⓔ	Prinz von Hessen 1997 Extra Brut
75	ⓔ	Reichsrat von Buhl 1998 Weissburgunder Dosage Zero
75	ⓔ	Hans Lang 1997 Johann Maximilian Extra Brut

| 72 | ℰ | Baron zu Knyphausen 1993 Herrlichkeit Knyphausen Extra Brut |
| 70 | ℰ | Winzerverein Deidesheim 1998 Deidesheimer Paradiesgarten Extra Brut |

Brut

80	ℰ	Markus Fries 1997 Noviander Klosterberg Brut
80	ℰ	Dr. Bürklin Wolf 1997 Chardonnay Brut
78	ℰ	Studert Prüm Maximinhof 1998 Maximiner Cabinet Brut
78	ℰ	Selbach-Oster 1997 Zeltinger Himmelreich Brut
78	ℰ	Wilhelmshof 1998 Siebeldinger Königsgarten Blanc de Noir Brut
77	ℰℰ	Reichsrat von Buhl 1994 Spätburgunder Blanc de Noir Brut
77	ℰℰ	Reichsrat von Buhl 1994 Spätburgunder Blanc de Noir Brut
75	ℰ	Carl Adelseck 1998 Juwel Brut
75	ℰ	St. Urbans-Hof 1998 Brut
75	ℰ	St. Laurentius Sektgut 1998 Chardonnay Brut
75	ℰ	Kloster Eberbach 1998 Rauenthaler Baiken Brut
75	ℰ	Mäurer's 1996 Chardonnay Classic Brut
75	ℰ	Bürgermeister W. Schweinhardt Nachf. 1998 Chardonnay Brut
75	ℰ	Schloss Schönborn 1994 Assmannshäuser Höllenberg Brut
74	ℰ	Freunde von Reinhartshausen NV Hattenheimer Deutelsberg Brut
74	ℰ	Wg. Lauffen 1996 Katzenbeißer Blanc de Noir Brut
74	ℰ	Gut Nägelsförst 1998 Blanc de Blanc Brut
73	ℰ	Staatsweingut Meersburg 1999 Pinot Brut
73	ℰ	Wilhelmshof 1999 Siebeldinger Königsgarten Blanc de Noir Brut
73	ℰℰ	Albert Heitlinger 1997 Heilinger Blanc et Brut
72	ℰ	Fürstlich Castell'sches Domänenamt NV Schloss Castell Brut
71	ℰ	Wg. Bickensohl 1999 Bickensohler Pinot blanc de Noir Brut
70	ℰ	C. Rumpel & Cie. 1998 Trabener Gaispfad Brut
70	ℰ	Max Ferd. Richter 1998 Mulheimer Sonnenlay Brut
70	ℰ	Heim'sche Privat-Sektkellerei 1999 Martin Heim Brut
70	ℰ	Eugen Schönhals 1999 Pinot Blanc de Noir Brut
70	ℰ	Joseph Deppisch 1998 Franken Silvaner Brut
70	ℰ	Badischer Winzerkeller 1996 Brut
70	ℰ	Dr. Pauly Bergweiler 1995 Zeltinger Himmelreich Brut
70	ℰ	Freunde von Reinhartshausen 1998 Schloss Reinhartshausen Brut

Trocken & Extra-Trocken

80	ℰ	Reis und Luft 1998 Blauer Spätburgunder Winzersekt Trocken
77	ℰ	Carl Adelseck 1998 Juwel Trocken
75	ℰ	Schales 1997 Weisser Burgunder Sekt Extra Trocken
74	ℰ	Winzerverein Deidesheim 1999 Spätburgunder Trocken Rotsekt
74	ℰ	Schmitt-Peitz 1999 Wallhäuser Pfarrgarten Trocken
72	ℰ	Edith Stein 1999 Riesling Gewürztraminer Trocken
70	ℰ	Winzerkeller Hex vom Dasenstein 1997 Trocken
70	ℰ	Weingärtner Flein-Talheim 1998 Trocken
70	ℰ	Winzersekt 1999 Rheinhessen Spätburgunder Weißherbst Extra Trocken
70	ℰ	Schloss Affaltrach, Dr. Reinhold Baumann GmbH & Co. 1998 Rose

Italy

The best response as always has come from Franciacorta, one of the few places in the world where high quality sparkling wine can be made in large volumes. At long last I am receiving full cooperation from Asti and Brachetto d'Acqui, thus the significant number of wines recommended from those appellations.

Remember!

75 Points
'Any sparkling wine other than Champagne that receives this score
is not just interesting, but good enough to grace the table of a
self-confessed Champagne addict.'
Tom Stevenson
Don't restrict your choice to 90 point wines – I don't!

Franciacorta

The only Italian sparkling wine appellation that must be made by méthode champenoise. Franciacorta also happens to be the only compact wine area producing world class sparkling wine in Italy. The overall quality was excellent, but an increasing number of Franciacorta are suffering from heavy-handed malolactic, which at best robs the wines of their finesse, while at worst results in off-putting aromas.

Franciacorta Extra-Brut

82	ⓔ	Ricci Curbastro NV Franciacorta Extra Brut
82	ⓔⓔ	Uberti NV Francesco I, Franciacorta Extra Brut
76	ⓔ	Monzio Campagnoni NV Franciacorta Extra Brut
74	ⓔ	Lo Sparviere NV Franciacorta Extra Brut
74	ⓔ	il Mosnel NV Franciacorta Extra Brut

Franciacorta Brut

85	ⓔ	Vezzoli 1997 Franciacorta Brut
85	ⓔⓔⓔ	Ca'del Bosco 1994 Cuvée Annamaria Clementi
83	ⓔ	Ricci Curbastro NV Franciacorta Satèn Brut
82	ⓔ	Barone Pizzini NV Franciacorta Satèn
82	ⓔ	Bagnadore Io 1995 Franciacorta Brut
82	ⓔⓔ	Villa 1995 Franciacorta Brut Selezione
80	ⓔ	Riccafana NV Franciacorta Satèn
80	ⓔ	Boschi NV Franciacorta Brut
80	ⓔ	San Cristoforo NV Franciacorta Brut
80	ⓔ	Castelveder 1996 Franciacorta Brut

80	ⓔⓔ	Bellavista 1997 Gran Cuvée Brut, Franciacorta
78	ⓔ	Bredasole NV Franciacorta Brut
78	ⓔⓔ	La Montina 1996 Franciacorta Brut
77	ⓔ	Barboglio DeGaioncelli NV Franciacorta Brut
77	ⓔ	Vigna Dorata NV Franciacorta Brut
77	ⓔ	La Boscaiola 1996 Franciacorta Brut
77	ⓔ	Monogram NV Cuvée Giunone, Franciacorta Brut
77	ⓔ	Ricci Curbastro NV Franciacorta Brut
77	ⓔ	il Mosnel 1997 Franciacorta Brut Satèn
76	ⓔ	Gatti NV Franciacorta Brut
76	ⓔ	Tenuta Castellino Bonomi NV Franciacorta Brut
76	ⓔ	Barone Pizzini NV Franciacorta Brut
76	ⓔ	Bersi Serlini NV Cuvée No.4, Franciacorta Brut
76	ⓔⓔ	Bellavista NV Cuvée Brut, Franciacorta
75	ⓔ	Cornaleto 1997 Franciacorta Brut Satèn
75	ⓔ	Monzio Compagnoni NV Franciacorta Brut
75	ⓔ	Faccoli NV Franciacorta Brut
75	ⓔ	Montorfano de Filippo NV Franciacorta Brut
75	ⓔ	il Mosnel NV Franciacorta Brut
75	ⓔ	Monzio Compagnoni NV Franciacorta Satèn
75	ⓔ	Bersi Serlini NV Franciacorta Brut
75	ⓔ	La Boscaiola NV Franciacorta Brut
75	ⓔ	Antica Cantina Fratta 1998 Franciacorta Brut
75	ⓔ	Contadi Castaldi NV Franciacorta Brut
75	ⓔ	Ca'del Bosco NV Franciacorta Brut
75	ⓔ	Contadi Castaldi 1997 Franciacorta Brut Satèn
75	ⓔ	Cornaleto 1992 Franciacorta Brut
75	ⓔⓔ	Ronco Calino 1996 Franciacorta Brut
75	ⓔⓔ	Uberti NV Magnificentia, Franciacorta Satèn
75	ⓔⓔ	Bellavista NV Gran Cuvée Satèn, Franciacorta
75	ⓔⓔ	Ca'del Bosco 1996 Franciacorta Satèn
74	ⓔ	Mirabella NV Franciacorta Brut
74	ⓔ	Gatti NV Franciacorta Satèn
74	ⓔ	Ferghettina NV Franciacorta Brut
74	ⓔ	Le Marchesine NV Franciacorta Brut
74	ⓔ	Tenuta Castellino Bonomi NV Franciacorta Satèn
74	ⓔ	Conti Bettoni Cazzago NV Tetellus, Franciacorta Brut
74	ⓔ	Monogram 1991 Franciacorta Brut
74	ⓔⓔ	Cavalleri NV Franciacorta Satèn Blanc de Blancs
74	ⓔⓔ	Monte Rossa NV Franciacorta Brut Satèn
73	ⓔ	Riccafana NV Franciacorta Brut
73	ⓔ	Enrico Serafino 1995 Cuvée Speciale per il Millennio, Brut Millesimato
73	ⓔ	Castelveder NV Franciacorta Brut
71	ⓔ	Batasiolo Dosage Zéro 1994 Millésimé

Franciacorta Sec & Extra-Sec

78	ⓔ	Barone Pizzini NV Franciacorta Extra Dry
77	ⓔ	Barboglio DeGaioncelli NV Franciacorta Extra Dry
72	ⓔ	Monte Rossa NV Franciacorta Sec

Franciacorta Rosé

The best of these wines have an elegance to rival most pink Champagnes.

80	ⓔ	Mirabella NV Franciacorta Rosé
80	ⓔ	Monte Rossa 1995 Cabochon, Franciacorta Rosé Brut
77	ⓔ	Faccoli NV Franciacorta Rosé Brut
75	ⓔ	Barone Pizzini NV Franciacorta Rosé
74	ⓔⓔ	Ca'del Bosco 1997 Franciacorta Rosé
72	ⓔⓔ	Bellavista 1997 Gran Cuvée Brut Rosé, Franciacorta

Asti

At long last I'm beginning to whittle Asti down to the true classics.

90	ⓔ	La Selvatica – Asti NV Caudrina, Romano Dogliotti
88	ⓔⓔ	De Miranda 1998 Asti Metodo Classico
87	ⓔⓔ	De Miranda 1997 Asti Metodo Classico
86	ⓔ	Cerutti NV Asti Cesare
85	ⓔ	Toso NV Asti Dolce
85	ⓔ	Tosti NV Asti Dolce
85	ⓔ	Vigne Regali NV Asti, Spumante Dolce
85	ⓔ	Capetta NV Asti Dolce
85	ⓔ	Conte di Cavour NV Asti
85	ⓔ	Casa Martelletti NV Tradizione Asti
85	ⓔ	Bava NV Malvasia di Castelnuovo don Bosco, Rosé Dolce
85	ⓔ	Vignaioli di S. Stefano 2000 Asti Spumante
84	ⓔ	Bersano NV Asti Dolce
75	ⓔ	Santero NV Asti Dolce

Brachetto d'Acqui

Red Asti for all intents and purposes, except that the aroma is more creamy-winey, less floral and never as intense as the peach or orange sometimes found on the best Asti.

85	ⓔ	I Ronchetti NV Brachetto d'Acqui
81	ⓔ	Tosti NV Brachetto d'Acqui
80	ⓔ	Marenco NV Brachetto d'Acqui Dolce
78	ⓔ	Arione NV Piemonte Brachetto Dolce
78	ⓔ	Rosa Regale 2000 Brachetto d'Acqui
78	ⓔ	Bersano NV Brachetto d'Acqui Dolce
78	ⓔ	Dezzani NV Brachetto d'Acqui Dolce

New Zealand

This country vies with Tasmania as the greatest sparkling wine area in the Southern Hemisphere and only the Loire and Burgundy share the same potential outside of Champagne in the Northern Hemisphere. It will be interesting to see who wins as New Zealand and Tasmania fight it out over the next couple of decades, although neither should worry about the French regions – the French producers don't.

Remember!

75 Points
'Any sparkling wine other than Champagne that receives this score is not just interesting, but good enough to grace the table of a self-confessed Champagne addict.'
Tom Stevenson
Don't restrict your choice to 90 point wines – I don't!

89	ⓔ	Hunter's 1996 Brut
89	ⓔ	Morton Estate 1995 RD, Marlborough
87	ⓔ	Miru Miru 1998 Hunter's
86	ⓔ	Miru Miru 1999 Hunter's
85	ⓔⓔ	Pelorus 1996 Marlborough
83	ⓔ	Lindauer NV Special Reserve
80	ⓔⓔ	Soljans Estate 1998 Sparkling Pinotage
80	ⓔ	Montana Deutz NV Marlborough Cuvée
80	ⓔ	Kim Crawford Rory NV Brut
80	ⓔ	Huia 1997 Brut
80	ⓔⓔ	Daniel No.1 NV Brut
80	ⓔⓔ	Pelorus NV Marlborough
78	ⓔ	Lindauer NV Rosé
78	ⓔ	Morton Estate NV Premium Brut, Marlborough
78	ⓔⓔ	Montana Deutz 1996 Blanc de Blancs
77	ⓔ	Palliser Estate 1997 Martinborough
75	ⓔ	Lindauer NV Brut
75	ⓔⓔ	Daniel le Brun 1996 Blanc de Blancs
75	ⓔⓔ	Alan McCorkindale 1999 Vintage, Waipara Valley
75	ⓔⓔ	Lindauer NV Grandeur
73	ⓔ	Daniel le Brun NV Brut

Spain

There are Cava fans out there who think that I hate Cava unless it has been crafted in the style of a Champagne, but I'm a Cava-sceptic, not a Cava-hater and I am perfectly willing to acknowledge quality in a Cava produced from Parellada, Macabéo and Xarel.lo grapes. The fact that most of the very best Cavas have been produced from Champagne grapes, whether pure or blended, can easily be explained. These varieties have established their credential as the best for sparkling wine throughout the world, whereas Cava's so-called traditional grapes have not. I taste hundreds of Cava every year and inevitably recommend more traditional-based products than Chardonnay-based. If I didn't I would suspect myself of being biased because that's the way the dice is loaded. Now, however, traditional-based Cava has reached a milestone (as far as this guide is concerned) because it is the first time that I have found such a Cava to be equal in quality to a very good Champagne. I have awarded 85-87 points to Cavas in previous editions, but they were all pumped-up with Chardonnay to one degree or another, but the Torre Galimany 1998 is made exclusively from the Holy Trinity of Parellada, Macabéo and Xarel.lo, with the emphasis on the last variety. Furthermore, all previous high-scorers – Raimat Gran Brut (87 points in the first edition), Jaume Codorníu (85 points in the 2000 edition) and once again the Raimat Gran Brut (85 points in the 2001 edition) – were from the Codorníu stable, whereas the Torre Galimany 1998 is the first Freixenet group Cava to break the quality barrier.

Remember!

75 Points
'Any sparkling wine other than Champagne that receives this score
is not just interesting, but good enough to grace the table of a
self-confessed Champagne addict.'
Tom Stevenson
Don't restrict your choice to 90 point wines – I don't!

Cava Brut Nature

Brut Nature is restricted to a maximum of three grams per litre of residual sugar. I have never recommended so many Brut Nature in any category of sparkling wine, including Champagne.

85	ⓔ	Torre Galimany 1998 Cava Brut Nature
80	ⓔ	Cristina Colomer NV Cava Brut Nature
80	ⓔ	Eudald Massana Noya NV Cava Brut Nature Mil.lenni
80	ⓔ	Gramona, III Lustros 1996 Cava Brut Nature
80	ⓔ	Gramona, III Lustros 1995 Cava Brut Nature
80	ⓔ	Gran Claustro 1998 Cava Brut Nature
80	ⓔⓔ	Maria Casanovas NV Cava Brut Nature Gran Reserva
78	ⓔ	Signat 1999 Cava Brut Nature
78	ⓔ	Raventós i Blanc 1998 Cava Brut Nature Gran Reserva

77	£	Alsina Sardà Sello 1996 Cava Brut Nature Gran Reserva
77	£	Titiana de Parxet NV Cava Brut Nature
76	£	Duc de Foix NV Cava Brut Nature
76	£	Mont-Ferrant Blanes Nature 1997 Cava Extra Brut
76	£	Juvé & Camps, Reserva de la Familia 1997 Cava Brut Nature
74	£	Castellblanch Brut Zero NV Cava Brut Reserva
74	£	Bohigas NV Cava Brut Nature
74	£	Duc de Foix NV Cava Brut Nature Rosado
73	£	Marques de Gelida NV Cava Brut Nature
72	£	Joan Raventós Rosell NV Cava Brut Nature
70	£	Sumarroca 1997 Cava Brut Nature Gran Reserva

Cava Extra-Brut

Extra-Brut may have up to six grams per litre of residual sugar.

| 80 | £ | Torreblanca 1999 Cava Extra Brut Reserva |
| 76 | £ | Masblanc NV Cava Extra Brut |

Cava Brut

Interestingly the four highest scoring wines are all non-vintage, as were the three highest-scoring Cavas from previous edition (see the main Cava introduction above).

80	£	Torreblanca NV Cava Brut
80	£	Raimat Chardonnay NV Cava Brut
80	££	Jaume de Codorníu NV Cava Brut
79	£	Vallformosa NV Cava Brut
79	£	Gramona, Imperial 1997 Cava Brut Gran Reserva
79	£	Gramona, Imperial 1998 Cava Brut Gran Reserva
78	£	Gala de Vallformosa 1998 Cava Brut
78	£	Codorníu Cuvée Raventós NV Cava Brut
77	£	Freixenet Cuvée D.S. 1996 Cava Brut
77	£	Naveran 1998 Cava Brut Reserva
77	£	Sumarroca 1998 Cava Brut Reserva
76	£	Castellblanch Gran Castell NV Cava Brut Gran Reserva
76	£	Marques de Gelida NV Cava Brut Reserva
76	£	Agustí Torelló Mata 1998 Cava Brut Reserva
75	£	Torre Oria NV Cava Brut Reserva
75	£	Eudald Massana Noya NV Cava Brut Nature Reserva
75	£	Ferret NV Cava Brut Reserva
75	£	Paul Cheneau NV Cava Brut
75	£	Cuvée 21 de Parxet NV Cava Brut
74	£	Castell de Vilarnau 1997 Cava Brut Gran Reserva
72	£	Cristalino NV Cava Brut
72	£	Chandon NV Cava Brut
70	£	Castillo de Perelada NV Cava Brut Reserva
70	£	Castell de Vilarnau NV Cava Brut

South Africa

For the very first time in three year two Cap Classique wines have matched the quality of a very good Champagne. In the first edition Nicky Krone achieved this with two vintages of Krone Borealis. This time Pieter Ferreira of Graham Beck has done the same. Cap Classique has the potential to develop internationally, but it won't do so until there are at least ten-times as many producers as there are now. Only when a critical mass of producers begin to push each other forward will we know what the true potential of Cap Classique actually is.

Remember!

75 Points
'Any sparkling wine other than Champagne that receives this score
is not just interesting, but good enough to grace the table of a
self-confessed Champagne addict.'
Tom Stevenson
Don't restrict your choice to 90 point wines – I don't!

85	(£)	Private Vintners Limited Release 1995 Pinot Noir, Cap Classique
85	(£)(£)	Graham Beck 1996 Brut Blanc de Blancs, Cap Classique
83	(£)	Krone Borealis 1994 Brut, Cap Classique
82	(£)	Graham Beck NV Pinot Noir – Chardonnay Brut, Cap Classique
80	(£)	Morgenhof 1997 Brut, Cap Classique
80	(£)	Graham Beck NV Cuvée Two Thousand, Cap Classique
78	(£)	J.C. Le Roux 1996 Chardonnay, Cap Classique
76	(£)	Villiera 1998 Brut Natural Chardonnay, Cap Classique
75	(£)	Villiera NV Tradition Brut, Cap Classique
75	(£)	Buitenverwachting NV Brut, Cap Classique
74	(£)	Krone Borealis 1998 Brut, Cap Classique
72	(£)	Villiera NV Brut Rosé, Cap Classique

United States of America

California was the first New World area in which a Champagne house set up a serious méthode champenoise operation, when Moët established Domaine Chandon in 1973. This state still leads the way, but with Washington and Oregon (not tasted this year) in the wings.

91	££££	Roederer Estate L'Ermitage 1994 Brut
91	£££££	Domaine Carneros by Taittinger 1995 Le Rêve
90	£££	Gloria Ferrer 1994 Royal Cuvée Brut
90	££££	Roederer Estate L'Ermitage 1996 Brut
90	£££££	Iron Horse 1991 Brut
89	£££	Gloria Ferrer 1993 Royal Cuvée Brut
89	£££££	Domaine Carneros by Taittinger 1994 Le Rêve Blanc de Blancs
88	£££	Iron Horse 1997 Blanc de Blancs
85	£££	Mumm Cuvée Napa 1994 Winery Lake
85	£££	Mumm Cuvée Napa NV Sparkling Pinot Noir
85	£££	Roederer Estate NV Rosé Brut
85	£££	Iron Horse 1995 Classic Vintage Brut
85	££££	Mountain Dome NV Cuvée Forté
85	££££	Mumm Cuvée Napa 1996 DVX Brut
85	££££	J 1994 Brut (*magnum*)
83	£££	Mountain Dome 1995 Brut
83	££	J 1996 Brut
82	£££	Schramsberg 1997 Blanc de Blancs
80	£££	Gloria Ferrer NV Carneros Rosé
80	£££	Mumm Cuvée Napa NV Brut Prestige
80	££	Roederer Estate NV Brut
80	£££	Domaine Carneros by Taittinger NV Brut
80	£££	Iron Horse 1996 Russian Cuvée
80	££££	Etoile NV Brut
79	£££	Thornton NV Cuvée de Frontignan
78	££	Mountain Dome NV Brut
78	£££	Jepson NV Blanc de Blancs
78	£££	Mumm Cuvée Napa NV Blanc de Noirs
77	£££	Mumm Cuvée Napa NV Blanc de Blancs
77	£££	Thornton NV Millennium Cuvée
77	£££	Iron Horse 1996 Classic Vintage Brut
76	£££	Mirabelle NV Brut, Schramsberg
76	£££	Gloria Ferrer NV Brut
76	£££	Thornton NV Brut Rosé
75	££	Mumm Cuvée Napa 1995 Brut
75	££	Domaine Chandon NV Blanc de Noirs
75	££	Korbel 1998 Natural Chardonnay Champagne
75	£££	Gloria Ferrer NV Blanc de Noirs
75	£££	Pacific Echo NV Brut, Mendocino County
75	£££	Iron Horse NV Brut Rosé
72	££	Chateau Frank 1996 Brut
70	££	Shadow Creek by Chandon NV Blanc de Noirs
70	£££	Thornton NV Natural Brut Reserve
70	£££	Chateau Biltmore 1998 Blanc de Blancs Brut

A-Z of Tasting Notes

In a number of notes I refer to the Annual Champagne Tasting and the SAA Champagne Tasting. The Annual Champagne Tasting is a trade event that is held in London at the end of March every year. Most of the big Champagne names are represented, but very few of the smaller growers attend. I do not rely on my notes from this event for various reason, not the least being that the tasting is not blind, but I find it useful to cross-reference notes with those made elsewhere. When comparing versions of the same cuvée at the London Annual Champagne Tasting to those submitted specifically to this Guide's tasting, any differences found in my notes are likely to be due to the former being an older disgorgement. In the case of non-vintage cuvées it might be exactly the same blend with just a few months more ageing after disgorgement (thus a few months less on yeast lees) or it could be the previous blend based on an earlier harvest. The SAA Champagne Tasting is organised by Michael Fridjhon on behalf of South African Airways. All the Champagnes are (or should be) designated Grand Cru and thus the emphasis is on smaller growers, the object being to select Champagnes for service on board. I give my services free.

Attention!

Champagne and sparkling wine producers:
If you are not already in contact with the author, but would like to submit wines for consideration in future editions, please contact Tom Stevenson at:

tom.fizz.stevenson@ntlworld.com

Warning:
Any other unsolicited mail received at this address will be ignored.

Please note that recommendation in this guide involves no charge whatsoever beyond the cost of the samples and their delivery.

Ackerman-Laurance

19 rue Léopold Palustre
St-Hilaire-St-Florent
49400 Saumur
France
Phone (241) 53.03.21
Fax (241) 53.03.29

72 Ackerman NV Cuvée Privée,
Crémant de Loire Brut
Far better on the palate than the
nose, with perfumed fruit and a
slightly fat finish.
Drink upon purchase.
Ⓔ Local Price **40FF**

74 Ackerman Laurance NV
Saumur 1811, Brut
This year's release is back on form
with a very fresh, light and crisply
fruity wine. A touch elevated, but
totally clean.
Drink upon purchase.
Ⓔ Local Price **30FF**

70 Ackerman Laurance NV
Privilège Brut, Crémant de Loire
Fresh and fruity.
Drink upon purchase.
Ⓔ Local Price **31FF**

74 Ackerman Laurance NV
1811 Vouvray Brut
A distinctly lighter cuvée than the
1811 Brut Saumur, with seemingly
younger, less elevated fruit.
Drink upon purchase.
Ⓔ Local Price **31FF**

75 Ackerman Laurance NV Cuvée
Excellence, Saumur Brut
Full and rich, yet crisp and clean.
Drink upon purchase.
Ⓔ Local Price **44FF**

74 Ackerman Laurance NV Cuvée
Excellence, Crémant de Loire Brut
Elevated fruit, very soft and
creamy on the finish, with a
somewhat sweet finish. Ideal for
those guests who talk dry, drink

sweet. Drink upon purchase.
Ⓔ Local Price **49FF**

71 Ackerman 1996 Cuvée
Jean-Baptiste, Saumur Brut
This 1996 is pushing the bounds
of its optimum shelf-life, but it
still has plenty of fruit and even
a touch a pepperiness.
Drink upon purchase.
Ⓔ Local Price **45FF**

Adelseck

Weingut Carl Adelseck
Saarstrasse 41
55424 Münster-Sarmsheim
Germany
Phone (6721) 97440
Fax (6721) 974422

75 Carl Adelseck 1998 Juwel Brut
Nicely lifted Riesling fruit with a
creamy aftertaste. (100% Riesling,
bottle-fermented, Nahe)
Drink now-2002.
Ⓔ Local Price **DM16**

77 Carl Adelseck 1998 Juwel Trocken
Mouth-tingling fresh, zippy-zingy
fruit. (100% Riesling, bottle-
fermented, Nahe)
Drink now-2002.
Ⓔ Local Price **DM16**

Affaltrach, Schloss

See Baumann

Agrapart

Champagne Agrapart
57 avenue Jean-Jaurès
51190 Avize
France
Phone (326) 57.51.38
Fax (326) 57.05.06

*Rarely seen on export markets,
but there is usually one cuvée
worth buying.*

85 Agrapart & Fils NV Brut
❗ Blanc de Blancs Grand Cru
I much preferred this rich
and delicious non-vintage to
Agrapart's 1995 vintage blanc
de blancs. Drink now-2004.
Ⓔ Local Price **91FF**

Albrecht

Lucien Albrecht
9 Grand'Rue
68500 Orschwihr
France
Phone (389) 76.95.18
Fax (389) 76.20.22

---

76 Lucien Albrecht NV Crémant
❗ d'Alsace Brut
Very fresh, with elevated fruit,
but needs more acidity for higher
score. Drink now-2002.
Ⓔ Local Price **43FF**

Alsina

Alsina & Sardà
Barri Les Tarumbes
S/N El Pla del Penedès
08733 Barcelona
Spain
Phone (93) 898.81.32
Fax (93) 898.86.71

---

77 Alsina Sardà Sello 1996 Cava Brut
❗ Nature Gran Reserva
Creamy-vanilla fruit, good acidity.
Drink now-2002.
Ⓔ Local Price **1,300 Ptas**

Anheuser

Weingut Paul Anheuser
Strombergerstrasse 15-19
55545 Bad Kreuznach
Germany
Phone (6714) 2571

---

74 Paul Anheuser 1996 Nahe Riesling
❗ Sekt Trocken
Fine, ripe Riesling fruit, quite
sweetish, but with an assertive
finish. (100% Riesling, tank-
fermented, Nahe) Now-2002.
Ⓔ Local Price **DM14**

Antica Cantina Fratta

Via Fontana
11 – 25040 Monticelli Brusati
Italy
Phone (30) 652661
Fax (30) 652661

---

75 Antica Cantina Fratta 1998
▶ Franciacorta Brut
The preview sample had very
fresh and clean fruit that was
well structured and potentially
complex, but would have
benefited from higher acidity,
lower pH. Drink 2002-2003.
Ⓔ Local Price **24,000 Lira**

Arione

Via Luigi Bosca 135
14053 Canelli
Italy
Phone (141) 823172
Fax (141) 835172

---

78 Arione NV Piemonte
❗ Brachetto Dolce
Not as sweet as other Brachetti,
this wine has a tangy, almost
acidic finish. Could be interesting
with food, particularly duck
with plum or cherry sauce.
Drink upon purchase.
Ⓔ

Attention!

*To submit samples for review
see page 52*

Arnould

Champagne Michel Arnould
& Fils
28 rue de Mailly
51360 Verzenay
France
Phone (326) 49.40.06
Fax (326) 49.44.61

87 Michel Arnould & Fils NV Brut
Grand Cru
I much preferred the fresh,
fruity new release not due to be
distributed until March 2002 to
the current one, which is too
oxidative. It is the new release
that is scored here.
Drink now-2002.
ⓔ Local Price 77FF

Arras

See BRL Hardy

Ayala

Champagne Ayala
2 Boulevard du Nord
51160 Aÿ-Champagne
France
Phone (326) 55.15.44
Fax (326) 51.09.04

*This former good-value grande
marque is back on form, but I
would like to see what its sous
marque Montebello is like
these days. Montebello is also,
technically, a former grande
marque and has always had
better exposure in the US than
anywhere else.*

84 Ayala NV Brut
Rather straightforward fruit, but
nonetheless enjoyable, fresh, crisp
and easy-drinking.
Drink upon purchase.

ⓔⓔ Local Price 135FF

85 Ayala 1996 Brut Blanc de Blancs
The beautifully fresh, floral-
perfumed Chardonnay aromas are
reflected in the fruit on the palate,
which is softer than most 1996s,
but that should suit some.
Drink now-2004.
ⓔⓔ Local Price 175FF

Badischer Winzerkeller

Burgunderplatz 1
77876 Kappelrodeck
Germany
Phone (7842) 99380
Fax (7842) 8763

70 Badischer Winzerkeller 1996 Brut
Entry level quality of Pinot
Blanc Sekt in a J. Schram
(of Schramsberg, California)
lookalike bottle and presentation.
(100% Weißburgunder, bottle-
fermented, Baden) Now-2002.
ⓔ Local Price DM24

Bagnadore

See Barone Pizzini

Balnaves

Balnaves of Coonawarra
Main Road
Coonawarra
SA 5263
Australia
Phone (8) 8737 2946
Fax (8) 8737 2945

84 Balnaves of Coonawarra 1999
Sparkling Cabernet
Heaps of blackcurrant overlaid
by a ton and a half of cedary oak
with a good smack of sweet fruit
on finish. Drink upon purchase.
ⓔⓔ Local Price A$28

Banfi

Principe Banfi
Via Per Iseo
25030 villa di Erbusco
Italy
Phone (30) 7750387
Fax (30) 7750387

78 Rosa Regale 2000
Brachetto d'Acqui
Very fresh and sweet with a nice
tangy finish.
Drink upon purchase.
ⓔ

Banrock Station

See BRL Hardy

Bara

Champagne Paul Bara
4 Rue Yvonnet
51150 Bouzy
France
Phone (326) 57.00.50
Fax (326) 57.81.24

88 Paul Bara NV Bouzy
Grand Cru Brut
Floral aromas, with very fine
fruit on the palate. Really quite
full-bodied following such a
delicate nose. Quite fat and lush
in the nicest sense. Will develop
gracefully. Drink now-2004.
ⓔ Local Price **91FF**

Barbero

Pietro Barbero
Via San Giuseppe 19
14050 Moasca
Italy
Phone (141) 856484
Fax (141) 856484

85 Conte di Cavour NV Asti
Really quite full-bodied for an
Asti, but the mousse is so smooth
and cushiony that the sweet
– rather than intensely sweet –
fruit remains light and elegant.
Drink upon purchase.
ⓔ Local Price **7,400 Lira**

Barboglio DeGaioncelli

See Gaioncelli

Bardfield Vineyard

The Great Lodge
Great Bardfield
Essex
CM74QD
Great Britain
Phone (1371) 810776
Fax (1371) 811398

75 Bardfield 1998 Extra-Brut
I never thought I would say
hooray for German crosses, but
this wine came after a trough of
dull and dirty Cava, so the fresh,
aromatic character was a blessed
relief! Follow this by a nicely
balanced dosage and nothing
hollow mid-palate (as can so
often happen with fizz made from
German crosses) and I have to say
this wine turned me from a
grumpy taster to a happy bunny
in no time at all.
Drink upon purchase.
ⓔ

Barfontarc

See Baroville

Barmes Buecher

Domaine Barmes Buecher
30 rue Ste Gertrude
68920 Wettolsheim
France
Phone (389) 80.62.92
Fax (389) 79.30.80

75 **Domaine Barmes Buecher 1998**
❢ **Crémant d'Alsace Brut**
Big, rich and tasty, with excellent
acidity and firm, but fine mousse.
Drink now-2003.
Ⓔ Local Price **54FF**

Baron Albert

Champagne Baron Albert
Grand Porteron
02310 Charly-sur-Marne
France
Phone (323) 82.02.65
Fax (323) 82.02.44

*The best performance in years
from this house.*

85 **Baron Albert NV Brut Tradition,**
❢ **Cuvée de l'An 2000**
What struck me most about this
wine was its soft, fluffy mousse,
which gives the fruit a billowy,
breezy freshness. Excellent acidity.
Drink now-2003.
ⒺⒺ

83 **Baron Albert NV Brut Carte d'Or**
❢ Firmer mousse supporting crisp
fruit. Drink upon purchase.
Ⓔ Local Price **80FF**

? **Cuvée Jean de la Fontaine
1995 Brut**
Unripe strawberry boiled-sweets!
Wait and see.
ⒺⒺ

85 **La Préférence de Baron Albert**
➤ **1994 Brut Millésime**
One of the better 1994s, ironically

this is cleaner and better focused
than other generally superior
vintages of La Préférence, with a
very crisp, clean finish.
Drink 2002-2004.
ⒺⒺ

Barone Pizzini

3 Via Brescia
25050 Timoline di Cortefranca
Italy
Phone (30) 984136
Fax (30) 9884650

76 **Barone Pizzini NV**
❢ **Franciacorta Brut**
Very fresh on the nose with
plenty of fruit on the palate and
a definite indication that this wine
will go toasty. Drink now-2002.
Ⓔ Local Price **21,000 Lira**

75 **Barone Pizzini NV**
❢ **Franciacorta Rosé**
Very fresh and silky with an
ultra-soft mousse of the finest
bubbles, although well-honed
palates might pick up a certain
touch of green and a hint of
pepperiness in the background.
Drink now-2002.
Ⓔ Local Price **21,500 Lira**

78 **Barone Pizzini NV**
❢ **Franciacorta Extra Dry**
The freshest and best Extra Dry
style of Franciacorta tasted this
year, this wine's mousse is so soft
and velvety it is more satèn than
most sold as satèn.
Drink now-2002.
Ⓔ Local Price **22,500 Lira**

82 **Barone Pizzini NV**
❢ **Franciacorta Satèn**
Toasty-mellow that's soft and
round, yet fresh and crisp.
Drink now-2002.
Ⓔ Local Price **29,500 Lira**

82 Bagnadore Io 1995
Franciacorta Brut
An unusual, but seductive peach
and coconut cream aroma is
followed through on the palate
where toasty aromas mingle with
the fresh, peachy-coconutty fruit.
Drink now-2002.
Ⓔ Local Price **30,600 Lira**

Baroville

Champagne G. de Barfontarc
Producteurs de Champagne de
la Côte des Bars
CV de la Region de Baroville
10200 Baroville
France
Phone (325) 27.07.09
Fax (325) 27.23.00

82 G. de Barfontarc NV Extra
Quality Brut
A fine, clean, delicately rich
Champagne that should go
biscuity. Drink now-2003.
ⒺⒺ

Barramundi

See Cranswick Estate

Batasiolo

Frazione Annunziata 87
12064 La Morra
Italy
Phone (173) 501301
Fax (173) 509258

71 Batasiolo Dosage Zéro
1994 Millésimé
Clean, fresh and much preferred
to the 1992. Drink upon purchase.
Ⓔ

Baumann

Schloss Affaltrach
Dr. Reinhold Baumann & Co
Am Ordensschloss 15-21
74182 Obersulm
Germany
Phone (7130) 474444

70 Schloss Affaltrach,
Dr. Rheinhold Baumann 1998
Rose Extra Trocken
Fresh, clran, zippy. (100%
Spätburgunder, transfer-method,
Württemberg) Drink upon
purchase.
Ⓔ Local Price **DM18**

Baumann Zirgel

5 rue du Vignoble
68630 Mittelwihr
France
Phone (389) 47.90.40
Fax (389) 49.04.89

72 Baumann Zirgel 1999
Crémant d'Alsace Brut
Crisp lemony fruit, lovely mousse,
very soft, microscopic bubble,
creamy texture, but pure, clean
fruit. Drink now-2002.
Ⓔ Local Price **45FF**

Baur

4 rue Roger Frémeaux
68420 Voegtlinshoffen
France
Phone (389) 49.30.97
Fax (389) 49.21.37

72 Baur 1998 Blanc de Noirs,
Crémant d'Alsace
Typical blanc de noirs colour,
fresh and tasty on the palate with
excellent Pinot fruit. However, this
wine threatens to go oxidative, so
if you do not care for that style,
drink it up while it is still fruit-

driven. Drink upon purchase.
ⓔ Local Price **38FF**

Bava

Strada Monferrato 2
14023 Cocconato
Italy
Phone (141) 907083
Fax (141) 907085

---

85 Bava NV Malvasia di Castelnuovo
ⓘ don Bosco, Rosé Dolce
Although still very much in the
sweet red Moscato vein, this
Malvasia is fresher and more
perfumed than most Brachetti
tend to be. Drink upon purchase.
ⓔ Local Price **14,000 Lira**

Bearsted Vineyard

Caring Lane
Bearsted
Maidstone
Kent
Great Britain
Phone (1622) 736974
Fax (1622) 736974

---

80 Bearsted NV Brut
➤ The current release was smooth
and fruity with a satisfying finish
and firm aftertaste (74 points),
but the pre-commercial sample
of next release was even better.
Due to be launched in May 2002
or thereabouts, it was
understandably young and
raw on the nose, but the palate
shouted a far superior quality
than that found in the current
cuvée. The fruit, acidity, balance
and mousse are all wonderful.
Drink 2002-2004.
ⓔⓔ Local Price **£13**

Beaumet

Champagne Beaumet
3 rue Malakoff
51207 Epernay
France
Phone (326) 59.50.10
Fax (326) 54.78.52

---

84 Beaumet NV Cuvée Brut
ⓘ A surprisingly good, if simple,
fruity style with no amylic aromas
to debase the quality.
Drink now-2003.
ⓔⓔ

85 Beaumet 1995 Cuvée Brut
ⓘ A lovely clean Champagne with
very rich, easy-drinking fruit.
Drink now-2005.
ⓔ ⓔ

Beaumont des Crayères

Champagne Beaumont des
Crayères
64 rue de la Liberté
Mardeuil 51318 Epernay
France
Phone (326) 55.29.40
Fax (326) 54.26.30

*Except for Nostalgie, this small
cooperative has not performed
as well as it normally does.*

---

84 Beaumont des Crayères
ⓘ **1995 Fleur de Prestige, Brut**
Preferred to the Nuit d'Or, which
threatens to go too oxidative.
Although this Champagne also
has an oxidative tendency, there is
an indication that it will also pick
up some true biscuity complexity.
Drink now-2004.
ⓔ Local Price **99FF**

84 Beaumont des Crayères
ⓘ **1995 Fleur de Rosé, Brut**
Creamy-cherry fruit. Should go
biscuity. Drink now-2003.

ⓔ Local Price **99FF**

83   Nostalgie 1995 Brut
➤ Potentially complex. Lovely
mousse. Drink 2002-2005.
ⓔⓔ Local Price **113FF**

Beblenheim

CV de Beblenheim
14 rue de Hoen
68980 Beblenheim
France
Phone (389) 47.90.02
Fax (389) 47.86.85

---

75   CV de Beblenheim NV
❢ **Heimberger, Crémant d'Alsace**
Fresh, fruity and easy to drink
with Alsation pure fruit flavours.
Drink upon purchase.
ⓔ Local Price **33FF**

75   CV de Beblenheim NV
❢ **Baron de Hoen, Crémant d'Alsace**
Sweet and ripe with some finesse,
the sweetness being of grapes, not
sugar. Drink now-2002.
ⓔ Local Price **35FF**

74   CV de Beblenheim 1998
❢ **Blanc de Noirs Heimberger,**
Crémant d'Alsace
Raspberry-ripple nose, nicely
balanced fruit and acidity on
palate, just let down by a short
finish. Drink now-2002.
ⓔ Local Price **38FF**

Beck, Graham

Graham Beck Wines
Robertson 6705
South Africa
Phone (23) 626 1214
Fax (23) 626 5164

*Gradually, relentlessly, Graham
Beck is establishing itself at the
very top of South Africa's Cap
Classique quality league.*

---

80   Graham Beck NV Cuvée Two
❢ **Thousand, Cap Classique**
Noticeably lifted aromas waft
around rich, strawberry'ish Pinot
fruit in this copper-tinged cuvée.
Drink now-2002.
ⓔ Local Price **R50**

82   Graham Beck NV Pinot Noir –
❢ **Chardonnay Brut, Cap Classique**
A touch less lifted than Beck's
Cuvée Two Thousand, this also
has a more classic structure, with
excellent acidity. Drink now-2002.
ⓔ Local Price **R50**

85   Graham Beck 1996 Brut
❢ **Blanc de Blancs, Cap Classique**
Absolutely classic nose, which is
bulging at the seams with great
autolytic finesse, followed by
excellent New World Chardonnay
fruit on the palate. Has the
potential to develop.
Drink now-2004.
ⓔⓔ Local Price **R57**

Becker

Jean Becker
68340 Zellenberg
France
Phone (389) 47.90.16
Fax (389) 47.99.57

*Becker's fizz is more of an
industrious effort than a
natural passion. This is not a
house where everything is pure
gold, but there are always
plenty of nuggets to be found
in the still wines by those who
are diligent enough to taste
through the entire range. The
real passion here is for vins
biologique, a relatively new
development, and some of the
wines from the 1999 vintage are
truly inspired.*

77 Jean Becker 1999 B de Becker,
Crémant d'Alsace
Fresh, floral aroma, very fine,
nicely crisp fruit, granny smith
apples on finish. Very soft, creamy
mousse. Drink now-2002.
Ⓔ Local Price **51FF**

Bellavista

Via Bellavista
5 – 25030 Erbusco
Italy
Phone (30) 7762000
Fax (30) 7760386

76 Bellavista NV
Cuvée Brut, Franciacorta
A very clever blend with a silky
mousse supporting fruit that is
one step away from having a green
edge, but works exceedingly well.
Drink now-2002.
ⒺⒺ Local Price **36,000 Lira**

75 Bellavista NV Gran
Cuvée Satèn, Franciacorta
Very fresh, creamy-malo fruit.
Should go biscuity.
Drink now-2002.
ⒺⒺ Local Price **50,000 Lira**

80 Bellavista 1997
Gran Cuvée Brut, Franciacorta
Fresh and elegant with lovely soft
fruit for current drinking.
Drink upon purchase.
ⒺⒺ Local Price **45,000 Lira**

72 Bellavista 1997 Gran
Cuvée Brut Rosé, Franciacorta
A Roederer-like pale rosé colour,
with fresh, soft fruit hinting of
poached pears.
Drink upon purchase.
ⒺⒺ Local Price **50,000 Lira**

Benoit Lahaye

See Lahaye

Bergweiler

Weingut Dr. Pauly Bergweiler
Gestade 15
54470 Bernkastel-Kues
Germany
Phone (6531) 3002
Fax (6531) 7201

70 Dr. Pauly Bergweiler 1995
Zeltinger Himmelreich Brut
Firm, zippy and youthful for its
age, yet will still benefit from
some post-disgorgement ageing.
(100% Riesling, bottle-fermented,
Mosel-Saar-Ruwer) Now-2003.
Ⓔ Local Price **DM29**

Bersano

Piazza Dante 21
14049 Nizza Monferrato
Italy
Phone (141) 721273
Fax (141) 701706

78 Bersano NV Brachetto d'Acqui
Dolce
Some red-winey character to this
intensely sweet, Moscato fizz.
Drink upon purchase.
Ⓔ

84 Bersano NV Asti Dolce
Very fresh and fluffy.
Drink upon purchase.
Ⓔ Local Price **9,900 Lira**

Attention!

*To submit samples for review
see page 52*

Bersi Serlini

Via Cerretto
7 – 25050 Provaglio di Iseo
Italy
Phone (30) 9823338
Fax (30) 983234

75   Bersi Serlini NV Franciacorta Brut
Perfumed fruit, not too brut,
but has a touch more finesse and
freshness than Bersi Serlini's cuvée
No. 4. Drink now-2002.
Ⓔ Local Price **19,900 Lira**

76   Bersi Serlini NV Cuvée No.4,
Franciacorta Brut
Very similar to the basic brut,
just a touch deeper in colour with
slightly richer and somewhat more
mellow fruit. Drink now-2002.
Ⓔ Local Price **25,000 Lira**

Besserat de Bellefon

Champagne Besserat de
Bellefon
19 Avenue de Champagne
51205 Epernay
France
Phone (326) 59.51.00
Fax (326) 59.51.19

84   Besserat de Bellefon NV
Brut Grande Tradition
Very clean, excellent acidity, nice
lean structure. Should go lemony-
toasty. Drink now-2003.
ⒺⒺ Local Price **150FF**

85   Besserat de Bellefon NV
Cuvée des Moines, Brut
Deeper fruit of more potential
complexity than the Grande
Tradition. Fine, pin-cushion
mousse. Drink now-2003.
ⒺⒺ Local Price **160FF**

80   Besserat de Bellefon 1995
Brut Grande Tradition
Will go toasty, but lacks the

finesse for a higher score.
Drink 2002-2004.
ⒺⒺ Local Price **170FF**

Bestheim

3 rue du Gal de Gaulle
68630 Bennwihr
France
Phone (389) 49.09.29
Fax (389) 49.09.20

70   Bestheim NV
Crémant d'Alsace Brut
A sweetish, light, fresh fruity
fizz that's absolutely clean and
not at all aggressive.
Drink upon purchase.
Ⓔ Local Price **38FF**

72   Bestheim 1998 Madame Sans
Gene, Crémant d'Alsace
Crisp, tangy fruit.
Drink now-2002.
Ⓔ Local Price **45FF**

Bettoni Cazzago, Conti

See Cazzago

Bianchi

See Villa di A. Bianchi

Bickensohl

Wg. Bickensohl
Neunlindenstrasse 25
79235 Vogtsburg-Bickensohl
Germany
Phone (7662) 93110
Fax (7662) 931150

71   Wg. Bickensohl 1999 Bickensohler
Pinot blanc de Noir Brut
A sweet, amylic centre to clean,

fresh fruit. (100% Spätburgunder, bottle-fermented, Baden.)
Drink now-2002.
Ⓔ Local Price **DM18**

Billecart-Salmon

Champagne Billecart-Salmon
40 rue Carnot
51160 Mareuil-sur-Aÿ
France
Phone (326) 52.60.22
Fax (326) 52.64.88

One of Champagne's best-known secrets.

88 Billecart-Salmon NV Brut Réserve
Fruit-driven all the way, yet not lacking in finesse or complexity. A very satisfying non-vintage. Drink now-2004.
ⒺⒺ Local Price **148FF**

89 Billecart-Salmon NV
Blanc de Blancs Brut Réserve
Really quite fat and yet deeply concentrated. Although easy to drink now, this will be a stunner in two years time. Drink now-2005.
ⒺⒺⒺ Local Price **221FF**

90 Billecart-Salmon 1995 Cuvée
Nicolas François Billecart, Brut
Wonderfully rich, complete and satisfying fruit of great complexity and finesse.
Drink now-2011.
ⒺⒺⒺ Local Price **345FF**

90 Billecart-Salmon 1995 Cuvée
Elisabeth Salmon, Brut Rosé
The wonderful finesse in this Champagne is emphasised by the ultra-smooth, velvety mousse, which underpins exquisitely fresh and soft cherry fruit.
Drink now-2006.
ⒺⒺⒺⒺ Local Price **510FF**

Biltmore Estate

One North Pack Square
Asheville
NC 28801
USA
Phone (800) 624 1575

70 Chateau Biltmore 1998
Blanc de Blancs Brut
In the four years since I last tasted Chateau Biltmore, it has gone from fresh and amylic, but lacking acidity and interest to being just as fresh, not as amylic, but still lacking acidity, although its fattish fruit and creamy aftertaste are interesting enough to warrant inclusion in this guide. Hopefully the progress will continue.
Drink upon purchase.
ⒺⒺ Local Price **$25**

Blanck

Domaine Paul Blanck
32 Grand'Rue
68240 Kientzheim
France
Phone (389) 78.23.56
Fax (389) 47.16.45

75 Domaine Paul Blanck 1999
Crémant d'Alsace, Extra Brut
Tasted on its lees. Fresh, floral aroma. Fuller and richer than most Crémant d'Alsace, but really needs more zippy acidity to age with finesse. Drink now-2002.
Ⓔ

Blin, H.

Champagne H. Blin
5 rue de Verdun
51700 Vincelles
France
Phone (326) 58.20.04
Fax (326) 58.29.67

88 **H. Blin & Co NV Brut Tradition**
I was not impressed by the estery, raw sample submitted this year, but earlier in 2001 I had tasted a hugely superior version of this cuvée at the Annual Champagne Tasting. It had lovely fruit and was so rich that it was almost sweet, with some biscuity complexity and a dusting of vanilla finesse. This nicely aged wine was obviously an earlier release with good landed age, yet it was still very fresh. If you can pick up a well-cellared bottle of the previous release, you will see that it deserves this high score. Drink now-2004.
Ⓔ Local Price **87FF**

86 **H. Blin & Co 1995 Brut**
A distinctive Champagne that will go biscuity-honeyed in a couple of years. Excellent acidity.
Drink 2003-2005.
ⒺⒺ Local Price **110FF**

Blin, R.

Champagne R. Blin
11 rue du Point du Jour
51140 Trigny
France
Phone (326) 03.10.973
Fax (326) 03.19.63

85 **R. Blin et Fils 1993 Brut Millésime**
Anyone who likes toast Champagne will adore this toasty going coffee cuvée and its intense flavour, assertive acidity and lean structure assure its long life.
Drink now-2006.
ⒺⒺ Local Price **105FF**

Attention!

To submit samples for review see page 52

Blondel

Champagne Th. Blondel
Les Monts Fournois
51500 Ludes
France
Phone (326) 03.43.92
Fax (326) 03.44.10

84 **Th. Blondel NV Brut Rosé, Premier Cru**
Very fresh aromas, a touch amylic, but that should disperse. Attractive red. Now-2002.
Ⓔ Local Price **90FF**

84 **Th. Blondel 1995 Vieux Millésime, Chardonnay Brut Premier Cru**
Soft and flowery with a pin-cushion mousse and a creamy finish. Drink now-2003.
ⒺⒺ Local Price **110FF**

Bloomsbury

See Ridgeview Estate

Blue Pyrenees Estate

Vinoca Road
Avoca
Vic. 3467
Australia
Phone (3) 5465 3202
Fax (3) 5465 3529

Rémy-Cointreau has owned this Victorian outpost since 1969 when, of course, the parent company was Rémy-Martin. The wines have shown glimpses of excellence over the last 10-12 years, but really should be doing better, more consistently, by now.

74 **Blue Pyrenees Reserve Brut NV Chardonnay**

Pinot Noir Pinot Meunier
Nice tasty tart fruit that will go
toasty. Drink 2002-2003.
ⓔ Local Price A$25

80 **Blue Pyrenees NV Midnight**
❢ **Cuvée Chardonnay**
Excellent richness, with classic
lean structure and lovely fresh
fruit. Drink now-2004.
ⓔⓔ Local Price A$30

Boesch

Domaine Léon Boesch
6 rue St. Blaise
68250 Westhalten
France
Phone (389) 47.01.83
Fax (389) 47.64.95

73 **Domaine Léon Boesch 1998**
❢ **Cuvée Réservée, Crémant d'Alsace**
Perfumed fruit, Pinot noir?
Drink now-2002.
ⓔ Local Price 58FF

76 **Domaine Léon Boesch 1996**
❢ **Cuvée Réservée, Crémant d'Alsace**
Rich, fruity with excellent acidity.
Drink now-2002.
ⓔ Local Price 70FF

Bohigas

Fermi Bohigas
Can Macia
08711 Odena
Spain
Phone (93) 8032366
Fax (93) 8032366

74 **Bohigas NV Cava Brut Nature**
❢ There is a fresh pepperiness to
the fruit in this soft, easy drinking
Cava (1999-based).
Drink upon purchase.
ⓔ Local Price 850 Ptas

Bohn

Bernard Bohn
1 chemin du Leh
67140 Reichsfeld
France
Phone (388) 85.58.78
Fax (388) 57.84.88

78 **Bernard Bohn 1995 Rosé,**
❢ **Crémant d'Alsace**
The darkest Crémant d'Alsace
rosé I've ever seen, this cherry-red
fizz has tart-cherry fruit and a
fearsome finish. Drink now-2003.
ⓔ Local Price 40FF

73 **Bernard Bohn 1992 Crémant**
❢ **d'Alsace Brut** (*magnum*)
Some peachiness, very fruit driven
still. Touch lavender on finish.
Drink upon purchase.
ⓔⓔ Local Price 110FF

Boilleau

Champagne Michel Boilleau
2 route Nationale
Les Orgneux 02650 Fossoy
France
Phone (323) 71.93.54
Fax (323) 71.93.54

85 **Michel Boilleau NV Brut Réserve**
❢ Very fresh, crisp and lively fruit.
Superb acidity. Only Champagne
can produce fruit of this structure.
Drink now-2005.
ⓔ Local Price 71FF

82 **Michel Boilleau NV Cuvée**
❢ **Prestige, Brut**
More perfumed than the Brut
Réserve, but less crispness,
structure and lift. Probably
because this was a blend of
unexciting 1994 and very good
1995, whereas the Brut Réserve
is a blend of very good 1995 and
truly great 1996. By this reckoning
next year's cuvée Prestige should

be stunning! Drink now-2002.
Ⓔ Local Price 80FF

Boizel

Champagne Boizel
14 rue de Bernon
51200 Epernay
France
Phone (326) 55.21.51
Fax (326) 54.31.83

85 Boizel NV Brut Réserve
➤ This cuvée was nothing short
of sensational at the Annual
Champagne Tasting in March
2001. It had a Charles Heidsieck
type of richness with plenty of
finesse and vanilla complexity on
the finish (88 points). The sample
submitted to the Guide tasting
was obviously a younger blend,
showing plenty of flowery autolysis
on the nose with serious fruit on
the palate, but not quite in the
same class and needing a good
year to settle down.
Drink 2002-2004.
ⒺⒺ Local Price 125FF

83 Boizel NV Rosé Brut
➤ Fresh and fairly tasty.
Drink 2002-2004.
ⒺⒺ Local Price 135FF

84 Boizel NV Chardonnay Brut
❗ **Blanc de Blancs**
The nose could be fresher, but
the creamy-toasty fruit is not just
fresh on the palate, it's really quite
elegant. Drink now-2003.
ⒺⒺ Local Price 155FF

87 Boizel 1991 Joyau de France, Brut
➤ Definitely some early-picked
grapes here, but they should settle
down and mellow into toasty
fruit. The early-picked element
certainly does not detract from
the finesse of this Champagne.
Drink 2003-2007.

ⒺⒺⒺ Local Price 295FF

88 Boizel 1990 Cuvée Sous Bois, Brut
➤ The fruit in this cuvée has
always been very high in quality,
with excellent acidity for great
longevity, but this has been
let down by the oxidative nose.
Whether this is a matter of
disgorgement dates or simply
that the style is well and truly
oxidative I have no idea, but in
order to find out I hope to taste
this wine directly off its lees plus
as many disgorgements as possible
before next years's edition.
Drink now-2008.
Ⓔ Local Price 250FF

Bollenberg

Domaine du Bollenberg
Bollenberg
68250 Westhalten
France
Phone (389) 49.67.10
Fax (389) 49.76.16

75 Domaine du Bollenberg 1999
❗ **Eugène, Crémant d'Alsace**
Elevated fruit, quite rich, full and
chewy. Drink now-2002.
Ⓔ Local Price 41FF

Bollinger

Champagne Bollinger
16 rue Jules Lobet
51160 Aÿ-Champagne
France
Phone (326) 54.33.66
Fax (326) 54.85.59

*For the last two years my
advice to anyone worried about
certain disgorgements of 1982
RD, 1985 RD, 1988 RD was to
leave it in your cellar a few
years because when these wines
were first disgorged as Grand
Année they scored between 94*

Bollinger (cont.)

and 96 points, thus the quality of the core wine was not in question. Most of these disgorgements were between 24 March and 14 October 1999 and I also had problems with the 1992 Grand Année and 1990 Grand Année Rosé disgorged around this time, although 1979 RD disgorged on 25 March 1999 is and always has been a superb specimen (95 points). Although I have never specifically recommended any of these dodgy RDs, I did believe they would get better, but having recently retasted them, it is absolutely clear this will not happen. In all cases they are getting worse.

The final straw came at Decanter's Fine Wine Encounter in London, where I was signing copies when the Bollinger Masterclass broke up and a few one-time fans of this Champagne told me that most of the wines were unpleasant and bore no relation to the descriptions given by Bollinger's Ghislain de Montgolfier, who hosted the Masterclass. It was, of course, no surprise to me and I told them it would have been no surprise to them had they purchased this guide! Apparently no one in the Masterclass challenged Montgolfier, but there was a lot of muttering. This conversation was overheard by Steven Spurrier, who was also was signing books, and I told him that I would be visiting Bollinger in a few weeks specifically to discuss the problem. It was a difficult visit. I genuinely believe that no one

Bollinger (cont.)

at Bollinger knew a problem existed (it's called 'cellar palate') and although there has been no acknowledgement that it ever did, Montgolfier listened to everything I said. I do not think it was coincidence that Bollinger arranged a tasting for a select group of wine writers at Mentzendorff in March 2001. All the problem vintages were included, every wine was disgorged subsequent to my meeting with Montgolfier and they were as clean as a whistle.

That is the good news, but what of those readers who have dodgy disgorgements in their cellars? The only option as far as I am concerned is to return them and demand a refund. In particular you should check out any bottles of 1988 and 1985 RD disgorged on 14 October 1999; 1985 & 1982 RD disgorged on 24 March 1999; and any 1990 Grand Année Rosé or 1992 Grand Année purchased in mid-2000.

85 **Bollinger NV Special Cuvée, Brut**
At a select Mentzendorff tasting in March 2001 this wine was what can only be described for Bollinger as fruit-driven. True, there was a slightly oxidative aroma on the nose, but nothing like the excessively oxidative character that has been Special Cuvée's call sign for almost as long as I can remember, and with heaps of fine, clean fruit on the palate. Drink now-2004.
ⒺⒺ Local Price **190FF**

90 **Bollinger NV Special Cuvée, Brut**
(*magnum*)
Bollinger magnums always have

been more fruit-driven and Lot No. L024909 is in that vein, albeit with an almost excruciating level of acidity and so much autolysis on the nose that it's likely to blow your olfactory bulb away. Usually I can recommend magnums of Bollinger Special Cuvée for immediate drinking, but this specific Lot should not be broached for at least three years, after which it should mature slowly into a great Champagne. Drink 2004-2007.
ⓔⓔⓔ Local Price **400FF**

97 Bollinger 1995 Grande Année, Brut
This was a preview of the next vintage (due to be released prior to publication) and I was spellbound by its instantly complex, hugely intense fruit infused by stone-fruit-like acidity and aromatic hints of peach, with a huge, rich, creamy finish. Drink now-2021.
ⓔⓔⓔⓔ Local Price **350FF**

91 Bollinger 1995 Grande Année Rosé, Brut
Oak is quite dominant on the nose of the preview sample of this Champagne, but it is jammed-pack with high-octane Pinot fruit on the palate. All redcurrants and crunchy-piquant acidity, yet so rich that it is not unpleasantly sharp. Probably the best Bollinger Rosé I've tasted. Drink now-2003.
ⓔⓔⓔⓔ Local Price **350FF**

88 Bollinger 1992 Grande Année, Brut
Crisp, oak-edged fruit. Absolutely clean. Although drinking well now, this has all the makings of evolving into a truly exceptional 1992, but I am told that it will not become an RD. Drink now-2006.
ⓔⓔⓔⓔ Local Price **350FF**

98 Bollinger 1992 Vieilles Vignes Françaises, Blanc de Noirs Brut
It is amazing what overripe grapes from ungrafted wines can do to the character of a vintage in Champagne and here they have produced super-ripe fruit with big, rich, strawberry, raspberry and cassis flavours. This wine does not suit being too chilled, as it emphasises the wood to the detriment of the fruit. Drink now-2004.
ⓔⓔⓔⓔ Local Price **1230FF**

89 Bollinger 1988 R.D. Extra Brut
Still not ready, essentially because the acidity has a relatively high malic content, making this too austere to drink comfortably without at least another year's post-disgorgement aging. Drink 2002-2007.
ⓔⓔⓔⓔ Local Price **490FF**

95 Bollinger 1985 R.D. Extra Brut
After two years of questionable quality, current disgorgements of this vintage have been as clean as a whistle and almost as stunning as the original Grande Année disgorgement (96 points). Great concentration and high acidity dictate a long life, while an immaculate, soft, cushiony mousse makes the fruit extremely accessible for current drinking. Drink now-2016.
ⓔⓔⓔⓔ Local Price **980FF**

92 Bollinger 1982 R.D. Extra Brut
The opulence of 1982 fruit dominates the current digorgements, although it will still improve if kept. Drink now-2011.
ⓔⓔⓔⓔ
Local Price **1600FF**

? Bollinger 1981 R.D. Extra Brut
I fear that Bollinger might have missed the boat on this one.

The rumour perpetuated by Bollinger is that this was never commercialised as a Grande Année, but kept and released for the Millennium celebrations. The truth, however, is that it was sold as a Grande Année on the Italian market, but was withdrawn after complaints that it was too acidic. I took an interest in this vintage from an early stage and it was served over dinner chez Bollinger on numerous occasions over a 12 year period. Always the question was 'Do you think it is ready to release?' and as far as I'm concerned its optimum disgorgement would have been in the early 1990s. The problem back then was that this would have required a full Brut dosage of 15g/l, although it would still have tasted every bit as dry as other Bollinger vintages. Bollinger was unable to contemplate any dosage beyond the Grande Année parameter of 7-9g/l, especially as by then it could only be released as an RD, the dosage for which had always been 3-4g/l. In the end it was released (in my judgement) some seven years after its optimum disgorgement window had shut tight and Bollinger forced itself to up the dosage to 5g/l. The result is not at all flattering, the nose being riddled with gamey aromas while the palate is gamey-oaky and the fruit, which in the early 1990s with a full brut dosage would have been electrifying, nowhere to be seen. Wait and see.
ⓔⓔⓔⓔ Local Price **1350FF**

97 **Bollinger 1979 R.D. Extra Brut**
❗ Current disgorgements of this library vintage show the most exquisite of fruit.
Drink now-2007.
ⓔⓔⓔⓔ Local Price **2000FF**

Bortoli

De Bortoli Road
Bilbul
NSW 2680
Australia
Phone (2) 6964 9444
Fax (2) 6964 9400

90 **Bonnaire 1996 Grand Cru**
❗ **Blanc de Blanc**
Wonderfully fresh and succulent fruit balanced by lively acidity.
Drink now-2005.
ⓔⓔ Local Price **160FF**

Bonnet

Champagne Alexandre Bonnet
138 rue du Général-de-Gaulle
10340 Les-Riceys
Phone (325) 29.30.93
Fax (325) 29.38.65

Part of the BCC group with Boizel, Chanoine, Abel Lepitre, Philipponnat and De Venoge.

83 **Alexandre Bonnet NV**
❗ **Cuvée Prestige Brut**
Very fresh, modern style, fruity Champagne that should appeal to those trying to step from New World fizz to Champagne.
Drink upon purchase.
ⓔⓔ

84 **Alexandre Bonnet NV Brut Rosé**
❗ Freshly perfumed, with crisp, clean fruit, nice acidity and length. An aperitif style rosé for a change? Drink now-2002.
ⓔⓔ

86 **Alexandre Bonnet NV**
➡ **Blanc de Noirs, Brut**
A bit of a blast of sulphur, but that will blow off and go toasty. Rich fruit on the palate. Drink 2002-2003.
ⓔⓔ

Bonnaire

Champagne Bonnaire
120 rue d'Epernay
51530 Cramant
France
Phone (326) 57.50.85

70 **Sacred Hill NV Brut Cuvée SEA**
Sekt-style (terpenes) but softer
and more fruity.
Drink upon purchase.
ⓕ

Boscaiola

La Boscaiola
Via Riccafana
19 – 25033 Cologne
Italy
Phone (30) 7156386
Fax (30) 715596

75 **La Boscaiola NV**
Franciacorta Brut
Biscuity-mature.
Drink upon purchase.
ⓕ Local Price **20,000 Lira**

77 **La Boscaiola 1996**
Franciacorta Brut
The first sample just did not seem
right. There was nothing specific,
such as an identifiable fault, and
in most other tasting situations
I would simply walk on by, but in
the unrushed atmosphere of my
own tasting unit I could call for
a second sample and it would be
chilled, opened and in position,
totally blind, within three
minutes. The back-up bottle
showed a clean, yeast-complexed
fruit that the first bottle only
hinted at. Drink now-2002.
ⓕ Local Price **23,000 Lira**

Boschi

Via Iseo
44/a – 25030 Erbusco
Italy
Phone (30) 7703096-7703097
Fax (30) 7703097

80 **Boschi NV Franciacorta Brut**
Go for the last release in the
slightly fatter bottle, with its
tangy fruit and mellow toasty
bottle aromas. The next release
(in a normal shaped bottle)
has an interesting, if somewhat
precocious, sweet-vanilla
non-oak-related character on the
palate, but I'm not convinced that
the nose will evolve attractively,
thus reserve opinion until next
year. Drink now-2002.
ⓕ Local Price **14,000 Lira**

Bouvet

Bouvet Ladubay
1 rue de l'Abbaye
St-Hilaire-St-Florent
49400 Saumur
France
Phone (241) 83.83.83
Fax (241) 50.24.32

Owned by Taittinger.

89 **Bouvet Ladubay 1998 Tresor,**
Brut Saumur
Classy Tronçais oak aromas
overlaying sweet, ripe fruit
followed by elegant fruit on the
palate, with exquisite acidity and
a finely tuned finish. When right
(as the 1998 in 2001 proved to be)
this is one of the greatest French
sparkling wines than not this
has been due to an ill-timed
disgorgement, which has ruined
an otherwise excellent wine. The
vintage, by the way, is located in
the top-right of the label, in the
tiniest digits and printed in gold.

Pretty good camouflage.
Drink now-2002.
ⓔ Local Price **84FF**

72 Bouvet 1998 Saphir Brut Vintage,
🍷 Saumur
As clean and as fresh as last year,
but the acidity is not as well
defined. Drink upon purchase.
ⓔ Local Price **56FF**

75 Zéro par Bouvet-Ladubay 1998
🍷 Extra Brut, Saumur
This pure Chenin fizz has a sweet-
oaky aroma, but is completely dry
on the palate, with more than
enough fruit not to require a
dosage, although it would have
had more finesse if it had received
a small dosage.
Drink upon purchase.
ⓔⓔ Local Price **103FF**

Breaky Bottom Vineyard

Rodmell
Lewes
Sussex
Great Britain
Phone (1273) 476427
Fax (1273) 476427

---

78 Breaky Bottom, Millennium
🍷 Cuvée Maman Mercier 1996
Cuvée Réservée Brut
The touch of greenness noted on
the finish last year was not present
in this year's sample, indicating
that it was released too early. I
have always maintained that Peter
Hall puts his fizz on the market
when they are far too young.
That's a compliment. There aren't
many English sparkling wines I
would recommend ageing five
years before release, but this 1996
is still extremely fresh and crisp,
with a very slow evolution to the
vitality of its fruit. This vintage is
the best that Peter has made so
far, jumping an amazing seven

percentile points over its score last
year. Drink 2002-2004.
ⓔⓔ

Bredasole

Bredasole di Ferrari Giacomo
Via S. Pietro
42 – 25030 Paratico
Phone (35) 910407
Fax (35) 910407

---

78 Bredasole NV Franciacorta Brut
🍷 Fresh and fruity with a classic lean
yet accessible structure. This sort
of quality and style cannot be
achieved in the New World, even
in areas that are cooler than
Franciacorta, which I confess still
confuses me! Drink now-2002.
ⓔ Local Price **15,000 Lira**

Brémont

Champagne Bernard Brémont
1 rue de Reims
51150 Ambonnay
France
Phone (326) 57.01.65

---

87 Bernard Brémont NV Brut
🍷 This youthful, fruit-driven
Champagne is let down by its
amylic aromas, which are not
dominant, but build in the glass.
Otherwise it might have scored
90! Drink now-2004.
ⓔⓔ

Brice

Champagne Brice
3 rue Yvonnet
51150 Bouzy
France
Phone (326) 52.06.60
Fax (326) 57.05.07

*Jean-Paul Brice was one of the
three owners of Barancourt*

Brice (cont.)

before it was sold to Vranken. A quiet, intellectual type, Jean-Paul specialises in what was the most successful concept of Barancourt in its heyday, a range of mono-cru Champagnes.

Bricout

Champagne Bricout
Ancien Château d'Avize
51190 Avize
France
Phone (326) 53.30.00
Fax (326) 57.59.26

Part of the group Financière Martin (see Delbeck).

---

87 Brice NV Bouzy Grand Cru Brut
Always the biggest and most complex of the Brice mono-crus, the Bouzy can sometimes lack finesse on the nose, but the palate stands out for its intense Pinot fruit flavours. Drink now-2004.
ⓔⓔ Local Price **145FF**

88 Brice NV Cramant Grand Cru Brut
Nicely perfumed Chardonnay aroma with a hint of oak to the fruit on the palate. I have no idea whether Jean-Paul Brice used any oak in the production of this cuvée, but it certainly gives that indication. Very fresh, delicate, ultra-clean fruit. This is the best Cramant I've tasted from Brice since the early-to-mid 1980s. Drink now-2003.
ⓔⓔ Local Price **145FF**

88 Brice NV Aÿ Grand Cru Brut
Lovely creamy-sweet rich fruit showing good maturity, with biscuity-toasty aromas. The gold colour and firm but not heavy structure suggest that this release is exactly the same wine as last year's cuvée, only more recently disgorged. Drink now-2005.
ⓔⓔ Local Price **145FF**

Attention!

To submit samples for review see page 52

81 Bricout NV Cuvée Réserve Brut
I was not very impressed by the two releases that were current in the first half of 2001, but the next release, which should be hitting the shelf about the same time as this edition is published, is much cleaner and fresher.
Drink now-2002.
ⓔⓔ

82 Bricout NV Cuvée Prestige, Brut Premier Cru
More fruity than the Cuvée Réserve. Drink now-2003.
ⓔⓔ

85 Bricout NV Cuvée Rosé, Brut
Mature yet fresh and clean fruit aromas followed by very fresh, nicely rich, cherry-tinged fruit on the palate.
Drink upon purchase.
ⓔⓔ

85 Bricout NV Cuvée Arthur Bricout, Brut Grand Cru
The preview sample of the cuvée to be released in September 2001 was stylishly light, rich and elegant, with a soft, fluffy mousse. Drink now-2004.
ⓔⓔⓔ

84 Bricout 1992 Cuvée Millésime Brut
Floral aromas followed by clean-cut fruit and a crisp, creamy finish. Drink now-2004.
ⓔⓔⓔ

86 **Bricout 1990 Brut Réserve**
This amazingly youthful 1990 has
bags of freshness and fruit.
Drink now-2004.
ⓔ ⓔ

BRL Hardy

Reynella Winery
Reynell Road
Reynella
SA 5161
Australia
Phone (8) 8392 2222
Fax (8) 8392 2202

---

76 **Banrock Station NV**
Sparkling Chardonnay
Excellent, fresh, easy drinking fizz
that shows tank-fermented does
not have to be low quality.
Drink upon purchase.
ⓔ Local Price **A$12**

74 **Flirt NV Fizz**
Fresh, fruit-driven and quite tasty,
but should be half the price.
Drink upon purchase.
ⓔ Local Price **A$11**

78 **Hardys NV R&R Classic Cuvée**
Tropical fruits, gentle sparkle,
smooth and creamy on the finish.
Really impressive for a cheap
tank-fermented fizz.
Drink upon purchase.
ⓔ Local Price **A$6**

72 **Hardys Stamp of Australia NV**
Sparkling Chardonnay Pinot Noir
Smooth and creamy.
Drink upon purchase.
ⓔ

79 **Omni NV**
Full, dry, nicely yeast-complexed
fruit. Drink now-2002.
ⓔ Local Price **A$9**

80 **Omni NV Red**
Pure raspberries. Drink upon
purchase.
ⓔ Local Price **A$9**

74 **Sir James Brut de Brut NV Pinot**
Noir Chardonnay
Nicely dosaged tart stone-fruits.
Drink now-2002.
ⓔ Local Price **A$12**

73 **Sir James Cuvée Brut NV Pinot**
Noir Chardonnay
For once I prefer the Brut de Brut,
although it is a very similar wine.
Drink now-2002.
ⓔ Local Price **A$12**

77 **Sir James 1995 Vintage**
For those who like coconutty-oak,
but it also has very crisp fruit
dominating. Drink now-2002.
ⓔ Local Price **A$24**

? **Arras 1995**
Why is BRL Hardy still pushing
the 1995 vintage of this hyped-up
upmarket fizz for the fourth year
running? Although it has received
many awards and rave reviews in
Australia, it is either not selling or
far too much has been made for it
to warrant such an exclusive
marketing pitch. Furthermore,
I have been unable to recommend
it. In the 2000 edition I noted
under a **?** sign that it was a 'very
malty brew ... full of unripe acid,
offering no hope of finesse
whatsoever'. I did not bother even
to reserve my opinion for the 2001
edition: it was simply too
foursquare and lacking in finesse
for such a premium price
Australian bubbly. I intend to taste
in great depth at BRL Hardy next
year, but if I don't get there until
the year after (I was in Australia
last year and need to visit the rest
of the world in between!), I hope
that BRL Hardy will submit
preview samples the next three
vintages to my next annual
tasting, whether they are still

flogging the 1995. Wait and see.
ⓔⓔ Local Price A$52

80 **Leasingham Classic Clare 1994**
❗ **Sparkling Shiraz**
Ribena on steroids!
Drink upon purchase.
ⓔⓔ Local Price A$43

Brown Brothers

Gorton Drive
Mystic Park
Vic. 3581
Australia
Phone (3) 5457 9233
Fax (3) 5457 9426

74 **Brown Brothers NV Pinot Noir**
❗ **& Chardonnay Sparkling,**
King Valley
For those who like oxidative-
biscuity fizz. Drink now-2002.
ⓔ Local Price A$16

Brugnon

Champagne P. Brugnon
16 rue Carnot
51500 Rilly-la-Montagne
France
Phone (326) 03.44.89
Fax (326) 03.46.02

84 **Philippe Brugnon 1996 Brut**
❗ Fresh, sherbety and not too brut,
this is a very easy drinking
Champagne for a 1996.
Drink now-2004.
ⓔⓔ

Attention!

*To submit samples for review
see page 52*

Bruisyard Vineyard

Church Road
Bruisyard
Saxmundham Suffolk
IP17 2EF
Great Britain
Phone 01728 638281
Fax 01728 638442

80 **Bruisyard NV Millennium**
❗ Last year's Millennium cuvée was
labelled 1998, but this year's is not
vintaged. Whether it's the same
wine I have no idea, but if it is,
then it has undergone an amazing
transformation, jumping 10
percentile points. Lots of lovely
fresh fruit with satisfying quality
that promises to slowly build hints
of vanilla on the finish. Another
English fizz that would benefit
from an informative back-label.
Drink now-2002.
ⓔ

Brun, Albert Le

Champagne Albert Le Brun
93 avenue de Champagne
BP204 51009 Châlons-sur-
Champagne
France
Fax (326) 21.53.31

83 **Albert Le Brun NV**
➥ **Vieille France, Brut**
The nose is raw and estery,
suggesting that it should not be
touched for at least a year,
probably two and possibly three!
However, the fruit underneath
has very good potential in what
should eventually become a
biscuity-rich style. What will
strike most people about this
Champagne, however, is the
bottle, which is a replica of the
earliest style of Champagne bottle
I have seen. Drink 2002-2005.
ⓔ Local Price 83FF

Brun, Cellier Le

Cellier Le Brun
Terrace Road
Renwick
Marlborough
New Zealand
Phone (3) 572 8859
Fax (3) 572 8814

73 Daniel le Brun NV Brut
Fresh, clean with a fullish, vanilla
finesse. Drink now-2002.
ⓔ Local Price **NZ$27**

75 Daniel le Brun 1996
Blanc de Blancs
It's amazing how this wine has
been tidied-up, going from not
recommendable (approximately 60
points) to 75 points. It's all in the
dosage, but that's the clever part.
Drink now-2003.
ⓔⓔ Local Price **NZ$36**

Brun, Edouard

Champagne Edouard Brun &
Cie
14 rue Marcel Mailly
51160 Aÿ-Champagne
France
Phone (326) 55.20.11
Fax (326) 51.94.29

84 Edouard Brun & Cie NV Réserve
1er Cru, Brut
Lifted fruit with good acidity.
Drink now-2003.
ⓔⓔ Local Price **105FF**

Brun Family Estate, Le

Rapaura Road
Rapaura
Blenheim
New Zealand
Phone (3) 572 9876
Fax (3) 572 9875

80 Daniel No.1 NV Brut
Very fresh, youthful Chardonnay
with clean, tropical fruit finish.
Drink now-2002.
ⓔⓔ Local Price **NZ$35**

? Daniel No.1 NV Reserve RD
Green, should be left in cellars.
Wait and see.
ⓔⓔ Local Price **NZ$35**

? Cuvée Virginie 1997 Marlborough
This is the second time I've tasted
this wine. Last year's preview
sample had superb promise.
This year it is hankering down
for some longterm development.
Needs time. Wait and see.
ⓔⓔ Local Price **NZ$40**

Buecher

Paul Buecher
15 rue Ste Gertrude
68920 Wettolsheim
France
Phone (389) 80.64.73
Fax (389) 80.58.62

72 Paul Buecher 1999 Prestige Rosé,
Crémant d'Alsace
Soft, perfumed Pinot Noir.
Drink upon purchase.
ⓔ Local Price **42FF**

Buhl

Weingut Reichsrat von Buhl
Weinstrasse 16-24
67146 Deidesheim
Germany
Phone (6326) 965019
Fax (6326) 965024

72 Reichsrat von Buhl 1999
Riesling Brut
Light, fruity, fresh and easy.
*(100% Riesling, bottle-fermented,
Pfalz)* Drink now-2002.
ⓔ

Local Price **DM20**

85 Reichsrat von Buhl 1999 Forster
❗ **Pechstein Riesling Brut** (*magnum*)
Beautifully expressive floral
aromas followed by excellent
bottle-mature Riesling fruit,
with excellent acidity and a fresh
creaminess on the finish. There
were only 200 magnums in stock
when I tasted this. After I left
Reichstrat von Buhl there were
just 194! My wife could not
believe that I would purchase
a case of Sekt when our cellar
is bulging at the seams with
top-notch Champagne. Certainly
it takes a special Sekt to make me
part with money. (100% Riesling,
bottle-fermented, Pfalz)
Drink now-2004.
ⓔⓔ Local Price **4DM60**

75 Reichsrat von Buhl 1998
❗ **Weissburgunder Dosage Zero**
This fresh, crisp, elegantly fruity
wine does not need any dosage.
(100% Weissburgunder, bottle-
fermented, Pfalz) Drink now-2002.
ⓔ Local Price **DM25**

77 Reichsrat von Buhl 1994
❗ **Spätburgunder Blanc de Noir Brut**
This tastes far younger than Von
Buhl's 1996 Blanc de Noirs, which
was over the hill and cannot be
recommended. It is not, however,
simply younger than an old wine
– it is very fresh and crisp in its
own right, with fresh, lively, easy
drinking strawberry and
redcurrant fruit. (100%
Spätburgunder, bottle-fermented,
Pfalz) Drink upon purchase.
ⓔⓔ Local Price **DM36**

Attention!

*To submit samples for review
see page 52*

Buitenverwachting

Klein Constantia Road
Constantia 7800
South Africa
Phone (21) 794 5190
Fax (21) 794 1351

75 Buitenverwachting NV Brut,
❗ **Cap Classique**
Mature nose followed by mellow
fruit on the palate with a lemony
finish. Good mousse.
Drink upon purchase.
ⓔ Local Price **R47**

**Bürgermeister W.
Schweinhardt Nachf.**

See Schweinhardt Nachf

Ca'del Bosco

Via Case Sparse
20 – 25030 Erbusco
Italy
Phone (30) 7766111
Fax (30) 7268425

75 Ca'del Bosco NV
❗ **Franciacorta Brut**
A light and elegantly fruit, early
drinking Franciacorta that should
appeal at a reception or as a
pouring fizz in a good restaurant.
Drink now-2002.
ⓔ Local Price **30,000 Lira**

74 Ca'del Bosco 1997
❗ **Franciacorta Rosé**
This wine's acidity gives its fruit
an assertive freshness.
Drink now-2002.
ⓔⓔ Local Price **50,000 Lira**

75 Ca'del Bosco 1996
❗ **Franciacorta Satèn**
Young for its age with sherbert-
lemon fruit, a smooth mousse and

a crisp, tangy finish.
Drink now-2002.
ⓔⓔ Local Price 55,000 Lira

85 Ca'del Bosco 1994
❢ **Cuvée Annamaria Clementi**
This cuvée is the best Italian
sparkling wine in the brut style
bar none. Last year the 1993 and
1990 both notched up 85 points
and the 1988 could still manage
a very special 80 points, whilst the
year before, when I was stunned
for the first time by Annamaria
Clementi, the 1992, 1993 and 1994
each received a thoroughly
deserved 85 points. I am now
beginning to speculate whether
the 1992 is not the best of all,
but to determine that I will have
to return to this magnificent
forest-clad property and do
another vertical blind. The pain
I go through for my readers ....
Drink now-2004.
ⓔⓔⓔ Local Price 92,000 Lira

Cadel

Champagne Guy Cadel
13 rue Jean Jaurès
51530 Mardeuil
France
Phone 326 55.24.49
Fax 326 54.63.15

---

85 Guy Cadel NV Carte Blanche
❢ I preferred this fresh, fruity
Champagne to Guy Cadel's 1995
vintage. Drink now-2002.
ⓔⓔ

82 Guy Cadel 1995 Brut
❢ Fresh, easy drinking, aperitif style.
Drink now-2004.
ⓔⓔ

Calino

Ronco Calino
Via Sala
88 – 25030 Erbusco
Italy
Phone (35) 477011
Fax (35) 477077

---

75 Ronco Calino 1996
❢ **Franciacorta Brut**
Extremely rich, elevated fruit.
Drink now-2002.
ⓔⓔ Local Price 36,000 Lira

Camel Valley Vineyard

Little Denby Farm
Nanstallon
Bodmin
Cornwall
PL30 5LG
Great Britain
Phone (1208) 77959
Fax (1208) 77959

Camel Valley 1999 Cornwall Brut
Almost water-white with a touch
green on the nose, this vintage
75 drops a percentile point over the
❢ 1998, yet the fruit is just as rich
and as serious on the palate,
suggesting it will get better.
Drink now-2002.
ⓔⓔ Local Price £14

Canard-Duchêne

Champagne Canard-Duchêne
1 rue Edmond Canard
Ludes le Coquet
51500 Rilly-la-Montagne
France
Phone (326) 61.10.96
Fax (326) 61.13.90

*Part of LVMH under the wing
of Veuve Clicquot*

84 Canard-Duchêne NV Brut
❗ Quite rich and full, with tangy-
toasty fruit. Drink now-2003.
€€ Local Price **110FF**

84 Canard-Duchêne NV Brut
❗ (*magnum*)
Lighter in structure than the 75cl
sample of the same cuvée, yet
toastier and significantly deep
in colour. Drink now-2003.
€€ Local Price **230FF**

86 Canard-Duchêne NV Charles VII
❗ Grande Cuvée, Rosé Brut
Mature, old-English style of
Champagne rosé, with plenty of
bottle-aged fruit and excellent
acidity. Not everyone's cup of tea
or indeed glass of rosé, but scored
for its style. Drink now-2002.
€€€ Local Price **250FF**

87 Canard-Duchêne NV
❗ Charles VII Grande Cuvée, Brut
Fine fruit underscored by biscuity
finesse. Drink now-2002.
€€€ Local Price **250FF**

84 Canard-Duchêne 1991 Brut
❗ A smelly example at the Annual
Champagne Tasting in March
2001 worried me, but the sample
submitted to my tastings was as
clean as a whistle. In fact it was
surprisingly fresh and crisp for
a mature example of a lesser
vintage, with nice fruit with light,
fresh toasty aromas.
Drink now-2004
€€€

Attention!

*To submit samples for review
see page 52*

Capetta

Ç.so Piave 140
S. Stefano Belbo
Italy
Phone (39) 0141 843282
Fax (39) 0141 843277

85 Capetta NV Asti Dolce
❗ Extremely fresh and fleshy,
succulently sweet fruit with
refreshing acidity on the finish.
Drink upon purchase.
€ Local Price **6,500 Lira**

Carneros

Domaine Carneros
1240 Duhig Road
Napa
CA 94558
USA
Phone (707) 257 0101
Fax (707) 257 3020

80 Domaine Carneros by Taittinger
❗ NV Brut
Good tasty fruit. Drink now-2003.
€€ Local Price **$22**

91 Domaine Carneros by Taittinger
❗ 1995 Le Rêve
A stunning wine. Sumptuous.
Drink now-2003
€€€€ Local Price **$50**

89 Domaine Carneros by Taittinger
❗ 1994 Le Rêve
Retasted one year on and this
wine has dropped just one
percentile point, thrashing the
1993 (which was fabulous at its
peak) for freshness, crispness and
finesse. Drink now-2002.
€€€€ Local Price **$50**

Casanovas

Maria Casanovas Roig
Montserrat 117
08770 Sant Sadurní d'Anoia
Spain
Phone (93) 8910812
Fax (93) 8911572

80 Maria Casanovas NV Cava Brut
⚑ Nature Gran Reserva
This seems extraordinarily young
on the nose for a Gran Reserva,
but quite weighty and rich with
a vanilla fullness on the palate.
Drink upon purchase
ⓔⓔ Local Price 3,000 Ptas

Castell'sches Domänenamt

Fürstlich Castell'sches
Domänenamt
Schloßplatz 5
97355 Castell
Germany
Phone (9325) 60160
Fax (9325) 60188

72 Fürstlich Castell'sches
⚑ Domänenamt NV Schloss
Castell Brut
Fresh, clean, zippy Riesling fruit.
(100% Riesling, bottle-fermented,
Franken) Drink now-2002.
ⓔ Local Price DM23

Castel Faglia

Loc. Boschi
3 – Fraz. Calino 25046 Cazzago
S.M.
Italy
Phone (59) 812411
Fax (59) 812424

77 Monogram NV
⚑ Cuvée Giunone, Franciacorta Brut
A sophisticated melange of fruit
and firm yet cushiony mousse.
Admirably the month of
disgorgement is printed on the
back label and this cuvée
obviously needs at least 6 months,
but will benefit from much more.
Drink now-2003.
ⓔ Local Price 25,000 Lira

74 Monogram 1991
⚑ Franciacorta Brut
A touch of greenness, but this is
not unpleasant, it is balanced by
elevated fruit and it has no doubt
kept the wine not just alive, but
fresh for a decade.
Drink upon purchase.
ⓔ Local Price 30,000

Castellane

Champagne de Castellane
57 rue de Verdun
51204 Epernay
France
Phone (326) 51.19.19
Fax (326) 54.24.81

*Owned by Laurent-Perrier,
De Castellane has consistently
provided excellent value
Champagnes.*

82 De Castellane NV Croix
⚑ Rouge Brut
Soft, sweet and fruity with
a fluffy-frothy mousse.
Drink upon purchase.
ⓔ Local Price 110FF

85 De Castellane NV Croix
⚑ Rouge Brut Rosé
Where did the colour go?
Obviously a mature Champagne
(Lot No. L948), but it's all fruit on
the nose and palate, without any
hint of oxidativeness or even
biscuitiness. Nectarines, cherries
and a hint of strawberry.
Drink upon purchase.
ⓔⓔ Local Price 130FF

85   De Castellane NV Chardonnay
▬   **Blanc de Blancs, Brut**
A big whiff of sulphur, but
this should turn toasty and the
Chardonnay fruit on the palate
is so rich and racy I just have to
recommend it. Drink 2002-2004.
ⓔⓔ Local Price **135FF**

85   De Castellane 1995 Croix
❗   **Rouge Brut Millésimé**
Mellow, lemony-toast fruit.
Drink now-2003.
ⓔⓔ Local Price **145FF**

Castellblanch

Castellblanch SA (Grupo
Freixenet)
Avda. Casetas Mir 2
08770 Sant Sadurní d'Anoia
Phone (93) 891.7025
Fax (93) 891.0126

---

74   Castellblanch Brut Zero NV
❗   **Cava Brut Reserva**
Crisper, higher acidity than
I remember it and without the
terpenes. Could age. Smart new
presentation. Drink now-2003.
ⓔ

76   Castellblanch Gran Castell NV
❗   **Cava Brut Gran Reserva**
Very fluffy, well structured, high
acids, could develop.
Drink now-2003.
ⓔ

Castellino

Tenuta Castellino
Via S. Pietro
46 – 25030 Coccaglio
Italy
Phone (30) 7721015
Fax (30) 7701240

---

76   Tenuta Castellino Bonomi NV
❗   **Franciacorta Brut**
Should be sweet and toasty by
Christmas 2001. The next release
has a superior, soft, silky mousse
and more finesse to the fruit (will
score 78). Drink now-2002.
ⓔ Local Price **19,000 Lira**

74   Tenuta Castellino Bonomi NV
▬   **Franciacorta Satèn**
The current release has rich fruit
with a hint of sweet-ripeness and
has been dosaged to develop a
toasty style, while the next release
is richer, softer and fatter.
Drink 2002.
ⓔ Local Price **23,500 Lira**

Castelveder

Via Belvedere
4 – 25040 Monticelli Brusati
Italy
Phone (30) 652308
Fax (30) 652308

---

73   Castelveder NV Franciacorta Brut
❗   This Franciacorta is very fruity
with an almondy aftertaste
and an orange presentation that
should give Veuve Clicquot
palpitations! Upon purchase.
ⓔ Local Price **16,800 Lira**

80   Castelveder 1996
❗   **Franciacorta Brut**
This would be a rich, biscuity
classic sparkling wine wherever
it came from. Good acidity and
extract determine that it has the
potential to develop.
Drink now-2004.
ⓔ Local Price **24,000 Lira**

Cattin

Cattin Frères
19 rue Roger Frémeaux
68420 Voegtlinshoffen
France
Phone (389) 49.30.21
Fax (389) 49.26.02

74 Cattin 1999
❗ **Crémant d'Alsace Brut**
Elevated fruit with vanilla on
finish. Very rich and clever blend.
Drink now-2002.
Ⓔ Local Price **45FF**

Cavalleri

Via Provinciale
96 – 25030 Erbusco
Italy
Phone (30) 7760217
Fax (30) 7267350

74 Cavalleri NV Franciacorta Satèn
❗ **Blanc de Blancs**
This Franciacorta has a ripeness
of fruit that's a touch sweet and
elevated. Drink now-2002.
ⒺⒺ Local Price **34,440 Lira**

Cavendish

See Ridgeview Estate

Cavour, Conte di

See Barbero

Attention!

*To submit samples for review
see page* 52

Cazzago

Conti Bettoni Cazzago
Via Marconi
6 – 25046 Cazzago S. Martino
Italy
Phone (30) 7750875
Fax (30) 7750875

74 Conti Bettoni Cazzago NV
❗ **Tetellus, Franciacorta Brut**
A serious, sturdy sparkler with
mature fruit, but needs more
finesse to score higher.
Drink now-2002.
Ⓔ Local Price **24,000 Lira**

Cerutti

Ca' Du Ciuvin Di Cerutti
Via Manzotti 6 bis
12053 Castiglione Tinella
Italy
Phone (141) 855127
Fax (141) 855127

86 Cerutti NV Asti Cesare
❗ Gone are the malo aromas that
spoiled the freshness of this
méthode champenoise Asti last
year, thus propelling the wine's
score forward by six points, but
there are geranium aromas
starting to build, thus it is not
as young as it should be. This is
a potential 90-pointer when
everything comes together just
right. Drink upon purchase.
Ⓔ Local Price **28,000 Lira**

Chandon (Argentina)

Bodegas Chandon Argentina
Ruta Prov. 15
Agrelo
Luján de Cuyo CP5509
Mendoza
Argentina
Phone (54) 261-4909900
Fax (54) 261-4909989

76   Chandon NV Brut Fresco
A rapidly improving South
American fizz with blowsy
Chardonnay aromas perked up
by citrus fruit on the palate.
Drink upon purchase.
Ⓔ

Chandon (Australia)

Domaine Chandon
Green Point
Maroondah Highway
Coldstream
Vic. 3770
Australia
Phone (3) 9739 1110
Fax (3) 9739 1095

---

80   Chandon NV Brut
This year's sample had a
noticeably deep, mature colour
with toasty aromas followed by
mellow, mouthfilling fruit. Really
quite rich. Drink upon purchase.
Ⓔ Local Price **A$19**

**85   Chandon Australia NV Sparkling
Red, Pinot Noir/Shiraz**
Sweet flowery Pinot fruit.
Drink upon purchase.
Ⓔ Local Price **A$23**

**85   Chandon Australia 1997 Vintage
Blanc de Blancs**
Lovely creamy-rich fruit, classic
lean structure. Far fresher and
more elegant than this year's
rendition of the standard Green
Point by Chandon 1997 vintage.
Drink now-2003.
ⒺⒺ Local Price **A$32**

**84   Green Point by Chandon 1997
Vintage Brut**
Fresh, bread dough aromas
mingling with crisp citrus fruits
of some finesse on the palate,
although the sample at the
centralised tasting had biscuity-
nutty fruit (77 points). If, as I

suspect, the latter was from the
same UK stock I tasted last year
(05 points), it has aged rapidly in
the intervening 12 months.
Drink now-2003
ⒺⒺ Local Price **A$26**

**83   Green Point by Chandon 1997
Vintage Brut Rosé**
The sample submitted to my
tasting was a bit oxidative, and
lacked the charm of some earlier
vintages, but was still way ahead
of most of Aussie pink fizz (77
point). However, the sample
tasted at the annual centralised
tasting of Australian fizz was not
at all oxidative. Its toasty-rich
brambly fruit had plenty of nice,
ripe acidity, rendering it full and
rich yet crisp. Comparing these
two to the second sample of the
same wine received last year, it
was obvious that the latter was
UK-landed stock, but unlike the
standard 1997 vintage brut, the
1997 Rosé has come on beautifully
over the last twelve months.
Drink upon purchase.
ⒺⒺ Local Price **A$30**

Chandon (California)

Domaine Chandon
1 California Dr.
Yountville
CA 94599
USA
Phone (707) 944 8844
Fax (707) 944 1123

**75   Domaine Chandon NV
Blanc de Noirs**
Vanilla-dusted red fruits floating
on a lovely pin-cushion mousse.
Drink upon purchase.
Ⓔ Local Price **$14**

80   Etoile NV Brut
The heavy special bottle this
deluxe cuvée used to be presented

in has been replaced by a standard bottle, with a very standard label and presentation.
Drink now-2002.
ⓔⓔⓔ Local Price **$29**

70 Shadow Creek by Chandon NV
❗ **Blanc de Noirs**
A bit green and not as fluffy as previous releases, this should however go quite toasty for lovers of that style. Drink now-2002.
ⓔ Local Price **$10**

Chandon (Spain)

Cavas Chandon
Mas Chandon
08798 Sant Cugat Sesgarrigues
Spain
Phone (93) 897.0505
Fax (93) 897.0459

It is a complete mystery to me why Chandon continues to dabble with Cava (or Sekt for that matter) when it has not bothered to put down roots in either New Zealand (even though it used to source a cuvée from there) or Franciacorta, two of the hottest sparkling wine areas in the world.

---

72 Chandon NV Cava Brut
❗ This is fresh, clean and marginally better than the 1992-based cuvées, which were the first Cava's of any interest under the Chandon label, but the rate of progress has been painfully slow. Time to call in the wine doctor, I think. If Tony Jordan, who has the best record for fast-tracking success in the Chandon empire, cannot do significantly better with Cava's so-called traditional varieties, and the political decision not to major on Champagne grapes still holds, then perhaps looking to see what

other Spanish grapes to save the day. Either that or call it a day.
Drink upon purchase.
ⓔ Local Price **1,450 Ptas**

Chanoine

Champagne Chanoine
Avenue de Champagne
51100 Reims
France
Phone (326) 36.61.60
Fax (326) 36.66.62

Part of the BCC group with Boizel, Alexandre Bonnet, Abel Lepitre, Philipponnat and De Venoge.

---

84 Chanoine NV
❗ **Grande Réserve Brut**
Very soft, gentle, elegant fruit with a violet-flowery smoothness. Should go toasty. Drink now-2002.
ⓔⓔ

86 Tsarine NV
❗ **Tête de Cuvée Brut, Chanoine**
Very similar in style to the Grande Réserve, but so surprisingly deeper it is almost sonorous, yet with a balance of fruit that is just as light and elegant.
Drink now-2003.
ⓔⓔ

85 Tsarine NV Rosé Brut, Chanoine
The nose needs possibly as long as one year to pull itself together, but plenty of freshness and elegance of fruit on the palate.
Drink 2002-2003.
ⓔⓔ

87 Tsarine 1995 Brut Millésime,
❗ Chanoine
Hints of malo and a lovely mellowness to the aroma and fruit. An excellent value and quite classy Champagne that will go creamy biscuity. Drink now-2005.

ⓔⓔⓔ

88   Chanoine 1990 Millésime Brut
❗ Distinctly mature Champagne of
some finesse and a big smack of
fresh fruit with a jolt of acidity on
the finish. Drink now-2004.
ⓔⓔ

Chapel Down

See English Wine Plc

Charbaut

Champagne Guy Charbaut
12 rue du Pont
51160 Mareuil-sur-Aÿ
France
Phone (326) 52.80.5
Fax (326) 51.91.49.9

84   Guy Charbaut 1995 Brut
 Excellent acidity, but needs a year
in bottle to fire on all cylinders.
Drink 2002-2004.
ⓔⓔ

Charlemagne

Champagne Guy Charlemagne
4 rue de la Brèche d'Oger
51190 Le-Mesnil-sur-Oger
France
Phone (326) 57.52.98
Fax (326) 57.97.81

83   Guy Charlemagne NV Réserve
❗ **Brut, Grand Cru Blanc de Blancs**
An overtly fruity style that will go
toasty. Drink now-2002.
ⓔ Local Price **90FF**

88   Guy Charlemagne 1996
❗ **Mesnillésime, Brut Grand Cru**
Blanc de Blancs
Fresh and fruity aroma with nicely
assertive, well-structured and

beautifully focused, fresh, citrussy
fruit on the palate. Pinhead
bubbles. Drink now-2004.
ⓔⓔ Local Price **142FF**

Charpentier

Champagne J. Charpentier
88 rue de Reuil
51700 Villers-sous-Châtillon
France
Phone (326) 58.05.78
Fax (326) 58.36.59

88   J. Charpentier 1996 Brut
❗ **Millésime**
A truly characterful, hand-crafted
Champagne, with scintillating
acidity and a soft, silky, pin-
cushion mousse. Drink now-2004.
ⓔ Local Price **95FF**

Chateau Biltmore

See Biltmore Estate

Cheneau

See Giró Ribot

Chiquet

Champagne Gaston Chiquet
912 avenue du Général-Leclerc
Dizy -51318 Epernay
France
Phone (326) 55.22.02
Fax (326) 51.83.81

*Cousins of the Chiquet family
that owns Jacquesson, Gaston
Chiquet is invariably big on
fruit and value.*

85   Gaston Chiquet NV Tradition,
❗ **Brut Premier Cru**

Lovely fresh, fruity Champagne that's a joy to drink. Drink now-2003.
ⓔ Local Price **97FF**

89 **Gaston Chiquet NV Blanc de Blancs d'Aÿ, Brut Grand Cru**
Stunningly fresh, fruity aromas with succulent easy-drinking fruit on the palate (L80017051). Drink now-2004.
ⓔⓔ Local Price **107FF**

Clément

See Colombé-le-Sec

Clérambault

Champagne Clérambault
Neuville-sur-Seine
10250 Mussy-sur-Seine
France
Phone (325) 38.20.10
Fax (325) 38.24.36

84 **Clerambault NV Cuvée Tradition, Brut**
The rich, succulent fruit in this Champagne should be quite toasty by Christmas 2001. Drink now-2003.
ⓔ Local Price **79FF**

82 **Clerambault NV Cuvée Carte Noire, Brut**
Pleasantly acidic fruit hinting of aniseed. Drink now-2003.
ⓔ Local Price **86FF**

Cleebourg

CV de Cleebourg
Route du Vin
67160 Cleebourg
France
Phone (388) 94.50.33
Fax (388) 94.57.08

74 **CV de Cléebourg NV Clérotstein, Crémant d'Alsace**
Sweet, ripe fruit, invigorating mousse of tiny bubbles. Drink now-2002.
ⓔ Local Price **39FF**

Cloudy Bay

Jacksons Road
Blenheim
New Zealand
Phone (3) 572 8914
Fax (3) 572 8065

Part of LVMH under the wing of Veuve Clicquot.

80 **Pelorus NV Marlborough**
Lovely clean fruit, really quite full, yet not at all heavy, with an extremely fruity finish. Drink now-2002.
ⓔⓔ Local Price **NZ$35**

85 **Pelorus 1996 Marlborough**
Last year's preview sample was spot-on (85 points), as we see with this year's commercial release, with the apricot turning to peach, classy, rich and long, with nice acidity. Drink now-2003.
ⓔⓔ Local Price **NZ$42**

Clouet

Champagne André Clouet
8 rue Gambetta
Bouzy 51150 Tours-sur-Marne
France
Phone (326) 57.00.82
Fax (326) 51.65.13

87 **André Clouet NV Grande Réserve Brut**
Very fresh with very clean, well-focused fruit and a crisp finish. Drink now-2002.
ⓔ Local Price **492F**

Codorníu

Gran Via Les Corts Catalanes
644
08007 Barcelona
Spain
Phone (93) 301.4600
Fax (93) 301.7129

78 Codorníu Cuvée Raventós
❗ NV Cava Brut
Fresh and stylish, with very good
acidity. Drink now-2002.
Ⓔ Local Price **1,800 Ptas**

80 Jaume de Codorníu
❗ NV Cava Brut
Lovely fruity nose, with complete
and satisfying fruit, excellent
acidity and freshness.
Drink now-2002.
ⒺⒺ Local Price **4,120 Ptas**

80 Raimat Chardonnay
❗ NV Cava Brut
This wine has lost its overt
Chardonnay character, which
quickly became toasty and set
itself apart from other Cavas in
the 1980s, but after going through
its wilderness years I am glad to
say that it has emerged as a much
fresher, truly excellent Cava with
a crisper more modern taste
profile. Drink now-2003.
Ⓔ Local Price **1,355 Ptas**

Collin

Champagne Charles Collin
27 rue pressoirs
10360 Fontette
France
Phone (325) 38.31.00

85 Charles Collin NV Brut
❗ Deep, mellow-rich fruit with
a touch of finesse from Charles
Collin Le Champagne du
Gentleman Vigneron! Stylish
presentation. Drink now-2002.
Ⓔ Local Price **74FF**

83 Charles Collin NV Tradition Brut
❗ Much more mature than the basic
non-vintage, with a hint of vanilla
on the finish. Its leaf-brown bottle
protects the wine more during the
ageing process that the regular
green Champagne bottle does.
Some people will prefer this.
Drink upon purchase.
Ⓔ Local Price **79FF**

Colombé-le-Sec

CV de Colombé-le-Sec
(Champagne)
rue St. Antoine
10200 Colombé-le-Sec
France
Phone (325) 92.50.70

84 Charles Clément NV
❗ Tradition Brut
Classic biscuity fruit, excellent
acidity. Drink now-2002.
Ⓔ Local Price **76FF**

85 Charles Clément NV
❗ Gustave Belon Brut
Biscuity-rich fruit lifted by a soft,
cushiony mousse and tangy on the
finish. Drink upon purchase.
Ⓔ Local Price **92FF**

Colomer Bernat

Diputacio 58
08770 Sant Sadurní d'Anoia
Spain
Phone (93) 891.0804
Fax (93) 891.0804

80 Cristina Colomer NV
❗ Cava Brut Nature
Very fresh and lush with creamy
fruit and despite the Cava-soft
acidity this wine has a good,
lengthy finish (1998-based).
Drink now-2002.

ⓔ Local Price **1,600 Ptas**

Contadi Castaldi

Fornace Biasca – Via Colzano
32 – 25030 Adro
Italy
Phone (30) 7450126
Fax (30) 7450322

75 Contadi Castaldi NV
❢ Franciacorta Brut
Soft, fresh-mellow, peachy fruit
enlivened supported by a firm
mouse of small bubbles.
Drink now-2002.
ⓔ Local Price **25,000 Lira**

75 Contadi Castaldi 1997
❢ Franciacorta Brut Satèn
A preview sample of this new
release was invigoratingly fresh
and crisp with a tad of early-
picked fruit on the palate. I never
like to pick up even a whisper of
early-picked fruit, despite it being
two levels removed from even the
slightest hint of green, but this
amount should quickly mellow
into a toasty aroma.
Drink now-2002.
ⓔ Local Price **30,000 Lira**

Conte di Cavour

See Barbero

Conti

Paul Conti Wines
529 Wanneroo Road
Woodvale
WA 6026
Australia
Phone (8) 9409 9160
Fax (8) 9309 1634

87 Nero NV Sparkling Shiraz
❢ Cedary nose, succulent Shiraz
fruit, nice tannic edge, with deep,
rich sweet fruity finish.
Drink now-2002.
ⓔ Local Price **A$22**

Conti Bettoni Cazzago

See Cazzago

Contratto

Giuseppe Contratto
Via G.B. Giuliani
56 Canelli
Italy
Phone (141) 823349
Fax (141) 824650

*Great Asti produced by the
Champagne method.*

88 De Miranda 1998
❢ Asti Metodo Classico
Slightly deeper in colour than
the older 1997 vintage. Exquisitely
perfumed, with very rich,
ultra-sweet fruit and a soft velvety
finish. Drink upon purchase.
ⓔⓔ Local Price **39,000 Lira**

87 De Miranda 1997
❢ Asti Metodo Classico
The peachy fruit in this vintage
has got richer and sweeter since
last year (87 points), but it still
does not have the finesse of the
1995 as tasted three or four years
ago. Drink upon purchase.
ⓔⓔ Local Price **39,000**

Attention!

*To submit samples for review
see page 52*

Cornaleto di Lancini Luigi

Via Cornaleto
2 – 25030 Adro
Italy
Phone (30) 7450507
Fax (30) 7450552

Cranswick Estate

Walla Avenue
Griffith
NSW 2680
Australia
Phone (2) 6962 4133
Fax (2) 6962 2888

75 **Cornaleto 1997**
❢ **Franciacorta Brut Satèn**
Rather firm mousse for a satèn,
but attractively fresh, crisp, tangy
stone-fruits on the palate.
Drink now-2002.
Ⓔ

76 **Barramundi Sparkling NV**
❢ Tropical fruits dominated by
pineapple. Fruity fizz par
excellence. Best release so far.
Drink upon purchase.
Ⓔ

75 **Cornaleto 1992 Franciacorta Brut**
❢ Very fruity with plenty of toasty
aromas, tangy acidity and a
smooth mousse. Drink now-2002.
Ⓔ Local Price **30,000 Lira**

72 **Cranswick NV Pinot Chardonnay**
❢ Terpenes, lemon and lavender.
Drink upon purchase.
Ⓔ

COVIDES

CV del Penedès Sociedad
Cooperativa Catalana
Ram Nostra Senyora 45
08720 Vilafranca del Penedès
Spain
Phone (93) 817.2552
Fax (93) 817.1798

Crawford

Kim Crawford Wines
Dominion Road
Auckland
New Zealand
Phone (9) 630 6263
Fax (9) 630 6293

76 **Duc de Foix NV Cava Brut**
❢ **Nature** Fresh and lemony, with
excellent structure and acidity
(1998-based). Drink now-2002.
Ⓔ Local Price **950 Ptas**

80 **Kim Crawford Rory NV Brut**
❢ Fine, full, firm biscuity-rich style
with yeast-complexed fruit and
vanilla on the finish. Drink now-
2002.
Ⓔ Local Price **NZ$30**

74 **Duc de Foix NV**
❢ **Cava Brut Nature Rosado**
A soft fruity rosé with hints
of cherry (1999-based).
Drink now-2002.
Ⓔ Local Price **1,020 Ptas**

Cristalino

See Serra

Cristina Colome

See Colomer Bernat

Attention!

*To submit samples for review
see page 52*

*To submit samples for review
see page 52*

Cristoforo

See San Cristoforo

Croser

See Petaluma

Curbastro

Ricci Curbastro
Via Adro
37 – 25031 Capriolo
Italy
Phone (30) 736094
Fax (30) 7460558

77 **Ricci Curbastro NV**
Franciacorta Brut
A combination of fresh, lifted and rich fruit with peppery hints and truly excellent acidity. In some ways this is mature, but the nose, palate and finish are all running at different speeds and need to come together. It is easy enough to drink now, but lovers of classic Franciacorta will keep this for at least 12 months. Drink 2002-2003.
ⓔLocal Price **25,000 Lira**

83 **Ricci Curbastro NV**
Franciacorta Satèn Brut
A firmer mousse than last year's release, but still nice, tiny pin-head bubbles. This barrique-fermented satèn deserves a special bottle and a better (understated) label. Drink now-2003.
ⓔ Local Price **25,000 Lira**

82 **Ricci Curbastro NV**
Franciacorta Extra Brut
Logic dictates that this would not be an older cuvée than that submitted last year and I would be amazed if I was told that it is a younger wine, thus last year's

release has matured extremely rapidly. It was very pale in colour with such a fresh autolytic aroma, yet it is quite yellow and relatively deep in colour, with mature oaky-satèn aromas and tangy but mellow fruit on the palate. Drink now-2002.
ⓔ Local Price **30,000 Lira**

Dagobert

Cave du Roi Dagobert
1 route de Scharrachbergheim
67310 Traenheim
France
Phone (388) 50.69.00
Fax (388) 50.69.09

75 **Cave du Roi Dagobert 1998 St.**
Eloi Rosé, Crémant d'Alsace
Attractive redcurrant-strawberry Pinot Noir fruit. Needs a little time to soften the mousse, but drinking well now fruit-wise. Drink now-2002.
ⓔ Local Price **37FF**

Danebury

Danebury House
Nether Wallop
Stockbridge
Hants
SO20 6JX
Great Britain
Phone (1264) 781851
Fax (1264) 782212

? **Danebury 1996 Cossack, Brut**
Pungent capsicum aroma pervades every nuance. I've come across this on other sparkling wines and although most of them get worse, some have lost all or part of this strange aroma after more time on yeast. In more than one of the latter cases it was put down to a high concentration of aspergine, which dropped off during

autolysis. Wait and see.
ⓔⓔ

70 **Danebury 1995 Cossack, Brut**
❗ Loads of lifted pineapple fruit on the palate, let down on the nose. Drink upon purchase.
ⓔⓔ

Daniel No.1

See Brun Family Estate, Le

Dasenstein

Winzerkeller Hex vom Dasenstein
Burgunderplatz 1
77876 Kappelrodeck
Germany
Phone (784) 299380
Fax (784) 28763

---

70 **Winzerkeller Hex vom Dasenstein**
❗ **1997 Trocken**
Excellent varietal fruit on nose. Soft. (100% Spätburgunder, bottle-fermented, Baden)
Drink upon purchase.
ⓔ Local Price **DM18**

Davenport

Limney Farm
Castle Hill
Rotherfield
East Sussex
TN6 3RR
Great Britain
Phone (1892) 852 380
Fax (1892) 852 381

---

86 **Davenport 1999 Brut Reserve**
❗ Not due to be released until July 2002 at the earliest, this represents a major step forward for Davenport sparkling wine and the first Davenport vintage was only

as recent as 1997. To tell the truth, I'm not sure when this should be commercially disgorged, but I am certain that whenever it is it will age very gracefully. This is a blend of Pinot Noir and Auxerrois and the early basic flavours are fantastic, the acidity even more impressive and I cannot wait to taste this wine as it develops, not to mention getting my hands on future vintages. Drink now-2005.
ⓔⓔ

72 **Davenport 1998 Brut**
❗ This is dramatically dry and crisp for an herbaceous-cum-aromatic fizz. Only two vintages (1997 & 1998) of this pure Faber cuvée have been and ever will be made. Drink upon purchase.
ⓔ Local Price £9

De Castellane

See Castellane

De Miranda

See Contratto

De Saint Gall

See Union Champagne

De Sousa

See Sousa

DeGaioncelli

See Gaioncelli

Delamotte

Champagne Delamotte
7 rue de la Brèche d'Oger
51190 Le Mesnil-sur-Oger
France
Phone (326) 57.51.65
Fax (326) 57.79.29

*Owned by Laurent-Perrier,
Delamotte is the sister
company of the great
Champagne Salon, which is
literally next door*

87 Delamotte NV
Blanc de Blancs Brut
Extremely rich, high acidity,
excellent fruit with peachy
aftertaste. The best Delamotte
NV in years. Drink now-2003.
€€ Local Price **160FF**

Delbeck

Champagne Delbeck
39 rue du Général Sarrail
51100 Reims
France
Phone (326) 77.58.00
Fax (326) 77.58.01

*Part of the group Financière
Martin, which is owned by
Pierre Martin, one of the three
original owners of Barancourt,
and includes Bricout.*

87 Delbeck NV Bouzy,
Brut Grand Cru
The nose really needs one more
year in bottle to catch up with the
soft, creamy strawberry-Pinot
fruit on the finish, but few bottles
will get this because it is currently
so easy to drink. Drink now-2004.
€€
Local Price **152FF**

84 Delbeck NV Cramant
Grand Cru Brut

A melange of ripe and
early-picked fruit that should
quickly go toasty. Drink now-
2003.
€€ Local Price **152FF**

85 Delbeck NV Aÿ Grand Cru Brut
This wine's youthful honeyed
finish should develop very quickly
into something quite special, but
I would not advise keeping it too
long. Drink now-2003.
€€
Local Price **152FF**

? Delbeck 1996 Brut Vintage
Perfumed aroma followed by
ripe-perfumed fruit on the palate.
This Champagne seems to be a bit
of a doughnut (that is to say it has
a hole in the middle of the palate
where there should be the most
fruit), but the best 1996s should
not be released for several years,
so if this is only a middling
example of the vintage (as
I suspect it is), it is probably
underperforming at the moment,
hence the **?** sign. Wait and see.
€€
Local Price **158FF**

87 Delbeck 1996 Cuvée Origines,
Brut (*magnum*)
The quality of this Champagne is
easier to discern than that of
Delbeck's standard 1996. No
doughnut here. In fact a bagful of
fruit and marked by a high level of
ripe acidity, which is the signature
of the 1996s. It is dosaged to go
toasty. However, if Delbeck has
more magnums to disgorge, I
hope they have the courage to use
less sulphur and perhaps one
gram more of sugar, which reduce
the precociousness of the toasty
aromas and allow the wine to
develop more biscuity complexity,
which despite the drop in sulphur
it should do slowly and gracefully
due to the unique acidity level of

this vintage. In which case it would jump up two or three percentile points.
Drink 2002-2005.
ⓔⓔⓔ Local Price **645FF**

89
Ⓣ **Delbeck 1995 Cuvée Origines, Brut** (*magnum*)
Beautiful, floral-fresh autolytic aromas followed by crisp, youthful fruit on a cushiony mousse.
Drink now-2007.
ⓔⓔⓔ Local Price **645FF**

86
Ⓣ **Delbeck 1990 Brut Vintage**
Extraordinarily fresh, lemon meringue fruit. Lovely.
Drink now-2003.
ⓔⓔ Local Price **158FF**

Demoiselle

See Vranken

Denois

Jean-Louis Denois
Domaine de l'Aigle
11300 Roquetaillade
France
Phone (468) 31.39.12
Fax (468) 31.39.14

Champenois expatriate making good in the south of France.

79
Ⓣ **Domaine de l'Aigle NV Jean-Louis Denois, Brut Tradition**
Oak aromas are noticeable, but not too dominant and add to the attraction of this wine. Much better acidity and structure than the Blanc de Blancs, but could do with a lighter touch to the balance, which would bring more finesse. Drink now-2003.
ⓔ

73
Ⓣ **Jean Louis Denois NV Blanc de Blancs Chardonnay Brut**
Dominated by cool-ferment aromas on both nose and palate, with soft, creamy-amylic Chardonnay on the finish.
Drink now-2002.
ⓔ

Deppisch

Weingut Joseph Deppisch
An der Röthe 2
97837 Erlenbach
Germany
Phone (9391) 5158

70
Ⓣ **Joseph Deppisch 1998 Franken Silvaner Brut**
This soft and perfumed fizz has a clean flavour with a hint liquorice to the fruit and although far too soft for most bubble-hunters, it is the best Silvaner fizz I've tasted this year, thus include it for those who are interested in this variety.
(100% Silvaner, bottle-fermented, Franken) Drink upon purchase.
ⓔ Local Price **DM20**

70
Ⓣ **Joseph Deppisch 1998 Franken Riesling Extra Trocken**
sherbety with elevated fruit.
(100% Riesling, bottle-fermented, Franken) Drink upon purchase.
ⓔ Local Price **DM25**

Déthune

Champagne Paul Déthune
2 rue du Moulin
51150 Ambonnay
France
Phone (326) 57.01.88
Fax (326) 57.09.31

84
Ⓣ **Paul Déthune NV Brut Rosé, Grand Cru**
A true pink rosé colour with a very fresh, simplistic fruity aroma

is accurately reflected on the palate and finish. Simplistic maybe, but this cuvée does not lack elegance and is certainly enjoyable. Drink upon purchase.
ⓔ Local Price **95FF**

85 **Princesse des Thunes NV Cuvée**
▬ **Prestige Brut, Grand Cru**
This needs a year in bottle for the nose to come together, but the potential is very clear on the palate, where the fruit is seductively soft and fluffed up with a fresh, breezy mousse. Drink 2002-2004.
ⓔⓔ Local Price **130FF**

Deutz

Champagne Deutz
16 rue Jeanson
51160 Aÿ-Champagne
France
Phone (326) 56.94.13
Fax (326) 58.76.13

Owned by Roederer, Deutz has been on a roll for the last few years, with a consistency of excellence across its entire range.

---

88 **Deutz NV Brut Classic**
❗ This seductively rich and biscuity Champagne has oodles of fresh, crisp fruit and is classic Champagne in every sense. Drink now-2005.
ⓔⓔ Local Price **160FF**

85 **Deutz 1996 Brut Rosé**
❗ Creamy-biscuity nose followed by creamy fruit and typically high acidity, which will enable this rosé to age for a few years yet. Drink now-2004.
ⓔⓔⓔ Local Price **150FF**

89 **Deutz 1995 Brut**
❗ Exquisitely rich fruit with

slow-building biscuity complexity. Drink now-2006.
ⓔⓔⓔ Local Price **220FF**

85 **Deutz 1995 Blanc de Blancs, Brut**
▬ Starting to go vanilla-toasty (absolutely no wood used here, though). Drink 2002-2005
ⓔⓔⓔ Local Price **300FF**

90 **Deutz 1995**
▬ **Cuvée William Deutz, Brut**
Complexity and finesse evident on the nose, followed by finely focused fruit floating on a luxuriantly soft and creamy mousse of the most minuscule bubbles. Drink 2002-2007.
ⓔⓔⓔⓔ Local Price **350FF**

91 **Amour de Deutz 1995 Blanc de**
❗ **Blancs, Brut**
This dream of wine is bursting with wonderfully fresh fruit of stunning finesse supported by a beautifully soft, cushiony mousse. Everything about this Champagne is a statement of class and taste except .... the capsule! I would not bother to mention it, except for the fact that this weighty item has a gilt finish, boasts a diamante and is even threaded with black cord so that you can hang it around your neck! Would Fabrice Rosset, the immaculately dressed directeur général of Deutz, wear one of these baubles? Of course not. So why does he think that Deutz drinkers would? Drink now-2006.
ⓔⓔⓔⓔ Local Price **650FF**

Devaux

Champagne Veuve A. Devaux
Domaine de Villeneuve
10110 Bar-sur-Seine
France
Phone (25) 38.30.65
Fax (25) 29.73.21

Devaux (cont.)

This year's samples failed to arrive, thus I can report on only one recommendable cuvée from the Annual Champagne Tasting.

84 Veuve A. Devaux NV Grande
❦ Réserve, Brut
Nice, fullish, fresh, fruit-driven style with refreshing, crisp finish.
Drink now-2004.
Ⓔ Ⓔ Local Price **115FF**

Dezzani

Via P. Giachino 140
14023 Cocconato d'Asti
Italy
Phone (141) 907044

78 Dezzani NV Brachetto
❦ d'Acqui Dolce
Very fresh, intensely sweet fruit with a fleeting glimpse of tannin on the finish.
Drink upon purchase.
Ⓔ

Divine

See Leclerc Briant

Dock

Christian Dock
20 rue Principale
67140 Heiligenstein
France
Phone (388) 08.02.69
Fax (388) 08.19.72

78 Christian Dock 1999
❦ Crémant d'Alsace Brut
Packs a lot of flavour for such a nicely light, fresh, easy-drinking

style. Drink now-2003.
Ⓔ Local Price **38FF**

77 Christian Dock 1998
❦ Crémant d'Alsace Brut
Big, rich, creamy-complex Champagne style.
Drink upon purchase.
Ⓔ Local Price **38FF**

Dogliotti

Azienda Agricola Caudrina di
Romano Dogliotti
Str. Brosia 20
12053 Castiglione Tinella Cn
Italy
Phone 141855126
Fax 141855008

90 La Selvatica Asti NV
❦ Caudrina, Romano Dogliotti
Very fresh, soft and peach fruit.
Lovely fresh acidity and an immaculate, cushiony mousse (bottled February 2001).
Drink upon purchase.
Ⓔ Local Price **18,000 Lira**

Dopff & Irion

1 cour du Château
68340 Riquewihr
France
Phone (389) 47.92.51
Fax (389) 47.98.90

73 Dopff & Irion 1998
❦ Crémant d'Alsace Brut
Fresh, crisp fruit. Drink now-2002.
Ⓔ Local Price **44FF**

Dopff Au Moulin

68340 Riquewihr
Frances
Phone (389) 49.09.69
Fax (389) 47.83.61

73 Dopff au Moulin NV
Cuvée Julien, Crémant d'Alsace
Light, fresh, pineapple fruit.
Drink upon purchase.
ⓔ Local Price **45FF**

73 Dopff au Moulin NV Rosé,
Crémant d'Alsace
Very fresh, clean, invigorating.
Drink now-2002.
ⓔ Local Price **54FF**

Drappier

Champagne Drappier
Grande Rue
10200 Urville
France
Phone (25) 27.40.15
Fax (325) 29.38.65

*I have long regarded Drappier
as one of the three best
producers in the Aube,
although only Grand Sendrée is
pure Aube to my knowledge,
but the Pinot Noir Zero
Dosage was a revelation.*

90 André et Michel Drappier NV
Brut Nature,
Pinot Noir Zero Dosage
One of the greatest, most
delightful and easily accessible
non-dosage Champagnes I've
tasted. This cuvée is made under
Drappier's traditional low-sulphur
regime (which in this instance
means no sulphur whatsoever
throughout the entire vinification
process), hence it will go biscuity
quite rapidly, but at the moment
it is pure Pinot fruit from the
strawberry aromas on the nose
through the rich, tangy palate
to the crisp and vital finish.
Drink now-2002.
ⓔⓔ Local Price **130FF**

84 Drappier NV Carte-d'Or Brut
As usual this is an overtly fruity,

user-friendly Champagne, but it
lacks a certain richness and could
do with a touch more acidity,
which is why under blind
conditions it dipped one percentile
point due. However, anyone who
finds all Champagnes too acidic
(stand up Jimmy Young) should
add at least another 10 points to
this score! Drink upon purchase.
ⓔⓔ Local Price **120FF**

86 Drappier NV Cuvée Signature,
Blanc de Blancs Brut
A luscious, mellow and yet
completely fresh tasting
Champagne of some finesse,
supported by a cushiony mousse
of pinhead bubbles.
Drink now-2004.
ⓔⓔ Local Price **140FF**

89 Drappier 1995
Grande Sendrée, Brut
Wonderfully fresh and fruity, this
Champagne typically goes creamy
biscuity. Lovely acidity.
Drink now-2005.
ⓔⓔ Local Price **195FF**

Duc de Foix

See COVIDES

Dumont

Champagne Daniel Dumont
11 rue Gambetta
51500 Rilly-la-Montagne
France
Phone (326) 03.40.67
Fax (326) 03.44.82

84 Daniel Dumont NV
Grande Réserve Brut
An inexpensive, succulently fruity,
easy-drinking Champagne.
Drink upon purchase.
ⓔⓔ

84 Daniel Dumont NV Grande
Réserve Brut
A reall developing Champagne
with a soft finish.
Drink now-2002.
ⓔⓔ

84 Daniel Dumont 1995 Brut
Réserve Millésime, Premier Cru
An overtly fruity, easy-to-drink
Champagne, but not special
enough to warrant vintage status.
However, because this is not an
expensive Champagne, it is
cheaper that some famous non-
vintage cuvées and scored on that
basis. Drink now-2003.
ⓔⓔ

Durbacher Wg.

Nachtweide 2
77770 Durbach
Germany
Phone (7819) 3660
Fax (7813) 6547

70 Durbacher Wg. 1998 Durbacher
Plauelrain Riesling Brut
High extract – needs at least
another year. (100% Riesling,
bottle-fermented, Baden)
Drink 2002-2003.
ⓔ Local Price **DM21**

Duval-Leroy

Champagne Fleur de
Champagne
69 avenue de Bammental
F-51130 Vertus
France
Phone (326) 52.10.75
Fax (326) 57.54.01

*If you thought that Margaret
Thatcher was the 'Iron Lady',
you have not met Carole
Duval!*

83 Duval-Leroy NV Fleur de
Champagne Brut
Really quite rich, deep and
complete for such a light, elegant
balance, but not quite the spark
on the nose or the crispness on the
finish that I have come to expect
from Duval-Leroy, thus it is two
percentile points down on last
year. Drink now-2002.
ⓔⓔ Local Price **110FF**

88 Duval-Leroy NV Fleur de
Champagne, Brut Premier Cru
Wonderfully light, fresh and
fragrant, this cuvée is back to how
it should be, with none of the
alien malo character that dogged
last year's release (although this
was still available at the beginning
of 2001). Drink now-2003.
ⓔⓔ Local Price **114FF**

84 Duval-Leroy NV Fleur de
Champagne, Rosé de Saignée Brut
Creamy summer fruits, but lacks
sufficient acidity for the dosage,
thus tastes a touch sweet. Some
will like this, and there is the
promise of creamy-biscuity
complexity in the future.
Drink now-2003.
ⓔⓔ Local Price **129FF**

85 Duval-Leroy 1996
Fleur de Champagne,
Blanc de Chardonnay Brut
Biscuity aromas on the nose
followed by creamy-rich fruit on
the palate. Relatively forward and
already complex. Drink now-2003.
ⓔⓔ Local Price **126FF**

88 Duval-Leroy 1995
Fleur de Champagne,
Blanc de Chardonnay Brut
This has evolved slowly since last
year. The finesse is remarkable.
Even more remarkable is that is,
I think, significantly better than
Duval-Leroy's 1995 of the same
cuvée. Drink now-2004.

€€ Local Price **126FF**

86 **Duval-Leroy 1995 Fleur de**
▬ **Champagne, Millésimé Brut**
Firm, with assertive lime fruit and
extract on the finish.
Drink 2002-2005.
€€ Local Price **133FF**

88 **Duval-Leroy 1995 Fleur de**
▬ **Champagne, Extra Brut Millésimé**
Extraordinary richness and
length for such an elegant style of
Champagne, slow-building
complexity will transform this
vintage into a food wine style.
Drink 2002-2004.
€€ Local Price **141FF**

87 **Duval-Leroy 1990 Cuvée des Roys**
❢ Fat and rich with sweet-juicy
fruit that promises to go
creamy-biscuity. Drink now-2002.
€€€ Local Price **260FF**

91 **Femme de Champagne**
❢ **1990 Brut Millésime**
On opening, this seems to be just
as oxidative as last year's release
and thus not a patch on the
original preview sample, but with
time in the glass the oxidativeness
is replaced by finer, fruitier
aromas of more finesse. Do not
over-chill. Drink now-2009.
€€€€ Local Price **475FF**

Einhart du Westerberg

Domaine Einhart du
Westerberg
15 rue Principale
67560
Rosenwiller
France
Phone (388) 50.41.90

---

75 **Domaine Einhart du Westerberg**
❢ **1998 Einhart, Crémant d'Alsace**
Creamy-malo serious style that
leans more towards Champagne in

style than Alsace in origin.
Drink now-2003
€ Local Price **41FF**

Elias i Terns

See Parató

English Wine Centre

Alfriston
East Sussex
BN26 5QS
Great Britain
Phone (1323) 870164
Fax (1323) 870005

---

73 **The English Wine Centre 1996**
❢ **House Bubbly, Brut RD 2000**
So herbaceously English on the
nose, with muscat-like fruit on
the palate. Nice now, but should
be drunk up. Grown and bottled
by Barkham Manor Vineyards.
Drink upon purchase.
€ Local Price **£10**

English Wine Plc

Tenterden Vineyard
Small Hythe
Tenterden
Kent TN30 7NG
Phone (1580) 763033
Fax (1580) 765333

*Formerly trading as Chapel
Down, this is one of the UK's
largest wine producers.*

---

73 **Chapel Down NV Epoch, Brut**
❢ Not as fresh as last year's cuvée,
but it does seem to pack more
weight of fruit. I just wish this
had the freshness, finesse, purity
and complexity of fruit that the
vintaged Epoch usually displays.
Drink upon purchase.

76 Chapel Down 1995
Epoch Vintage Brut
Yet another exotic, peachy Epoch vintage. My only criticism is that this cuvée should be released at least one year earlier. Two years would be preferable. Chapel Down no doubt believes it should sell its older vintages first, but by doing that they fail to get this wine on the shelf at the optimum moment in its development and thus fail to maximise its potential. They should grasp the nettle and sell off two older vintages to a supermarket at a knockdown price. Drink upon purchase.
€

Ermel

David Ermel
30 route de Ribeauvillé
68150 Hunawihr
France
Phone (389) 73.61.71
Fax (389) 73.32.56

70 David Ermel 1998 Brut David
Ermel, Crémant d'Alsace
Clean, soft, smooth, fruity
Drink now-2002.
€ Local Price **42FF**

Etoile

See Chandon (California)

Eymann

Weingut Rainer Eymann
Ludwigstrasse 35
67161 Gönnheim
Germany
Phone (632) 22808
Fax (632) 268792

75 Rainer Eymann 1998
Riesling Sekt Brut
Lovely bottle-aromas on both nose and palate, with rounded fruit that's ready to drink. (100% Riesling, bottle-fermented, Pfalz)
Drink upon purchase.
€ Local Price **DM19**

Faccoli

Faccoli Cascina Ronco
Via Cava
7 – 25030 Coccaglio
Italy
Phone (30) 7722761
Fax (30) 7722761

75 Faccoli NV Franciacorta Brut
An overtly fruity Franciacorta that should go toasty. Drink now-2003.
€ Local Price **18,000 Lira**

77 Faccoli NV Franciacorta
Rosé Brut
A pale-salmon coloured rosé with red fruits, pears and crab apples on the palate. Drink now-2002.
€ Local Price **19,000 Lira**

Ferghettina

Ferghettina di Roberto Gatti
Via Case Sparse 4
25030 Erbusco
Italy
Phone (30) 7760120
Fax (30) 7768098

74 Ferghettina NV Franciacorta Brut
Fresh, light and fruity fizz in an easy-drinking style.
Drink upon purchase.
€ Local Price **18,000 Lira**

Attention!

To submit samples for review see page 52

Ferret

Mateu Jose
Avda. Penedès 27.bo.la Rapita
08730 – Santa Margarida I Els
Monjos
Spain
Phone (93) 898.0105
Fax (93) 898.0584

75 **Ferret NV Cava Brut Reserva**
Fresh and fluffy with sherbety fruit. Drink now-2002.
Ⓔ Local Price **1,200 Ptas**

Feuillatte

Champagne Nicolas Feuillatte
CV de Chouilly
Chouilly 51206 Epernay
France
Phone (326) 54.50.60
Fax (326) 55.33.04

Anyone who has followed my scoring over the years will have noticed that I have been under-whelmed by the vast majority of Champagnes produced by this cooperative. In fact the only great Champagne it has produced was the 1985 Palmes d'Or Brut. The very first vintage of this prestige cuvée, I hoped it would mark the start of an upturn in quality, but it did not. The wines since have all lacked finesse, including all the follow-on vintages of Palmes d'Or. Until last, that is, when the 1995 Blanc de Blancs became the highest-scoring Nicolas Feuillate since the 1985 Palmes d'Or Brut. Although the jury is still out on the 1996 Cuvée Palmes d'Or Rosé that was launched in mid-2001, the magnums of 1992 Palmes d'Or Brut are truly fine and the new trio of mono-cru Champagnes represent an exciting,

Feuillatte (cont.)

imaginative departure for this cooperative.

? **Nicolas Feuillatte 1996 Cuvée Palmes d'Or Rosé, Brut**
This pure Pinot Noir rosé de saignée is made from 50% Bouzy, 50% les Riceys and boasts bags of cherry fruit flavour, but seems to lack finesse. It also does not have typical 1996 acidity. However, since the best 1996s should not be released just yet and this is supposed to be a prestige cuvée, I will give this the benefit of doubt and reserve judgement for a while. Wait and see.
ⒺⒺⒺⒺ
Local Price **1200FF**

84 **Nicolas Feuillatte 1995 Chouilly**
At the SAA Champagne Tasting this cuvée had a distinctive malo-style on palate leading to a toffee finish, but it is now the fruitiest of Feuillatte's four new mono-cru Champagnes, with hardly any toffee showing (which is a good thing). It is also the simplest, least potentially complex. Drink now-2002.
ⒺⒺⒺ

87 **Nicolas Feuillatte 1995 Mesnil**
The complexity and structure was truly Pinot-like at the SAA tasting and in the final fight-off its extraordinary finesse made this my clear favourite. Several months down the line, all these new cuvées have developed and it has become my second favourite. It has the greatest potential finesse, complexity and longevity of all the Chardonnay Grands Crus in this new range.
Drink now-2004.
ⒺⒺⒺ

89 Nicolas Feuillatte 1995 Verzy
❗ This displayed vivid Northern Montagne richness at the SAA Champagne Tasting and by June it had built up great finesse. Lovely fresh fruit and cushiony mousse. Drink now-2004.
£££

86 Nicolas Feuillatte 1995 Cramant
❗ This was fresh and juicy at the SAA Tasting, but promised to build up a biscuity complexity. A fresh and tasty new disgorgement and I'm still waiting for the biscuitiness, although I have no doubts that it will come. Drink now-2003.
£££

85 Nicolas Feuillatte 1995 Blanc de Blancs Millésime, Brut Premier Cru
❗ Last year this became the best-scoring Champagne produced by this cooperative since the 1985 Palmes d'Or. It was noted for its classic structure and fruit, with biscuitiness building. The same applies this year, except that the biscuitiness is now a lovely creamy-biscuitiness. Drink now-2002.
££ Local Price 127FF

84 Nicolas Feuillatte 1992 Brut Millésimé, Premier Cru
❗ This vintage has continued the relatively fast evolution noted last year and already has a mature, biscuity nose. It might even be too mature for some, but there is an attractive sour-creaminess on the finish. Drink now-2002.
££ Local Price 127FF

84 Nicolas Feuillatte 1992 Cuvée Palmes d'Or, Brut
❗ Paler, younger colour when compared to the 1992 Brut Millésimé, but equally mature on the nose and less creaminess,

more fruit on the finish. Drink now-2003.
£££ Local Price 345FF

85 Nicolas Feuillatte 1992 Cuvée Palmes d'Or, Brut (*magnum*)
➡️ So much fresher than the regular 75cl bottle of Palmes d'Or. All fruit and freshness without a hint of biscuitiness. Is it the magnum effect or is there a big difference in the disgorgement dates? Drink 2002-2004.
££££ Local Price 800FF

Flein-Talheim

Weingärtner Flein-Talheim
Römerstrasse 14
74223 Flein
Germany
Phone (7131) 59520
Fax (7131) 595250

70 Weingärtner Flein-Talheim 1998 Trocken
❗ Soft and sweet. (100% Samtrot, bottle-fermented, Württemberg) Drink upon purchase.
£ Local Price DM19

Flirt

See BRL Hardy

Fontaine, Jean de la Fontaine

See Baron Albert

Foix, Duc de

See COVIDES

Frank

Chateau Frank
9749 Middle Road
Hammondsport
NY 14840
USA
Phone (800) 320 0735
Fax (607) 868 4884

*Late, great Konstantin Frank,
who opened up America's
Atlantic Northeast to vinifera
varieties.*

72 **Chateau Frank 1996 Brut**
Fresh, clean and sherbety with
rounded mid-palate fruit.
Drink upon purchase.
ⓔ

Freixenet

Pza Joan Sala 2
08770 Sant Sadurní d'Anoia
Spain
Phone (93) 891.7000
Fax (93) 818.3095

? **Freixenet Trépat 1999 Cava Brut**
Copper glints, chewy fruit, quite
fat and clear as a bell in some
respects, yet suggests it will go
oxidative in others. I include this
wine even though I'm not
convinced how it will evolve
because the use of Trépat is
another innovative step for
Freixenet and it is
pre-commercial sample, so I must
give it the benefit of doubt. I do,
however, fear that this experiment
will be as uninspiring as the
Monastrell-Xarel.lo. Wait and see.
ⓔ

77 **Freixenet Cuvée D.S.**
1996 Cava Brut
Bags of fruit, excellent acidity and
as clean as a whistle.
Drink now-2002.

ⓔ

Frey Sohler

72 rue de l'Ortenbourg
67750 Scherwiller
France
Phone (388) 92.10.13
Fax (388) 82.57.11

76 **Frey Sohler 1999 Blanc de Blancs,**
Crémant d'Alsace
Soft and creamy, nice acidity,
hint of vanilla on finish.
Drink upon purchase.
ⓔ Local Price **41FF**

72 **Frey Sohler 1998 Riesling,**
Crémant d'Alsace
Jammy-Riesling nose followed by
raspberry jam on the palate.
Not my cup of tea, but I had to
include this curiosity!
Drink upon purchase.
ⓔ Local Price **45FF**

Fries

Weingut Markus Fries
Zum Brauneberg 16
54484 Maring-Noviand
Germany
Phone (6535) 493
Fax (6535) 1505

80 **Markus Fries 1997**
Noviander Klosterberg Brut
Really soft, seductive Peach-stone
fruit floating on a lovely mousse
of creamy bubbles and anchored
by great acidity. (100% Riesling,
bottle-fermented, Mosel-Saar-
Ruwer) Drink now-2004.
ⓔ Local Price **DM16**

Fürstlich Castell'sches Domänenamt

See Castell'sches Domänenamt

Gaioncelli

Barboglio de Gaioncelli
Via N. Sauro
25040 Colombaro di
Cortefranca
Italy
Phone (30) 9826831
Fax (30) 9826831

77 **Barboglio DeGaioncelli NV**
♟ **Franciacorta Extra Dry**
Apricots and custard with firm
structure and good acidity.
Drink now-2003
ⓔ Local Price **11,500 Lira**

77 **Barboglio DeGaioncelli NV**
♟ **Franciacorta Brut**
Fresh, upfront fruity aromas. Firm
mousse, small bubbles. Should
develop surprisingly well over
the next few years.
Drink now-2004.
ⓔ Local Price **13,000 Lira**

Gallimard

Champagne Gallimard
18-20 rue du Magny
10340 Les Riceys
France
Phone (25) 29.32.44
Fax (25) 38.55.20

85 **Gallimard Père & Fils 1997 Cuvée**
◗ **Prestige, Brut Millésime**
Too young to drink, but the fruit
promises to build in depth with
a biscuity complexity and vanilla
finesse on the finish.
Drink 2003-2005.
ⓔ Local Price **89FF**

Attention!

*To submit samples for review
see page 52*

Gardet

Champagne Gardet
13 rue Georges Legros
51500 Chigny-les-Roses
France
Phone (326) 03.42.03
Fax (326) 03.43.95

85 **Georges Gardet NV Brut Spécial**
♟ At the Annual Champagne
Tasting, this cuvée had elevated
fruit (82 points), but the sample
submitted to my tastings was a
classic non-vintage quality with
crisp, crisp fruit and high acidity.
Drink now-2003.
ⓔⓔ Local Price **90FF**

86 **Georges Gardet NV Brut Rosé**
♟ With cherries, cream and vanilla,
this is a serious, yet fresh and
absolutely enjoyable rosé to drink
now or keep for a couple of year.
Clean and focused with no
oxidative tendencies.
Drink now-2004.
ⓔ Local Price **96FF**

90 **Cuvée Charles Gardet 1996 Brut**
♟ It might sound sacrilegious for a
wine from possibly the greatest
Champagne vintage of the century,
but drink this wonderfully fresh,
mind-blowingly complex cuvée
now! Great acidity, seductive
mousse. Drink upon purchase.
ⓔⓔ Local Price **125FF**

87 **Cuvée Charles Gardet 1995 Brut**
◗ Excellent extract, very crisp.
Needs time. Drink 2003-2007.
ⓔⓔ Local Price **125FF**

Gardet, Charles

See Gardet

Garrett

Andrew Garrett Vineyard
Estates
134a The Parade
Nowrood
SA 5067
Australia
Phone (8) 8379 0119
Fax (8) 8379 7228

78 McLarens on the Lake NV
☖ Sparkling Red Shiraz
Whacky label for an equally
whacky overtly raspberry
flavoured red fizz.
Drink upon purchase.
ⓔⓔ

Gatti

Gatti Enrico di Gatti Lorenzo
Via Metelli
9 – 25030 Erbusco
Italy
Phone (30) 7267157
Fax (30) 7760539

76 Gatti NV Franciacorta Brut
☖ Toasty rich fruit, lovely acidity
and length. Drink upon purchase.
ⓔ Local Price **15,000 Lira**

74 Gatti NV Franciacorta Satèn
☖ The preview sample of the next
release was really quite toasty
with a creamy, almost chewy-
creamy, richness of fruit. A toast-
lover's Franciacorta, but I would
not recommend keeping it very
long unless your toast-loving is
an extreme fetish.
Drink upon purchase.
ⓔ Local Price **17,000 Lira**

Gauthier

See Marne et Champagne

Gelida, Marques de

See Vins El Cep

Giersberger

See Ribeauvillé

Gimonnet

Champagne Pierre Gimonnet
& Fils
1 rue de la République
51530 Cuis
France
Phone (326) 59.78.70
Fax (326) 59.79.84

*This young grower gets more
impressive with every vintage.*

85 Pierre Gimonnet & Fils NV
➤ Blanc de Blancs Brut, Cuis 1er Cru
Really young with a low dosage,
has potential. Very fresh and crisp.
This turned out to be a blend of
85% 1998, 5% 1997 and 10%
1993, with just 8g/l dosage.
Drink 2002-2005.
ⓔ Local Price **95FF**

88 Pierre Gimonnet & Fils NV
☖ Cuvée Oenophile,
Blanc de Blancs, Extra-Brut
Although not vintaged, this is
pure 1993, but its beautifully fresh
floral aroma, crisp citrus and
apple-blossom Chardonnay fruit
and electrifyingly brut finish belie
its age. And all but 6% of the
blend comes from grand cru
vineyards. Best drunk at the table
and not kept.
Drink upon purchase.
ⓔⓔ Local Price **125FF**

86 Pierre Gimonnet & Fils 1997
Gastronome,
Blanc de Blancs Brut, 1er Cru
Very young on the nose, but quite
rich and fat, making it a relatively
early developer. The fatness of
this wine is unusual for
Gimonnet. Early in 2001 there
was even what seemed to be some
Pinot fruit developing, which is
not only unusual for Gimonnet,
but absolutely bizarre for a blanc
de blancs! By mid-June, however,
these developmental oddities were
beginning to disappear as the
wine pulled itself together,
making itself ideal for drinking
by Christmas 2001.
Drink now-2004.
ⒺⒺ Local Price 125FF

87 Pierre Gimonnet & Fils 1996
Premier Cru-Chardonnay, Brut
Initially this might seem to
lack fruit and appeal, but the
undeveloped extract on the
finish promises to develop into
a Champagne of great hazelnut-
walnut complexity. This Club de
Viticulteurs cuvée makes the 1996
Gastronome seem like ready
drinking in comparison, although
they should both start to open up
at about the same time. After the
covers came off, I wondered if
I had marked this too low, but
that's blind tasting for you, so I'll
stick with 87 points for this year
at least. Drink 2003-2005.
ⒺⒺ Local Price 115FF

88 Pierre Gimonnet & Fils 1996
Gastronome,
Blanc de Blancs Brut, 1er Cru
This won't even hint at its true
potential for a couple of years yet.
Drink 2003-2007.
ⒺⒺ Local Price 125FF

88 Pierre Gimonnet & Fils 1995
Fleuron, Blanc de Blancs Brut,
1er Cru

Lovely, fresh, breezy fruit. Should
be perfect for Christmas 2001.
A true brut, but not at all austere,
which is remarkable considering
its very low dosage (5g/l).
Drink now-2006.
ⒺⒺ Local Price 115FF

91 Pierre Gimonnet & Fils,
Millésime de Collection 1995
Les Cuvées de l'An 2000,
Brut (*magnum*)
Seductively fruity aromas with
limes and lemon-blossom in the
high-ripe-acid fruit. A very fruity
style that has lots of ageing
potential. Drink now-2006.
ⒺⒺⒺ Local Price 400FF

90 Pierre Gimonnet & Fils,
Millésime de Collection 1990
Les Cuvées de l'An 2000,
Brut (*magnum*)
This is fabulously good and
ridiculously young!
Drink now-2011.
ⒺⒺⒺ Local Price 400FF

Ginglinger

Paul Gingliner
8 Place Charles de Gaulle
68420 Eguisheim
France
Phone (389) 41.44.25
Fax (389) 24.94.88

---

76 Paul Ginglinger 1998
Crémant d'Alsace Brut
A fresh and very fruity wine of
some finesse. Drink now-2002.
Ⓔ Local Price 45FF

Giró Ribot

CIGRAVI
Finca El Pont s/n
08792 Santa Fe del Penedès
Spain
Phone (93) 8974050
Fax (93) 8974311

75 Paul Cheneau NV Cava Brut
Fresh and fruity, with plenty
of easy going, Cava-soft acidity
(1998-based).
Drink upon purchase.
€ Local Price **427 Ptas**

Gisselbrecht

Willy Gisselbrecht
5 route du Vin
67650 Dambach/ville
France
Phone (388) 92.41.02
Fax (388) 92.45.50

70 Willy Gisselbrecht 1999
Blanc de Noirs, Crémant d'Alsace
Too fat for most sparkling wine
lovers, but scrapes in for those
who find sparkling wine to harsh
because this certainly isn't!
Drink upon purchase.
€ Local Price **43FF**

Glaetzer

34 Barossa Valley Way
Tanunda
SA 5352
Australia
Phone (8) 8563 0288
Fax (8) 8563 0218

80 Glaetzer NV Barossa Valley
Sparkling Shiraz
Relatively dry cedary-Shiraz fruit.
Drink now-2002.
€€€ Local Price **A$60**

79 Glaetzer 1996 Barossa Valley
Sparkling Pinot Noir
Very fine, crisp fruit with a soft,
pin-cushion mousse.
Drink now-2003.
€€

Glenara

126 Range Road North
Upper Hermitage
SA 5131
Australia
Phone (8) 8380 5056
Fax (8) 8380 5056

78 White Quartz, Adelaide Hills
1997 Organic Sparkling Pinot
Noir Chardonnay
Classic structure, very fresh,
elegant fruit. Drink now-2003.
€€

Gloria Ferrer

23555 Highway 121
Sonoma
CA 95476
USA
Phone (707) 996 7256
Fax (707) 996 0378

76 Gloria Ferrer NV Bru
The 1998-based blend (298 on the
bottle) has elegant sherbety-
strawberry fruit, is very soft and
fine, with a lovely creamy mousse.
Drink upon purchase.
€€ Local Price **$15**

75 Gloria Ferrer NV Blanc de Noirs
Light, fresh and crisp.
Drink upon purchase.
€€ Local Price **$15**

80 Gloria Ferrer NV Carneros Rosé
The 498 release has a delicate
pale-peach colour with a vibrantly
fresh and fruity nose, very elegant,
ripe acid-charged Bartlett pear
fruit on a pin-cushion mousse.
Drink now-2002.
€€ Local Price **$15**

90 Gloria Ferrer 1994
Royal Cuvée Brut
Beautifully integrated, deliciously
soft, silky fruit. Will slowly

intensify and assume a mellow
sweetness on the finish.
Drink now-2003.
ⓔⓔ Local Price **$18**

89   Gloria Ferrer 1993
Ⓨ **Royal Cuvée Brut**
A super-silky mousse, adds finesse
to the very fresh, silky-smooth
fruit. Excellent. Drink now-2002.
ⓔⓔ Local Price **$18**

Goerg

Champagne Paul Goerg
4 Place du Mont Chenil
51130 Vertus
France
Phone (326) 52.15.31
Fax (326) 52.23.96

---

84   Paul Goerg NV Blanc de Blancs,
Ⓨ **Brut Premier Cru**
Perfumed Chardonnay aromas,
quite floral and citrus, this cuvée
will develop a creamy-nutty-
biscuity complexity.
Drink now-2003.
ⓔ Local Price **80FF**

84   Paul Goerg 1996 Millésimé,
▬ **Brut Premier Cru**
Fresh and perfumed fruit, good
acidity. Drink 2002-2004.
ⓔⓔ Local Price **100FF**

Gonet

Champagne Philippe Gonet
1 rue de la Brèche d'Oger
51190 Le-Mesnil-sur-Oger
France
Phone (326) 57.51.07
Fax (326) 57.51.03

---

82   Philippe Gonet NV Brut
▬ Estery aromas followed by rich
Chardonnay fruit suggest that this
release has been disgorged too
early, but should mellow with age.

It must cost a lot of money to
envelop this bottle in such a crass
plastic coating. Presented in blue
plastic coated bottle!
Drink 2002-2003.
ⓔⓔ

Gosset

Champagne Gosset
69 rue Jules Blondeau
51160 Aÿ-Champagne
France
Phone (326) 55.14.18
Fax (326) 51.55.88

---

85   Gosset NV Excellence Brut
Ⓨ (*magnum*)
This wine in the standard 75cl
bottle has never squeezed more
than 83 points out of me under
blind conditions and did not
manage that at the Annual
Champagne Tasting in March
2000. However, this is my first
experience of Gosset Excellence
in magnum and it seems to be a
different animal, with very fresh,
fine aroma followed by crisp,
clean fruit of some depth and
excellent acidity. I think a
magnum is the only way I will
drink this wine in future.
Drink now-2004.
ⓔⓔ Local Price **150FF**

90   Gosset NV Grande Réserve Brut
▬ (*magnum*)
The autolysis on the nose bodes
well for the future finesse of this
Champagne, while a fleeting
bitterness of undeveloped extract
on the finish promises great
complexity. It really would be
infanticide to drink this for
at least three years.
Drink 2004-2009.
ⓔⓔⓔ Local Price **500FF**

89   Gosset NV Grand Rosé Brut
Ⓨ Deliciously rich and nicely mellow

with a creamy aftertaste.
Drink now-2006.
ⓔⓔⓔ Local Price **250FF**

97 Gosset 1996 Grand Millésime Brut
With such great extract, acidity
and finesse, this vintage promises
to be one of Gosset's greatest ever.
When in a masochistic mood I
love drinking the electrifying fruit
in this wine now, but don't
over-chill this and if you really like
Gosset, keep it five years or more.
Drink now-2021.
ⓔⓔⓔ Local Price **327FF**

93 Gosset Celebris 1995 Brut
It is only in comparison to
Gosset's 1996 that this vintage of
Celebris seem a touch fat, forward
and ready because on it's own it
is almost excruciating in its
application of acidity to fruit.
This is another great, very great
Gosset. Drink now-2016.
ⓔⓔⓔⓔ Local Price **445FF**

89 Gosset 1993 Grand Millésime Brut
This vintage is only just beginning
to develop a touch of vanilla on
its finish. Gosset fans will keep
this at least two years.
Drink 2002-2007.
ⓔⓔⓔ Local Price **327FF**

Goutorbe

Champagne Henri Goutorbe
9 rue Jeanson
51160 Aÿ-Champagne
France
Phone (326) 55.21.70
Fax (326) 54.85.11

85 Henri Goutorbe NV
Cuvée Tradition, Brut
Lifted fruit aroma followed by
rich, sharp fruit on the palate.
Drink now-2003.
ⓔ Local Price **77FF**

87 Henri Goutorbe 1996
Brut Grand Cru
Powerful autolytic aromas
followed by rich, tangy, strawberry
boiled-sweet fruit. Serious
Champagne drinkers will keep
this two years at least.
Drink 2002-2005.
ⓔⓔ Local Price **118FF**

91 Goutorbe 1995 Brut Grand Cru
A big bruiser of a Champagne.
Huge flavour, yet not lacking
elegance and finesse. Great
extract. Will be a truly great
Champagne. Drink now-2011.
ⓔ Local Price **92FF**

Gramona

Industria 36
08770 Sant Sadurní d'Anoia
Spain
Phone (93) 8910113
Fax (93) 8183284

79 Gramona, Imperial 1998
Cava Brut Gran Reserva
Promises to be even rich than
the 1997. Drink upon purchase.
ⓔ Local Price **1,850 Ptas**

79 Gramona, Imperial 1997
Cava Brut Gran Reserva
Definitely going for the fuller,
more complex, rich-biscuity
Champagne style and not doing a
bad job considering the varietal
hurdles! Drink upon purchase.
ⓔ Local Price **1,600 Ptas**

80 Gramona, III Lustros 1996
Cava Brut Nature
Fresh, firm and well-structured
with an underlying vanilla
smoothness to the fruit. This
pre-commercial bottling was
ready in early 2001 and should be
released before terpenes develop.
Drink now-2002.
ⓔ Local Price **2,500 Ptas**

80 Gramona, III Lustros 1995
Cava Brut Nature
The 1995 is virtually
indistinguishable from the
1996. Perhaps the acidity is
more pronounced, but that could
well be nothing more than my
imagination trying to discern
a difference. Drink now-2002.
ⓔ Local Price **2,500 Ptas**

Grand Siècle

See Laurent-Perrier

Gratien

Champagne Alfred Gratien
30 rue Maurice Cerveaux
51201 Epernay
France
Phone (326) 54.38.20
Fax (41) 51.03.55

86 Alfred Gratien NV Brut
Acidulated apple purée fruit with
a lovely soft mousse.
Drink now-2004.
ⓔⓔ Local Price **167FF**

83 Alfred Gratien 1991 Brut
This vintage has developed a
marked oxidativeness since last
year, hence its drop of two
percentile points. The optimum
disgorgement date is vital here
and I have not yet tasted it, so it
could fetch a much higher score
in a future edition.
Drink now-2004.
ⓔⓔⓔ Local Price **256FF**

Green Point

See Chandon (Australia)

Gruss

Domaine Gruss
25 Grand'Rue
68420 Eguisheim
France
Phone (389) 41.28.78
Fax (389) 41.76.66

75 Domaine Gruss 1998 Brut
Prestige, Crémant d'Alsace
Creamy-lemony fruit, very soft,
gentle, but nicely ripe acidity
carries the length, fruity
aftertaste. Drink upon purchase.
ⓔ Local Price **47FF**

Haegelin Materne

45-47, Grand'Rue
68500 Orschwihr
France
Phone (389) 76.95.17
Fax (389) 74.88.87

74 Haegelin 1996 Chardonnay,
Crémant d'Alsace
The best Chardonnay Crémant
d'Alsace from 1996, a notoriously
high malic acid vintage that as
a signature stink on most wines,
but this is clear, fresh and fruity.
Drink now-2002.
ⓔ Local Price **45FF**

Hale Valley

Boddington East
Hale Lane
Wendover
Bucks HP22 6NQ
Great Britain
Phone (1296) 623730

70 Hale Valley 1998 Brut
This aromatic fizz should really
have far higher acidity, but it will
at least appeal to those who do
not like their wines too crisp.
The label needs redesigning.

Drink upon purchase.
Ⓔ

and a fatter finish when compared to the SG-6, but equal in pure quality terms. Drink now-2002.
Ⓔ

Harbonville

See Ployez-Jacquemart

Hardys

See BRL Hardy

Harris

Andrew Harris
Mudgee
Sydney Road
Mudgee
NSW 2850
Australia
Phone (2) 6373 1213
Fax (2) 6373 1296

84 Andrew Harris 1997 Double Vision Mudgee Sparkling Shiraz
Exceedingly dry for sparkling Shiraz! Drink now-2002
ⒺⒺ Local Price **A$45**

Hartenberg

See Pfaffenheim

Haselgrove

Sand Road
McLaren Vale
SA 5171
Australia
Phone (8) 8323 8706
Fax (8) 8323 8049

80 Haselgrove NV
McLaren Vale Garnet SG-7
More dry tannins, less cranberries

Hauses Württemberg

Weingut des Hauses
Württemberg
Schloß Monrepos
71634 Ludwigsburg
Germany
Phone (7141) 221060
Fax (7141) 22106260

70 Des Hauses Württemberg 1998 Maulbronner Eilfingerberg Riesling Sekt Trocken
Saved by high acidity, but needs a little time. (100% Riesling, bottle-fermented, Württemberg)
Drink 2002-2003.
Ⓔ Local Price **DM20**

Heidsieck, Charles

Champagne Charles Heidsieck
4 Blvd. Henry Vasnier
51100 Reims
France
Phone (326) 84.43.50
Fax (326) 84.43.99

90 Charles Heidsieck NV Brut Réserve, Mis en Cave en 1997
Disgorged in the second quarter of 2000, this Mis en Cave is currently dominated by intense fruit of great finesse and complexity. The intensity of the fruit indicates considerably more complexity to come, thus its score could increase in future. Don't forget that this is the 1996-based blend. Drink now-2005.
ⒺⒺ Local Price **145FF**

91 Charles Heidsieck NV Brut Réserve, Mis en Cave en 1996
Disgorged in the second quarter

of 1999, this Mis en Cave is an absolute stunner, full of glorious fruit impregnated with wonderfully gentle toasty nuances and supported by the most velvety and cushiony of mousses. Drink now-2004.
ⒺⒺ Local Price **145FF**

89 **Charles Heidsieck NV Brut**
Ⓘ **Réserve, Mis en Cave en 1995**
Disgorged in the first quarter of 2000, this Mis en Cave shows classic Charles Heidsieck vanilla-coated fruit with toast and a touch of coffee grinds on the aftertaste. Drink now-2003.
ⒺⒺ Local Price **145FF**

Heidsieck Monopole

Champagne Heidsieck & Co Monopole
17 avenue de Champagne
51205 Epernay Cedex
France
Phone (326) 59.50.50
Fax (326) 51.87.07

---

83 **Heidsieck Monopole**
Ⓘ **NV Blue Top Brut**
A sweet and creamy Champagne for the masses. Surprisingly well made. Drink now-2002.
ⒺⒺ Local Price **115FF**

82 **Heidsieck Monopole 1995**
Ⓘ **Gold Top Brut**
The 1995 onboard Air France business class to San Francisco was not exceptional, but palatable and strangely superior to the 1995 on the general market in early 2001. Drink now-2003.
ⒺⒺ Local Price **170FF**

Attention!

To submit samples for review see page 52

Heim

CV de Westhalten
52 route de Soultzmatt
68250 Westhalten
France
Phone (389) 78.09.08
Fax (389) 49.09.20

---

78 **Heim NV Imperial,**
Ⓘ **Crémant d'Alsace**
1st corked. 2nd bottle very nice indeed, with fresh, piquant fruit and a perfectly balanced dosage. Drink upon purchase.
Ⓔ Local Price **40FF**

Heim'sche

Privat-Sektkellerei Heim'sche
Maximilianstrasse 32
67433 Neustadt/Weinstrasse
Germany
Phone (6321) 39260
Fax (6321) 392610

---

70 **Heim'sche Privat-Sektkellerei**
Ⓘ **1999 Martin Heim Brut**
A crisp, clean, entry level Riesling Sekt for sparkling wine aficionados. (100% Riesling, bottle-fermented, Pfalz)
Drink upon purchase.
Ⓔ Local Price **DM19**

Heitlinger

Weingut Albert Heitlinger
Am Mühlberg
76684 Östringen-Tiefenbach
Germany
Phone (7259) 91120
Fax (7259) 911299

---

73 **Albert Heitlinger 1997**
Ⓘ **Heilinger Blanc et Brut**
A fresh-tasting melange of Riesling, Pinot Gris and Pinot Noir. Easy to drink classic style with a Germanic lift to its sweetish

finish. (41% Riesling, 30%
Grauburgunder, 29%
Spätburgunder; bottle-fermented,
Baden) Drink now-2003.
ⓔⓔ Local Price **DM39**

Henriot

Champagne Henriot
3 Place des Droits de l'Homme
51100 Reims
France
Phone (326) 89.53.00
Fax (326) 89.53.10

---

86 **Henriot NV Brut Souverain**
▮ This fresh yet mature cuvée is on
top form with a completeness
and touch of finesse to its fruit.
Should age gracefully.
Drink now-2005.
ⓔⓔ Local Price **145FF**

87 **Henriot NV Blanc de Blancs Brut**
▮ This stood out from a row
of 20 blanc de blancs grower
Champagnes. Not because of
quality, but because of style. I had
not thought about it before, but
just as most (not all) houses tend
to rely on malolactic for a stable
product that has to undergo the
rigours of global transportation,
so most (but not all) growers tend
to avoid malolactic or at least not
to emphasise it, probably because
their Champagnes are not used to
being transported to all four
corners of the globe. Lover of
mature creamy-biscuity blanc
de blancs will snap this up and
probably cellar it a couple of
years. Drink now-2005.
ⓔⓔ Local Price **155FF**

86 **Henriot 1995 Brut Millésime**
▬ The buttery-malo aroma on this
Champagne is reflected by vanilla
on the finish, but with time both
these characteristics will merge
into a creamy-biscuity complexity

of some finesse. Drink 2003-2007.
ⓔⓔ
Local Price **190FF**

88 **Henriot 1990 Brut Millésime**
▬ The apricot-Chardonnay aromas
noted two years ago have turned
into seductively mellow toast and
coffee aromas, yet still young and
closed on the palate, with a
sweetish, vanilla-dusted finish.
This wine needed time two
editions and still needs time to
swell out the fruit mid-palate,
its optimum drinking period the
same then as now.
Drink 2002-2012.
ⓔⓔ Local Price **190FF**

? **Henriot 1989**
Cuvée des Enchanteleurs, Brut
A goodish Champagne that could
have been great if it was released
two years ago, when it showed
'great finesse from the biscuity
aromas through the fabulously
rich yet classically lean fruit to the
exquisite mousse and great finish'.
All this has gone because no one
at Henriot had the savvy to
release the 1989 vintage of this
cuvée before the 1988. The wine
now is a shadow of its former self,
which is a great shame, and the
1988 is only just opening out.
Madness! Wait and see.
ⓔⓔⓔⓔ Local Price **450FF**

89 **Henriot 1988**
▮ **Cuvée des Enchanteleurs, Brut**
A lovely, biscuity-mature
Champagne on the nose, but still
a little unrelenting on the palate,
where the fruit is lean and even a
little green. Don't get me wrong,
these elements do come together,
particularly with food, but they
also demonstrate what a bright
future this vintage has. Put it this
way, I took this home to go with
some supper, but poured the 1989
(technically superior two years

ago) down the drain!
Drink now-2006.
ⒺⒺⒺⒺ Local Price **450FF**

Hérard et Fluteau

Champagne G. Fluteau
5 Rue de la Nation
10250 Gyé-sur-Seine
France
Phone (325) 38.20.02
Fax (325) 38.24.84

86 **G. Fluteau NV Brut Carte Blanche**
The preview sample of the blend
due to be released in September
2001 looks like a blanc de noirs
New World style, which is to say a
very pale rosé as opposed to the
champenois ideal of no colour
whatsoever. If it was actually
labelled Blanc de Noirs I would
wonder at the influence of
Jennifer Fluteau, who is
American, but it's not and I've
never noticed any coloration
before, although Carte Blanche is
sometimes marked by redcurrant
Pinot Noir fruit. Anyway, this
release is excellent in a very soft,
silky, fresh, not too brut style,
with sugar-dusted red fruits on
the finish. Drink now-2002
Ⓔ Local Price **71FF**

87 **G. Fluteau 1997 Cuvée Prestige,**
Blanc de Blancs Brut
A precocious 1997 that is
nevertheless extremely fine, with
an immaculate mousse of
minuscule bubbles, tastefully
presented in a dead-leaf brown
bottle. Drink now-2003
Ⓔ Local Price **88FF**

Attention!

To submit samples for review
see page 52

Hertz

Albert Hertz
3 rue du Riesling
68420 Eguisheim
France
Phone (389) 41.30.32
Fax (389) 23.99.23

72 **Victor Hertz 1996**
Crémant d'Alsace Brut
Sweet creamy fruit on the nose,
perfumed fruit, high acidity. Not
sure how this will develop, but
worth watching 1-2 years or so.
Drink now-2002
Ⓔ Local Price **45FF**

74 **Victor Hertz 1995**
Rosé d'Alsace, Crémant d'Alsace
A very mature-looking, Tavel Rosé
colour, but with fresh, cherry
Pinot fruit underneath.
Drink upon purchase.
Ⓔ Local Price **45FF**

Hessen

Weingut Prinz von Hessen
Johannisberg/Rheingau
65366 Geisenheim
Germany
Phone (672) 28172
Fax (672) 250588

80 **Prinz von Hessen 1997 Extra Brut**
Nice perfumed Riesling bottle
aromas with fresh, citrussy fruit
on the palate, and mouthwatering
acidity on the finish. Beautifully
clear fruit and well-focused.
(100% Riesling, bottle-fermented,
Rheingau) Drink now-2002.
ⒺⒺ Local Price **DM39**

Hinkel

Weingut Dr. Hinkel
Kirchstrasse 53
55234 Framersheim
Germany
Phone (6733) 368
Fax (6733) 1490

72 **Dr. Hinkel 1999 Framersheimer
Hornberg Halbtrocken**
Sekt meets Asti! (100% Morio
Muskat, bottle-fermented,
Rheinhessen)
Drink upon purchase.
ⓔ Local Price **DM15**

Huia

Boyces Road RD3
Blenheim
Renwick
New Zealand
Phone (3) 572 8326
Fax (3) 572 8331

80 **Huia 1997 Brut**
Biscuity crème anglaise!
Drink now-2002.
ⓔ Local Price **NZ$32**

Hunawihr

CV de Hunawihr
48 route de Ribeauvillé
68150 Hunawihr
France
Phone (389) 73.61.67
Fax (389) 73.33.95

70 **CV de Hunawihr NV
Calixte Brut, Crémant d'Alsace**
Very fruity, but needs more acidity.
Drink upon purchase.
ⓔ Local Price **38FF**

Hunter's

Rapaura Road
Blenheim
New Zealand
Phone (3) 572 8489
Fax (3) 572 8457

86 **Miru Miru 1999 Hunter's**
Soft, fruity and so easy to drink.
Drink now-2003.
ⓔ Local Price **NZ$30**

87 **Miru Miru 1998 Hunter's**
Even easier to drink than the 1999,
finer quality, more graceful.
Drink now-2003.
ⓔ Local Price **NZ$30**

89 **Hunter's 1996 Brut**
Richly flavoured, pure and classy
now, this vintage will be truly
splendid if kept a few years.
Drink now-2004.
ⓔ Local Price **NZ$30**

Hutt

Pierre Hutt
24 rue Principale
67140 Heiligenstein
France
Phone (388) 08.50.52
Fax (388) 08.59.77

73 **Pierre Hutt NV
Crémant d'Alsace Brut**
Spiced fruit with liquorice
richness. Must have some mature
reserve wines in this blend.
Now-2002.
ⓔ Local Price **40FF**

I Ronchetti

See Martelletti

Ingersheim, CV de

CV de Ingersheim
45 rue de la République
68040 Ingersheim
France
Phone (389) 27.05.96
Fax (389) 27.51.24

70 CV d'Ingersheim NV Crémant
❢ d'Alsace Brut
Fresh and light with clean fruit
and nicely crisp finish.
Drink upon purchase.
ⓔ Local Price 35FF

70 CV d'Ingersheim NV Brut
❢ Prestige, Crémant d'Alsace
Sweet, creamy fizz. Needs more
acidity if it is to score higher.
Drink upon purchase.
ⓔ Local Price 37FF

Iron Horse

9786 Ross Station Road
Sebastopol
CA 95472
USA
Phone (707) 887 1507
Fax (707) 887 1337

75 Iron Horse NV Brut Rosé
❢ Exuberant mature fruit, but l'm
still waiting for the wacky
crimson-pink rosé that Iron Horse
first made its rosé reputation
with. Drink upon purchase.
ⓔⓔ Local Price $27

88 Iron Horse 1997 Blanc de Blancs
❢ Beautiful creamy-nutty-biscuity
fruit. Classy stuff.
Drink now-2002.
ⓔⓔ Local Price $26

77 Iron Horse 1996
▬ Classic Vintage Brut
Hard-edged, but promises to
develop into a toasty style.
Drink 2002-2004.

ⓔⓔ Local Price $25

80 Iron Horse 1996 Russian Cuvée
❢ Smooth, seamless fruit and
sweetness. Drink now-2003.
ⓔⓔ Local Price $25

85 Iron Horse 1995
❢ Classic Vintage Brut
The same disgorgement as last
year (80 points) has really come
on with an additional 12 months
post-disgorgement ageing. In the
last edition I noted that there was
'lots of malo, lots of extract and
promise, but you will have to
wait'. Well those with patience
will be rewarded because the
extract has started to loosen up,
swelling out the fruit and
subduing the malo to the point
where it is purely of a textural
nature, contributing creaminess
to the back of the palate. The
mousse is lovely and cushiony, yet
there's terrific acidity, which will
ensure that it gets even better,
although it has already leaped up
five percentile points.
Drink now-2004.
ⓔⓔ Local Price $25

90 Iron Horse 1991 Brut
❢ A rich, complex wine, yet with
such elegance and a wonderfully
smooth mousse there is no feeling
of heaviness. With no overt malo
character the full finesse of this
wine is realised. Drink now-2004
ⓔⓔⓔⓔ Local Price $54

J Wine Company

11447 Old Redwood Highway
Healdsburg
CA 95448
USA
Phone (707) 431 5400
Fax (707) 431 5410

83 J 1996 Brut
High acids. Very tight.
Potentially exciting. Needs time.
Drink 2002-2004.
Ⓔ Local Price $26

85 J 1994 Brut (*magnum*)
This vintage has taken on
some real gravitas in magnum.
A serious sparkling wine with
freshness and complexity.
Drink now-2004.
ⒺⒺⒺ Local Price $72

Jacob's Creek

See Orlando Wyndham

Jacquart

Champagne Jacquart
6 rue de Mars
51066 Reims
France
Phone (326) 07.20.20
Fax (326) 57.78.14

*Is Brut de Nominée the first 90-
point Champagne from a
cooperative to appear on these
pages? I think it is and the fact
that it is a non-vintage cuvée is
all the more amazing.*

---

83 Jacquart NV Demi-Sec
Still a bit sugary, but good extract
promises better things to come.
Drink 2002-2005.
ⒺⒺ Local Price 125FF

72 Jacquart NV Brut Mosaïque
The release in the UK at the
beginning of 2001 was malty
and would not have qualified for
recommendation in this guide,
but the next release was better.
The nose could have been more
appealing, but on the palate the
fruit was fresh, attractive and
easy to drink. It was also much
preferred this year to the same
cuvée in magnum.
Drink now-2003.
ⒺⒺ Local Price 125FF

87 Jacquart NV Brut Mosaïque Rosé
The nose is mature, but pale
peach colour and fresh,
creamy-strawberry fruit on the
palate make this very seductive.
Drink now-2002.
ⒺⒺ Local Price 150FF

90 Jacquart NV Brut de Nominée
Brilliant quality and tasteful
packaging for this new deluxe
quality cuvée presented in a bottle
made from heavy-weight dark
glass, with a tastefully understated
ticket label. This is a 50/50
Chardonnay/Pinot Noir blend
from the best crus and although
not a vintage Champagne, the
back label does claim that it is
principally from the 1996 harvest.
Selection is the hallmark of this
great Champagne and it is
currently expressed through the
clarity and finesse of the fruit,
and the future promises
exceptional complexity. After
such a lacklustre record for the
vintaged Nominée Brut, I could
not be more surprised or more
pleased that Jacquart has struck
gold with this non-vintage
version. Drink now-2006.
ⒺⒺⒺ Local Price 250FF

**88 Jacquart 1996 Blanc de Blancs,
Brut Mosaïque**
Lovely clean-cut, citrussy fruit
that's a delight to drink now, but
will improve. Drink now-2006.
ⒺⒺ Local Price 160FF

Attention!

*To submit samples for review
see page 52*

Jacquesson

Champagne Jacquesson & Fils
68 rue du Colonel Fabien
51200 Dizy
France
Phone (326) 55.68.11
Fax (326) 51.06.25

93 Jacquesson & Fils NV Mémoire
‼ du XX ème Siècle, Brut
Released for the Millennium celebrations and consisting primarily of the very good 1995 vintage and truly outstanding 1996, it was dosaged with a wine containing 22 vintages spanning the 20th century (1990, 1989, 1988, 1985, 1983, 1982, 1981, 1979, 1978, 1976, 1975, 1973, 1971, 1970, 1964, 1961, 1953, 1952, 1942, 1928 and 1915). As exotic as this might sound, it was simply amylic last year and I was forced to reserve my opinion in the 2000 edition. I've been bullying Jacquesson for another sample ever since. The nose is now dominated by autolytic aromas, which makes me suspect that it has been recently disgorged, when I would have preferred to see how the original disgorgement had developed. I could be wrong; in some very special Champagnes the autolytic aromas can dominate for up to 10 years after disgorgement and this is indeed shaping into something special. It has a profoundly deep, complete and satisfying flavour that is full of finesse and capable of great complexity. This Champagne amazes me, whether it is the same disgorgement or not. Drink now-2011.
ⓔⓔⓔⓔ

87 Jacquesson & Fils 1995
➤ Blanc de Blancs, Brut Grand Cru
I have experienced a couple of off-bottles, but most examples are very good, but still quite tight and concentrated. Drink 2002-2007.
ⓔⓔⓔ Local Price **260FF**

? Jacquesson & Fils 1993
Grand Vin Signature
A beautiful mousse, lovely fruit on the palate, but it needs another tasting of this preview sample to convince me about its aromatic qualities. Wait and see.
ⓔⓔⓔ Local Price **330FF**

89 Jacquesson & Fils 1988
‼ Grand Vin Signature
The 1988s are long-distance runners, as the preview sample of this ultra-smooth biscuity cuvée demonstrated. Due to be released in September 2001.
Drink now-2005.
ⓔⓔⓔⓔ Local Price **400FF**

Jamain

Champagne Pierre Jamain
1 rue des Tuileries
51260 La Celle-sous-Chantemerle
France
Phone (326) 80.21.64
Fax (326) 80.29.32

84 Pierre Jamain NV
‼ Cuvée Caroline, Brut
Elevated youthful fruit.
Drink now-2002.
ⓔ Local Price **78FF**

88 Pierre Jamain NV Brut Rosé
‼ Lovely pale rosé with soft, vanilla-dusted red fruits on the palate.
Drink now-2002.
ⓔ Local Price **78FF**

87 Pierre Jamain 1996 Brut Millésimé
‼ Beautifully clean, clear, bright fruit with nice acidity, but nothing like the high ripe acids found in most Champagnes from this vintage. Perhaps the Sézannais 1996s are softer? Not due to be released until December 2001.

Drink now-2003
ⓔ Local Price **83FF**

Jansz

See Smith

Jean de la Fontaine

See Baron Albert

Jepson

10400 South Highway 101
Ukiah
CA 95482
USA
Phone 800 516 7342
Fax 707 468 0362

78 Jepson NV Blanc de Blancs
Very fruity indeed. Creamy stone
fruit. Lovely mousse.
Drink now-2002.
ⓔⓔ Local Price **$18**

Joseph

See Primo Estate

Juvé & Camps

Sant Venat 1
08770 Sant Sadurní d'Anoia
Spain
Phone (93) 8911000
Fax (93) 8912100

76 Juvé & Camps, Reserva de la
Familia 1997 Cava Brut Nature
Bags of fruit for a Cava. Firm
structure, good acidity.
Drink now-2002.
ⓔ Local Price **1,850 Ptas**

Kallfelz

Weingut Albert Kallfelz
Hauptstrasse 60-62
56856 Zell-Merl/Mosel
Germany
Phone (6542) 93880
Fax (6542) 938850

72 Albert Kallfelz 1999 Kallfelz
Riesling Sekt Brut
Although this has more flavour
than finesse, its richness, varietal
character and acidity put it ahead
of many other Sekte. (100%
Riesling, bottle-fermented,
Mosel-Saar-Ruwer)
Drink now-2003.
ⓔ Local Price **DM17**

Klein

J.Marie et Françoise Klein
Route du Haut Koenigsbourg
68590 St. Hippolyte
France
Phone (389) 73.00.41
Fax (389) 73.04.94

70 Klein 1997 Extra Brut Blanc de
Blancs, Crémant d'Alsace
Creamy-biscuity Champagne
style, but needs much more acidity
and (then) a larger dosage to work
properly. Drink upon purchase.
ⓔ Local Price **55FF**

70 Klein 1996 Extra Brut Blanc de
Blancs, Crémant d'Alsace
This just scrapes through, but
it's decidedly champenois style.
Would have been enhanced by
a large dosage to balance the
extremely high typical 1996
acidity. Drink now-2004.
ⓔ Local Price **55FF**

Klein Constantia

Constantia 7848
South Africa
Phone (21) 794 5188
Fax (21) 794 2464

? **Klein Constantia NV Brut Triple
Zero, Cap Classique** (*magnum*)
Only its high acidity has kept this
hugely toasty fizz fresh. Certainly
the cork has not. If the tiny cork
protecting the magnum I tasted
is representative of the entire lot,
there is not much time left so
owners should drink up.
Wait and see.
ⓔⓔ

Klingenfus

Robert Klingenfus
60 rue de Saverne
67120 Molsheim
France
Phone (388) 38.07.06
Fax (388) 49.32.47

70 **Robert Klingenfus NV
Crémant d'Alsace Brut**
Too fat for purists (either purist
sparkling wine lovers or purist
Alsace fans), but would suit a
large reception of mixed guests.
Drink upon purchase.
ⓔ Local Price **46FF**

Kloster Eberbach

Hessische Staatsweingüter
Kloster Eberbach
Schwalbacherstrasse 56-62
65343 Eltville
Germany
Phone (6123) 92300
Fax (6123) 923090

75 **Hessische Staatsweingüter
Kloster Eberbach 1998
Rauenthaler Baiken Brut**
Soft and sultry Riesling aromas
mingling around a firm fruit core.
(100% Riesling, transfer-method,
Rheingau) Drink now-2003.
ⓔ Local Price **DM23**

Klur

Vignoble Klur
105 rue des 3 Epis
68230 Katzenthal
France
Phone (389) 80.94.29
Fax (389) 27.30.17

70 **Vignoble Klur 1999 Klur Clement,
Crémant d'Alsace**
Fresh and clean, very soft,
technically correct, ideal for those
who find sparkling wines too
acidic. Drink upon purchase.
ⓔ Local Price **44FF**

Knyphausen

Weingut Baron zu Knyphausen
Klosterhof Dreis
65346 Erbach im Rheingau
Germany
Phone (6123) 62177
Fax (6123) 4315

72 **Baron zu Knyphausen 1993
Herrlichkeit Knyphausen
Extra Brut**
The perfumed Riesling aromas
are amazingly fresh for its age,
but this wine is now edging
past its best and should any
undisgorged stocks remain, it
would be advisable for longevity
not necessarily balance to dosage
them as Brut, not Extra-Brut.
(100% Riesling, bottle-fermented,
Rheingau) Drink upon purchase.
ⓔ Local Price **DM27**

Korbel

Korbel Champagne Cellars
13250 River Road
Guerneville
CA 95446
USA
Phone (707) 824 7000
Fax (707) 869 2506

*This is only the third
Korbel wine I've ever been able
to recommend (the fizzy red is
under-appreciated).*

75 **Korbel 1998 Natural
Ⓨ Chardonnay Champagne**
Fresh, clean and crisp.
Drink upon purchase.
Ⓔ Local Price $14

Krone Borealis

See Twee Jonge Gezellen

Krug

Champagne Krug
5 rue Coquebert
51100 Reims
France
Phone (326) 84.44.20
Fax (326) 84.44.49

*Part of LVMH under the wing
of Veuve Clicquot. Anyone
who has recently walked
through the barrel room of this
famous house will have been
struck by the gleam of
stainless-steel. Not that Krug is
forsaking its beloved barriques
(or pièces in champenois) of
Argonne oak. These tanks are
for blending, not fermenting,
and should ensure greater
homogeneity for each cuvée in
the future. It is not the first
stainless-steel at Krug, since
smaller tanks can be found*

Krug (cont.)

*deep in its cellars, but those are
for reserve wines. I also noted
gyropalettes. It seems that not
even Krug can avoid progress!*

95 **Krug Grande Cuvée NV Brut**
Ⓨ When tasted blind with other
Champagnes this truly is an exotic
creature, with masses of oaky
fruit. Drink now-2006.
ⒺⒺⒺⒺ Local Price **600FF**

85 **Krug Rosé NV Brut**
Ⓨ The colour of the sample
submitted (L3013174) was old gold,
with no hint of pink and, on the
nose and palate, there is certainly
none of the exuberant red-fruits
shown by this cuvée in the last
two editions. The dominant
character is oak and it is almost
back to the old stock style that
made me put a **?** sign on it three
years ago. Drink upon purchase.
ⒺⒺⒺⒺ Local Price **1300FF**

? **Krug Clos du Mesnil 1990 Brut
Blanc de Blancs Brut**
This obviously has an excellent
potential, but there is a straw-like
character that blurs the clarity of
the fruit, preventing me from
making any specific comments.
It probably is nothing more than
one of many developmental
characteristics that are never
found in the final commercial
and the disgorgement of the
preview sample was simply
unfortunate timing. Since the
Clos du Mesnil 1990 will not
be released until after the Krug
Vintage 1990 and that itself is
not due to be released for at least
a year, I am happy to reserve my
opinion for another year.
Wait and see.
ⒺⒺⒺⒺ

99   **Krug Vintage 1990 Brut**

Krug has captured the essence of 1990, one of the dozen greatest vintages of the 20th century, in this wine. If any two words can sum up 1990 it must be outstanding balance and here Krug has achieved almost perfect balance. The integration of fruit and mousse is particularly impressive, producing a creamy-velouté Champagne in which it is so difficult to discern the difference between the velvety feel of the mousse and the ultra-luxuriant texture of the fruit. This is my first tasting of a wine that will improve greatly and yet I have left myself no room to increase the score (a perfect 100 being impossible in my book). I apologise for this paradox, but I am myself imperfect and I could not score the wine any less or any more. Not due to be released until 2002. Drink now-2019.

ⓔⓔⓔⓔ

96   **Krug Vintage 1989 Brut**

This showed the greatest amount of autolysis out of the trio of 1988, 1989 and 1990 in both Vintage and Clos du Mesnil. It was also lighter in colour than either the 1988 or 1990 Vintage, which is remarkable considering that 1989 is renowned for a tinge of colour in its cuvées. Theoretically this should go into decline long before the 1988, but I'm not so sure. It is just so unbelievably fresh and unquestioningly great. Drink now-2019.

ⓔⓔⓔⓔ Local Price **900FF**

95   **Krug Clos du Mesnil 1988 Brut Blanc de Blancs Brut**

Rich creamy, hazelnut and brazilnut aromas pervade every nook and cranny of this wine, which would seem to be ageing faster than the 1989 Clos du Mesnil. However, after once having written off the 1979 Clos du Mesnil only to see it rise like a Phoenix to even greater heights, I have no intention of repeating that particular mistake. Especially as even Henri Krug admits to being confounded by the evolution of this single-vineyard Champagne. Furthermore, on paper at least, this wine has the acidity and overall balance to mature slowly for several decades under ideal storage conditions. Drink now-2021.

ⓔⓔⓔⓔ Local Price **1600FF**

97   **Krug Clos du Mesnil 1988 Brut Blanc de Blancs Brut**

Whether this vintage will always outshine the 1988 Clos du Mesnil is anybody's guess, but there is no doubt that it is at a far more flattering point in its development. Although scores in this guide are based on both actual and potential quality, they are openly biased towards current drinking, thus for the time being the 1989 ranks two percentile points above the 1988. Drink now-2009.

ⓔⓔⓔⓔ Local Price **1600FF**

97   **Krug Vintage 1988 Brut**

Just such extraordinary finesse. Drink now-2012.

ⓔⓔⓔⓔ Local Price **1000FF**

92   **Krug Collection 1982 Brut**

I tasted two different disgorgements of this future Collection vintage (due to be released in 2002) and much preferred the October 1999 disgorgement to the July 1990 disgorgement. Normally I favour more post-disgorgement ageing to less, as does Henri Krug, and as this was part of a tasting to reinforce the point, I can only assume that the July 1990

disgorgement was not a representative bottle, thus the score below relates exclusively to the October 1999 disgorgement. Extremely fresh and pale-coloured with rich, crystal-clear, honeyed fruit and lovely toasty aromas of great finesse. Unfortunately no disgorgement dates are given on Collection bottles.
Drink now-2008.
ⒺⒺⒺⒺ Local Price **3500FF**

98 Krug Collection 1981 Brut
One of Krug's greatest vintages. I tasted ... strike that, I drank a fair bit of this wine (disgorged June 1988) over lunch with Henri Krug. This is one of his favourites too and we have both remarked how well it has been drinking in recent years, so it was a great pleasure to share a bottle with him over a simple lunch chez Krug. After a quarter of a century of analysing Champagne, the toasty aromas I used to wax lyrical about are now beginning to bore me, yet the slow-evolving toasty aromas in Krug 1981 never fail to seduce me. This is classic mature Champagne in the most sumptuous of styles, possessing fabulous finesse. Drink now-2010.
ⒺⒺⒺⒺ

98 Krug Collection 1979 Brut
Last year I wrote 'To die for!' about the Krug 1988 Vintage and I've died and gone to heaven for this wine, the Krug Collection 1979. They are two superb vintages that share impeccable finesse and in the case of the 1979 this has kept the fruit uppermost. Both vintages were also slow-developers, albeit for different reasons. The 1988 was not released until after the 1989 because of its relatively high malic acidity, whereas the 1979 simply possessed a classic lean,

unyielding structure.
Drink now-2007.
ⒺⒺⒺⒺ Local Price **2250FF**

97 Krug Collection 1953 Brut
No longer commercially available, even as a Krug Collection, a very small number of 1953s remain in the Krug library. I tasted two disgorgements, one disgorged in 1965, the other in 1986 and although both had evolved into very similar wines, the former had the edge, being deeper and longer in flavour and lasting longer in glass. An exquisitely rich Champagne with plenty of creamy, crumbly-biscuit, honeyed-fruit. If you come across a perfectly cellared bottle of this wine, snap it up. Drink now-2010.

Kuentz Bas

14 Route des Vins BP 7
68420 Husseren Les Chateaux
France
Phone (389) 49.30.24
Fax (389) 49.23.39

70 Kuentz Bas NV Tradition, Crémant d'Alsace
Soft and easy to drink.
Drink upon purchase.
Ⓔ Local Price **53FF**

80 Kuentz Bas 1991 Chardonnay Brut, Crémant d'Alsace
Biscuity rich, tasted on its lees. Needs a light dosage (5-6 g/l). Quite complex.
Drink upon purchase.
ⒺⒺ

80 Kuentz Bas 1991 Chardonnay Brut RD, Crémant d'Alsace (*magnum*)
Biscuity-rich in a distinctive Champagne-type style. Complexity demands food. Ideal for immediate drinking. Drink upon purchase.

ⓔⓔⓔ Local Price **216FF**

Kuntz

Weingut Sybille Kuntz
Moselstrasse 25
54470 Lieser
Germany
Phone (6531) 91000
Fax (6531) 91001

72 Sybille Kuntz 1999
🍷 **Riesling Sekt Brut**
Rich and flavoursome
Riesling Sekt. (100% Riesling,
bottle-fermented, Mosel-Saar-
Ruwer) Drink now-2002.
ⓔ Local Price **DM22**

L'Aigle

See Denois

Labastide

Labastide de Lévis Cellars
81150 Marssac
Phone (563) 53.73.73
Fax (563) 53.73 74

73 Cave de Labastide de Lévis NV
🍷 **Gaillac Brut**
If you're looking for the ultimate
fizz to give or serve to someone
who finds all dry sparkling wines
too acidic, this is it. Its fresh,
apple-blossom fruit has a certain
charm but virtually no acidity to
speak of, so if this is also
considered to.
Drink upon purchase.
ⓔ

Attention!

*To submit samples for review
see page 52*

Lahaye

Benoit Lahaye
33 rue Jeanne d'Arc
51150 Bouzy
France
Phone (326) 57.03 05
Fax (326) 52 79 94

88 Benoit Lahaye NV Brut
🍷 A youthful, fruit-driven
Champagne with excellent
balance and finesse.
Drink now-2004.
ⓔⓔ

Lallier

Champagne René James Lallier
4 place de la Libération
BP5 51160 Aÿ-Champagne
France
Phone (326) 55.32.87
Fax (326) 55.79.93

84 René James Lallier NV
🍷 **Grande Réserve Brut**
A very fruity style that is light,
fresh and crisp on the finish.
Drink now-2002.
ⓔⓔ

85 René James Lallier NV Blanc de
▬ **Blancs, Brut**
The nose is really quite young and
raw, but it will come together and
the fruit is nice and crisp and
zesty. Drink 2002-2003.
ⓔⓔ

85 René James Lallier NV Brut Rosé
🍷 Fresh, assertive raspberry fruit
with a crisp, clean, slightly
sweetish finish. Although a delight
now, this cuvée would benefit
from an extra year in bottle to
smooth out the mousse.
Drink now-2003.
ⓔⓔ

Lang

Weingut Hans Lang
Rheinallee 6
65347 Eltville-Hattenheim
Germany
Phone (6723) 2475
Fax (6723) 7963

75 Hans Lang 1997 Johann
► Maximilian Extra Brut
Nice Riesling bottle aroma, with
attractively crisp acidity on the
palate, but there is still has a core
of undeveloped extract that needs
time. (100% Riesling, bottle-
fermented, Rheingau)
Drink 2002-2003.
ⓔ Local Price **DM29**

Langlois-Château

3 rue Léopold Palustre
St-Hilaire-St-Florent
49400 Saumur
France
Phone (241) 40.21.40
Fax (241) 40.21.49

72 Langlois NV
! Crémant de Loire, Brut
Much preferred to Quadrille de
Langlois-Chateau, the 1995 of
which follows in the same mouldy
vein as the previous vintage. The
straight Crémant is fresh and
clean. Drink upon purchase.
ⓔ Local Price **52FF**

74 Langlois NV Crémant de Loire,
! Brut Rosé
Lovely pale colour, very fresh,
light-bodied, absolutely clean
red-fruits on the palate and a
crisp finish. Drink now-2002.
ⓔ Local Price **54FF**

Lanson

Champagne Lanson
12 Boulevard Lundy
51100 Reims
France
Phone (326) 78.50.50
Fax (326) 78.50.99

*Since Lanson's change of
ownership, which involved the
loss of its vineyards, new
masters Marne et Champagne
have been very adamant that
the company has contracted
more than enough top-rated
vineyards to guarantee not only
the continuity of quality, but
also character. The style of
a vintage Champagne is much
harder to replicate than a
certain level of quality,
especially when
it depends on the character of
specific vineyards that are no
longer available. This is why
commentators have been
waiting for the first truly great
vintage under Marne et
Champagne to judge the future
of Lanson on. Lanson made a
disappointing 1994, but 1994
was itself a disappointing
vintage, and although the 1993
was very good for the year, it
was not a truly great vintage.
The first truly great vintage
since Lanson's acquisition was
1995 (although 1996 was, of
course, even greater) and
Lanson has passed the test
with flying colours.*

? Lanson Black Label NV Brut
Excellent acidity, but the fruit
is less complex than it has been
in recent years, and there is an
indication that it will go
oxidative. This would scrape in
with 80 points, but I am uncertain
what is happening here, thus the
? sign is applied and I will reserve

judgement until next year. Wait and see

££ Local Price **160FF**

88   Lanson Gold Label 1995 Brut

This is the vintage we've all been waiting for and it is a truly great Champagne, with classic fruit structure, exquisite acidity and great potential depth. It will be at least another four or five years before we experience its full potential, but that is part and parcel of Lanson's traditional vintage style. Drink 2003-2009.

££ Local Price **190FF**

87   Blanc de Blancs de Lanson 1994 Brut

I'll have to ask whether there is more fruit from Le Mesnil in this vintage. Certainly tastes as if there is. Promises to go creamy-biscuity with brazil nuts. Must drink with food for at least two years, after which it will still be preferable, but no longer necessary. Drink now-2006.

££££ Local Price **450FF**

89   Noble Cuvée de Lanson 1989 Brut

Fine and floral with exceptional acidity and lean structure for the year (due in part no doubt because Lanson has a policy not to put the wines through malolactic). Drink now-2008.

££££ Local Price **450FF**

84   Massé 1995 Brut

Quite broad, yet with high acidity, this Champagne will go toasty in two years. Drink 2002-2005.

££ Local Price **115FF**

Attention!

To submit samples for review see page 52

Larmandier

Champagne Guy Larmandier
30 rue du Général Koenig
51130 Vertus
France
Phone (326) 52.12.41
Fax (326) 52.19.38

85   Guy Larmandier NV Brut Premier Cru

Very fresh, crisp, tangy fruit supported by a lovely soft, silky mousse. This wine benefits from not being over-chilled.
Drink now-2003.

£ Local Price **79FF**

88   Guy Larmandier NV Blanc de Blancs, Brut Grand Cru

Floral-perfumed Chardonnay aroma followed by very fine, beautifully crisp fruit. Very fresh and sherbety with a soft, pin-cushion mousse.
Drink now-2004.

£ Local Price **88FF**

87   Guy Larmandier, Cramant Millésime 1996 Blanc de Blancs Cuvée Prestige, Brut Grand Cru

Plenty of fresh, zippy fruit with a creaminess on the finish that promises to go biscuity.
Drink now-2004.

££ Local Price **115FF**

Lauffen

Wg. Lauffen
In Brühl 48
74348 Lauffen
Germany
Phone (7133) 1850
Fax (7133) 18560

74   Wg. Lauffen 1996 Katzenbeißer Blanc de Noir Brut

Excellent mousse, young for its age. (100% Spätburgunder, bottle-fermented, Baden)

Drink upon purchase.
Ⓔ Local Price **DM21**

Laurent-Perrier

Champagne Laurent-Perrier
Domaine de Tours-sur-Marne
51150 Tours-sur-Marne
France
Phone (326) 58.91.22
Fax (326) 58.77.29

*The Laurent-Perrier group also
includes Salon, Delamotte and
De Castellane.*

---

95 Grand Siècle NV La Cuvée, Brut
This firm and youthful Grand
Siècle has great extract and
intensity of fruit on the finish,
which will need two or three
years to evolve slowly into a great
Champagne. Since last year's La
cuvée still needs another year and
the year before's probably two
more years, you'll have to drink
something else in the meantime!
That said it accompanies food
well and although you will be
missing much of its potential, this
Champagne already makes
excellent drinking.
Drink now-2006.
ⒺⒺⒺⒺ Local Price **380FF**

87 Laurent-Perrier NV Brut L.P.
At the Annual Champagne
Tasting, this cuvée had a touch of
green fruit on the palate offset by
a nice vanilla finish. The sample
submitted to the Guide's tasting
had no hint of green or vanilla.
It had a very fine aroma,
beautifully fresh fruit and a lovely
crisp finish, putting L.P. back on
tip-top form. Drink now-2004.
ⒺⒺ Local Price **160FF**

87 Laurent-Perrier NV
Cuvée Rosé Brut
This year's release (no Lot number

visible!) is one of the few times
that I have been able to enjoy
Laurent-Perrier's rosé with its
famous FT-coloured label. Usually
there is a pepperiness that needs
to be smoothed out or, quite
simply, insufficient fruit. Almost
always, however, this wine turns
into a very classy rosé after one
or two years. Indeed, every time
I taste a current release I have to
go back and taste a cellared
version to reassure myself of this
metamorphosis, but I'm seldom
disappointed. This time I can
enjoy it from the very beginning!
Drink now-2004.
ⒺⒺⒺ Local Price **230FF**

88 Laurent-Perrier 1993 Brut Vintage
Fine aromas with the barest hint
of pepperiness (toned down from
quite peppery at the beginning of
2001) reflected in the fruit on the
palate, supported by a lovely
cushiony mousse. Promises to
develop into a complex
Champagne of great finesse.
Drink now-2006.
ⒺⒺⒺ Local Price **200FF**

91 Laurent-Perrier 1990 Brut Vintage
My own stocks of this beautiful
wine are rapidly diminishing.
Drink now-2010.
ⒺⒺⒺ Local Price **200FF**

? Grand Siècle 1990 Lumière du
Millénaire, Brut
The current release of this
wine has shed almost all of its
pepperiness and now has a
lemony fruit that will develop
greater finesse and complexity.
However, last year's release is still
peppery (difference in dosage base
wine?) and both need quite a bit
of time before they will live up to
the wine's true potential. I could
score this, but I know that it will
eventually be a lot better than any
score I could legitimately give at

this time. Wait and see.
ⓕⓕⓕⓕ Local Price 630FF

89 **Grand Siècle 1990 Alexandre**
❗ **Rosé, Brut**
Fine, ripe, bottle-matured Pinot
aromas followed by fresh fruit on
the palate, with just a hint of the
pepperiness noted in the Grand
Siècle 1990 Brut and Grand Siècle
1990 Lumière du Millénaire. This
wine has crept up one percentile
point since last year and I expect
a further jump when the
pepperiness disperses.
Drink now-2006.
ⓔⓔⓔⓔ Local Price 750FF

Leasingham

See BRL Hardy

Leclerc Briant

Champagne Leclerc Briant
67 rue Chaude Ruelle
51204 Epernay
France
Phone (326) 54.45.33
Fax (326) 54.49.59

85 **Leclerc Briant NV**
❗ **Cuvée de Réserve**
This fresh, elegant fruity
Champagne is the best Leclerc
Briant Brut non-vintage I've
tasted in a long while.
Drink now-2002.
ⓔⓔ Local Price 145FF

85 **Divine 1988 Brut**
❗ I could not recommend the less
than Divine 1989 because it was
dog-tired, but this vintage is as
fresh as a daisy. In fact it is so
unbelievably fresh it even has a
touch of amylic aroma on the
nose. Not a great wine, but any
Champagne that remains so fresh

for so long must have some future
to play out. Drink now-2004.
ⓔⓔⓔ Local Price 232FF

Ledru

Champagne Marie-Noelle
Ledru
5 place de la Croix
51150 Ambonnay
France
Phone 326 57.09.26
Fax 326 58.87.61

83 **Marie-Noelle Ledru**
❗ **NV Brut Grand Cru**
The softest of all three Marie-
Noelle Ledru cuvées submitted.
Softest in acidity and mousse.
Drink now-2003.
ⓔ Local Price 86FF

85 **Marie-Noelle Ledru NV**
❗ **Cuvée du Goulté, Brut Grand Cru**
Quite a bit of autolytic finesse
on the nose with lovely, crisp fresh
fruit on the palate, supported by
a nice cushiony mouse.
Drink now-2004.
ⓔⓔ Local Price 110FF

84 **Marie-Noelle Ledru 1996**
❗ **Brut Millésime Grand Cru**
Typically high acidity. Could
do with more finesse, especially
on the nose, but capable of ageing
into toasty richness. I much
preferred a 50/50 blend of this and
the cuvée du Goulté, which would
have scored 87 points, while one
third each of these two
Champagnes and the basic Grand
Cru Brut would have been 89
points! Obviously the potential is
there. Drink now-2005
ⓔⓔ Local Price 100FF

Legras

Champagne R.&L. Legras
10 rue des Partelaines
Chouilly 51200 Epernay
France
Phone (326) 54.50.79
Fax (326) 54.88.74

88 R.&L. Legras NV
Blanc de Blancs Brut
Quite a firm style considering its
youthful aromas. Lots of flavour
building. Some vanilla.
Drink now-2004.
££ Local Price **125FF**

Lehmann

Peter Lehmann Wines
Para Road
Tanunda
SA 5352
Australia
Phone (8) 8563 2500
Fax (8) 8563 3402

85 The Black Queen
1996 Sparkling Shiraz
Drier than most. Nice Shiraz
fruit, touch menthol. Excellent.
Drink now-2003.
££ Local Price **A\$30**

Lemaire

Champagne R.C. Lemaire
19 rue Pasteur
51200 Damery
France
Phone (326) 58.41.31
Fax (326) 58.39.28

85 R.C. Lemaire NV
Sélect Réserve, Brut
Very fruity with good acidity, this
release is going toasty and should
pick up a hint of coffee along the
way. Drink now-2003.
££

84 R.C. Lemaire NV
Cuvée Trianon, Brut Premier Cru
Very fresh and fruity with a
crisp, attractively acidic finish.
Drink now-2003.
££

90 R.C. Lemaire 1996 Chardonnay,
Millésime Premier Cru Brut
Gentle oaky aromas do not
interfere with the zippy-zingy
citrussy fruit on the palate, which
has scintillating acidity on the
finish. I suggest those who like
Selosse try this. Drink now-2004.
££

Lindauer

See Montana

Lorentz

Gustave Lorentz
35 Grand'Rue
68750 Bergheim
France
Phone (389) 73.22.22
Fax (389) 73.30.49

70 Gustave Lorentz 1999
Crémant d'Alsace Brut
Fresh, lemony fizz.
Drink now-2002.
£

Loriot-Pagel

Champagne Joseph Loriot
Pagel
33-40 rue de la République
51700 Festigny
France
Phone (326) 58.33.53
Fax (326) 58.05.37

86 Joseph Loriot-Pagel
❢ NV Brut Blanc de Blancs
Slightly elevated, succulent
Chardonnay fruit. Excellent value.
Drink now-2002.
££

87 Joseph Loriot-Pagel
❢ 1996 Brut Cuvée de Réserve
Rich, rich fruit. So succulent.
Adorable now! Drink now-2002.
££

Mailly

Champagne Mailly
28 rue de la Liberation
51500 Mailly-Champagne
France
Phone (326) 49.41.10
Fax (326) 49.42.27

---

88 Mailly Grand Cru NV
❢ Blanc de Noirs, Brut
Although I noted this to be well
structured with some impressive
weight at the SAA Champagne
Tasting, it lacked a certain finesse
and would not have scored much
above 80 points. On the other
hand, the sample submitted for
my Guide tastings (Lot number
B569D) had quite a bit of finesse
and the fruit was far fresher and
better focused, with hints of
strawberry on the aftertaste.
Drink now-2003
££ Local Price **154FF**

90 Mailly Grand Cru 1996
❢ La Terre, Brut
Complex autolytic aromas
of great finesse are already
developing on this Champagne,
which has soft yet deeply-
flavoured, profound fruit bobbing
up and down on a soft, fluffy
mousse. This has come a long
way since the SAA Champagne
Tasting, when it was rather solid
and foursquare. If you want to

know how this will develop, drink
a glass or two, then re-seal the
bottle and leave it in the fridge
for 24 hours. Presented in a metal
case. Drink now-2005.
£££ Local Price **209FF**

86 Mailly 1992 Deux Mille
❢ A rich biscuity-complex
Champagne for current drinking.
Drink now-2003.
££

88 Mailly Grand Cru 1988
❢ Cuvée Les Echansons, Brut
Truly complex, heaps of fruit,
great intensity and great finesse.
Presented in a gift box.
Drink now-2005.
£££ Local Price **315FF**

Malard

Champagne Jean-Louis Malard
19 Rue Jeanne d'Arc
51200 Epernay
France
Phone (326) 57.77.24
Fax (326) 52.75.54

---

86 Jean-Louis Malard NV
❢ Pinot Noir & Chardonnay Brut
Very young and fresh, quite full
yet elegant, with crisp fruit and
a creamy mousse.
Drink now-2004.
££

Mandois

Champagne Henri Mandois
66 rue du Gal-de-Gaulle
51200 Pierry
France
Phone (326) 54.03.18
Fax (326) 51.53.66

*Impressively consistent in value
and quality.*

85 Henri Mandois NV
Cuvée de Réserve, Brut
Fresh, elegant, lifted fruit with
classic structure and acidity.
Drink now-2003.
ⓔ Local Price **68FF**

87 Henri Mandois NV
Brut Rosé, Premier Cru
Lovely concoction of strawberries
and cherries with a touch of
redcurrants for piquance.
Drink now-2002.
ⓔ Local Price **73FF**

85 Henri Mandois NV
Chardonnay, Brut Premier Cru
Easy drinking, but not yet as
hedonistically enjoyable as most
Mandois cuvées tend to be. This
release (no Lot number visible)
also needs six months for the nose
to catch up with the crisp, fruity
palate. Drink now-2004
ⓔ Local Price **77FF**

89 Henri Mandois 1996
Millésimé, Brut Premier Cru
Make no mistake, this is a great
Champagne. Mandois might be
a master of the easy drinking
Champagne that overflows with
fruit, and here we have it by the
bucket-load, but we also have
complexity and finesse, and at
a bargain price! Drink now-2004.
ⓔ Local Price **76FF**

91 Henri Mandois 1996
Cuvée Victor Mandois, Brut
Even better than Mandois 1996
Millésimé, this has more finesse,
more complexity and more
distinction. Although wonderful
to drink now, with its very
more'ish fruit, there is so much
undeveloped extract on the finish
that just how god it will.
Drink now-2011.
ⓔ Local Price **93FF**

Mann

Domaine Albert Mann
13 rue du Château
68920 Wettolsheim
France
Phone (389) 80.62.00
Fax (389) 80.34.23

74 Domaine Albert Mann
1998 Baron de Castex Brut,
Crémant d'Alsace
Fresh and clean with neutral fruit,
which should go biscuity.
Drink now-2002.
ⓔ Local Price **46FF**

Marchesine

Marchesine di Biatta Giovanni
Via Vallosa 31
25050 Passirano
Italy
Phone (30) 657005
Fax (30) 6857933

74 Le Marchesine NV
Franciacorta Brut
A creamy-biscuity fizz that would
have scored higher had there been
more finesse and freshness to the
fruit. Drink now-2002.
ⓔ Local Price **19,000 Lira**

Marenco

Marenco Srl Casa Vinicola
Piazza V. Emanuele 10
15019 Strevi
Italy
Phone (144) 363133
Fax (144) 363909

80 Marenco NV
Brachetto d'Acqui Dolce
Fresh, perfumed moscato aroma
followed sweet, perfumed, cherry
fruit on the palate.
Drink upon purchase.
ⓔ

Margaine

Champagne A. Margaine
3 avenue de Champagne
51380 Villers-Marmery
France
Phone (326) 97.92.13
Fax (326) 97.97.45

83 A. Margaine NV
❢ Brut Premier Cru
A touch lifted on the palate, with
crisp, clean fruit. Aperitif style.
Drink now-2003.
Ⓔ Local Price **75FF**

85 A. Margaine 1995 Special Cuvée
❢ Club, Blanc de Blancs
A rich and biscuity Champagne
that has a welcome plumpness of
fruit on mid-palate and a fresh,
crisp finish. Drink now-2004.
ⒺⒺ Local Price **119FF**

Marguet-Bonnerave

Champagne Marguet-
Bonnerave
14 rue de Bouzy
51150 Ambonnay
France
Phone (326) 57.01.08
Fax (326) 57.09.98

87 Marguet-Bonnerave
❢ NV Brut Tradition
Delicate, youthful aromas with
just the slightest amylic hint
(which does not detract and
should fade by publication) and
some substantive flavours locked
away on the palate, which should
gradually build into a complex
Champagne of some finesse.
Drink now-2004.
Ⓔ Local Price **75FF**

82 Marguet-Bonnerave
❢ NV Rosé Grand Cru, Brut
Lovely fresh floral aromas
followed by somewhat simplistic,
albeit easy-drinking fruit on the
palate. Drink now-2002.
Ⓔ Local Price **80FF**

88 Marguet-Bonnerave
❢ NV Brut Réserve, Grand Cru
Excellent quality Champagne in
a full, serious style that should go
biscuity. Drink now-2004.
Ⓔ Local Price **84FF**

87 Marguet-Bonnerave
➤ NV Anciens Vintages 1995-1996,
Brut Grand Cru
I cannot get my head around the
concept of 1995 and 1996 being
designated anciens, especially as
there are hardly any 1997s
released at the time of writing,
but there was little problem
getting this Champagne down my
throat. Under blind conditions
I noted young, raw aromas, which
suggested it should not be
disgorged for at least another
year. However, it is very easy to
drink and there is no denying the
quality of fruit. Just an illogical
name, that's all. Drink 2002-2004.
ⒺⒺ Local Price **100FF**

Marne et Champagne

22 rue Maurice-Cerveaux
51205 Epernay
France
Phone (326) 78.50.50
Fax (326) 54.55.77

*The owners of Lanson, Marne
et Champagne also produces
Champagne in three different
qualities under 200-odd
different labels, plus 100-odd
own-label brands. The top
quality is represented here as
Gauthier, but the same
Champagne will be found
under various other names such
as Alfred Rothschild, Pol
Gessner, Eugène Cliquot (sic)
and Geismann & Co.*

83 Gauthier NV
Grande Réserve Brut
Keep this inexpensive Champagne
for a couple of years to go toasty
and rich. Drink 2003-2004.
ⓔⓔ Local Price **120FF**

86 Gauthier 1993 Brut Millésime
Mature vintages of Gauthier,
one of Marne et Champagne's
top-rank yet inexpensive brands,
are always a bargain for lovers of
toasty Champagne, and this wine
has the acidity to improve and
remain fresh for several years.
Drink now-2005.
ⓔⓔ Local Price **150FF**

Marques de Gelida

See Vins El Cep

Martel

Champagne GH Martel
69 avenue de Champagne
51318 Epernay Cedex
France
Phone (326) 51.06.33
Fax (326) 54.41.52

84 G.H. Martel & Co.
NV Brut Prestige
This fresh, light aperitif-style
Champagne may not be earth-
shattering in quality, but it is clean
and vif, and happens to be the
first release of Martel's Brut
Prestige I have been able to
recommend. Drink now-2003.
ⓔ Local Price **96FF**

85 G.H. Martel & Co.
1996 Cuvée Victoire, Brut
This very crisp and correct
1996 needs time to open out.
Drink 2002-2007.
ⓔⓔ Local Price **119FF**

Martelletti

Corso P. Giachino 142
14023 Cocconato
Italy
Phone (141) 907044
Fax (141) 907372

85 Casa Martelletti NV
Tradizione Asti
Very fresh and sherbety.
Drink upon purchase.
ⓔ Local Price **11,800 Lira**

85 I Ronchetti NV Brachetto d'Acqui
Rowntrees Fruit Gums: the red
ones! Very fresh, smooth and
perfumed-fruity.
Drink upon purchase.
ⓔ Local Price **16,000 Lira**

Martinolles

Domaine de Martinolles
Vignobles Vergnes
11250 – Saint-Hilaire
Phone (468) 69.41.93
Fax (468) 69.45.97

80 Cuvée Maistre Antoine NV
Blanquette de Limoux Brut
Well I suppose someone has
been waiting for it: oak-fermented
Blanquette de Limoux. Actually
it's pretty good, with tangy fruit
lifted by a lovely pin-cushion
mousse. Drink now-2002.
ⓔ Local Price **90FF**

Masblanc

See Torreblanca

Attention!

*To submit samples for review
see page 52*

Massana Noya

Finca Maset del Lleó s/n
08739 Sant Pau d'Ordal
Spain
Phone (3) 899 4124
Fax (3) 899 4139

75 Eudald Massana Noya NV
Cava Brut Nature Reserva
Lacks the chewiness of the
Mil.lenni, but has developed more
complexity, although exactly the
same age (1998-based).
Drink upon purchase.
Ⓔ Local Price **1,155 Ptas**

80 Eudald Massana Noya NV
Cava Brut Nature Mil.lenni
There is a chewy-creamy richness
to the 1998-based blend of this
non-vintage cuvée.
Drink upon purchase.
Ⓔ Local Price **1,800 Ptas**

Massé

See Lanson

Mäurer

Mäurer's Sekt- und Weingut
In den Weinbergen 10
67273 Dackenheim/Pfalz
Germany
Phone (6353) 7842

75 Mäurer's 1996
Chardonnay Classic Brut
Rich and flavoursome, full and
fat. (100% Chardonnay, bottle-
fermented, Pfalz) Drink now-2002.
Ⓔ Local Price **DM25**

Mayerling

See Turckheim

McCorkindale

Alan McCorkindale
Waipara Valley
Omihi Road
Waipara
New Zealand
Phone (800) 423 532
Fax (3) 351 4925

75 Alan McCorkindale 1999
Vintage, Waipara Valley
Oak underpinning crisp fruit.
Should be interesting to age.
Drink now-2003.
ⒺⒺ Local Price **NZ$39**

McLarens on the Lake

See Garrett

Melton

Charles Melton
Krondorf Road
Tanunda
SA 5352
Australia
Phone (8) 8563 3606
Fax (8) 8563 3422

90 Charles Melton NV Barossa
Valley Sparkling Red
Fresh, sweetish, seductive, vibrant
Shiraz fruit. Drink upon purchase.
ⒺⒺ

Mercier

Champagne Mercier
68/70 avenue de Champagne
51200 Epernay
France
Phone (326) 51.22.00
Fax (326) 54.84.23

*Part of LVMH under the wing
of Moët & Chandon.*

87 Eugène Mercier NV
Cuvée du Fondateur, Brut
Wonderfully elegant, flowery-
autolytic aromas and delightfully
fresh fruit on the palate, this
release scores as highly as it did
three years ago, albeit for a
different, far less fat style. Two
years ago it dropped to 83 points
and last year I refused to
recommend it, so I had better
qualify this year's praise with the
relevant Lot number LHCFUS
(strange though this lasered code
appears to be). Drink 2002-2004.
ⓔⓔ

84 Mercier NV Brut
Not very interesting at the Annual
Champagne tasting, the next
release was significantly better,
with more lemony fruit with
good acidity. Drink now-2003.
ⓔⓔ

? Mercier 1996 Vendange
Bit too much malolactic. Won't
go smelly, but will go butterscotch
with an exotic twist to the fruit,
which will appeal to some New
World consumers. It is therefore
included for consideration by
those who would like a stepping-
stone to more traditional
Champagnes. Wait and see.
ⓔⓔ

84 Mercier 1995 Vendange Brut
Toasty-rich aromas on the nose
and in the fruit. Drink now-2004.
ⓔⓔ

Merret

See Ridgeview Estate

Metz

Hubert Metz
3 rue du Winzenberg
67650 Blienschwiller
France
Phone (388) 92.43.06
Fax (388) 92.62.08

75 Hubert Metz 1997 Réserve
de la Dome, Crémant d'Alsace
Spiced and fruity. Authentic
Alsace fizz. Drink upon purchase.
ⓔ Local Price **40FF**

Metz Laugel

102 rue du Général de Gaulle
67521 Marlenheim
France
Phone (388) 59.28.60
Fax (388) 87.67.58

70 Metz Laugel 1998 Riesling,
Crémant d'Alsace
Neutral nose (ie, not aromatic),
fresh neutral palate.
Drink upon purchase.
ⓔ Local Price **35FF**

Meyer Fonné

Domaine Meyer Fonné
24 Grand'Rue
68230 Katzenthal
France
Phone (389) 27.16.50
Fax (389) 27.34.17

70 Domaine Meyer Fonné 1999
Crémant d'Alsace, Brut Extra
Clean, firm with lots of foamy
mousse, crisp finish.
Drink now-2002.
ⓔ Local Price **41FF**

Mignon & Pierrel

Champagne Mignon & Pierrel
24 Rue Henri Dunant
51200 Epernay
France
Phone (326) 51.93.39
Fax (326) 51.69.40

83 **Pierre Mignon NV Brut Rosé**
Too young and raw on the nose,
but excellent fresh fruit acidity
on the palate. Keep nine months
before drinking. Drink now-2002.
ⓔⓔ

Milan

Champagne Milan
6 route d'Avize
51190 Oger
France
Phone (326) 57.50.09
Fax (326) 57.78.47

83 **Jean Milan NV Brut Spécial,**
Blanc de Blancs, Grand Cru
The current release is fresh, light
and fine, but the preview sample
of the next release (not due to
be released until March 2002)
promises to be significantly finer,
with extremely elegant pineapple
fruit (88 points). In fact, I would
release it straight away!
Drink now-2003.
ⓔ Local Price **86FF**

83 **Terres de Noël An 2000 Brut**
Sélection 1995 Grand Cru
Blanc de Blancs, Milan
Tasted one year on the high-tone
element to the front palate has all
but disappeared and the citrussy
fruit has gained in finesse.
However, the nose would benefit
from another year in bottle.
Drink 2002-2003.
ⓔⓔ

Mills Reef

Mills Reef Winery
143 Moffat Road
Bethlehem
Tauranga
New Zealand
Phone (7) 576 8800
Fax (7) 576 8824

? **Mills Reef NV Hawkes Bay**
This coconutty-oaky fizz can
only be recommended to those
who like a plank of 4x2 rammed
down their throat!
Drink upon purchase.
ⓔ Local Price **NZ$19**

? **Mills Reef 1995 Hawkes Bay**
Yet more coconutty-oaky fizz.
Drink now-2002.
ⓔ Local Price **NZ$30**

Mirabella

Via Cantarane
2 – 25050 Rodengo Saiano
Italy
Phone (30) 611197
Fax (30) 611388

74 **Mirabella NV Franciacorta Brut**
Fresh, fluffy fruit.
Drink upon purchase.
ⓔ Local Price **16,500 Lira**

80 **Mirabella NV Franciacorta Rosé**
This wine has a very pale apricot
colour with exquisitely fresh fruit,
but will someone please tell the
owners that this sort of labelling
went out with the Ark and even
then it was deemed to be very
unsophisticated! Drink now-2002.
ⓔ Local Price **16,500 Lira**

Attention!

To submit samples for review
see page 52

Miranda

Miranda Barossa
Barossa Valley Highway
Rowland Flat
SA 5352
Australia
Phone (8) 8524 4537
Fax (8) 8524 4066

80 **Miranda 1994 Sparkling Shiraz,**
🍷 **Barossa Old Vine Reserve**
Touch alcoholic, but lovely cedary
Shiraz fruit with a firm sweet
finish and dry tannins.
Drink now-2002.
Ⓔ

Miranda, De

See Contratto

Miru Miru

See Hunter's

Moët & Chandon

Champagne Moët & Chandon
20 avenue de Champagne
51200 Epernay
France
Phone (326) 51.20.00
Fax (326) 51.20.37

The launch of three single-vineyard grand cru Champagnes is a great idea, spoilt only by a lack of vintage. The idea is not new; Leclerc Briant launched three single-vineyard Champagnes in the early 1990s (albeit premieres, not grandes, crus), but it is a particularly great idea for Moët & Chandon because the larger the house, the more it needs to express

Moët & Chandon (cont.)

individuality if it is to retain its reputation as well as size. The trio launched by Leclerc Briant also made the mistake of not being vintaged and this was a major factor in why these Champagnes failed to make their mark even within Leclerc's limited customer base. At £50 a bottle, Moët's trilogy is obviously aimed at serious collectors, but how can these Champagnes be cellared and their development followed when there is nothing to distinguish one bottling from another? Georges Blank, Moët's new Chef de Cave, told me that there was much internal debate over whether these cuvées should be vintage or not. Above everything else, the aim was to express 'terroir, terroir, terroir' Georges insisted, 'and a vintage would only detract from this'. He also said that the blending flexability of a non-vintage Champagne would help guarantee a consistent product each year and here is where the argument falls down, because the result will not be a pure expression of terroir. Terroir can only be expressed in a wine of a single vintage.

81 **Moët & Chandon**
▶ **NV Brut Impérial**
A hint only of the floweriness that
used to mark the world's best-selling Champagne, but that's a
hint more than last year, hence –
I suppose – the extra percentile
point. I expect this wine to score
83 or 84 points most years and it
will always get better with just
12 months extra cellaring, if
toastiness is what you're after.

However, neither this year's cuvée, nor the established Moët non-vintage style come anywhere near the exciting quality that lurked beneath this label just two years ago, when I gave the wine 88 points under blind conditions. Call me a cynic, but the inventories purchased by Moët in recent years make me wonder what exactly it was that we were drinking under this label in 1999/2000. Drink 2002-2003.
ⓔⓔ Local Price **145FF**

86 | **Moët & Chandon**
❗ | **NV Brut Premier Cru**

Rich, smooth and toasty, this is either a significant step up on last year's submission or more mature stocks. Whatever, it's damn good! Drink now-2003.
ⓔⓔ Local Price **165FF**

88 | **Moët & Chandon NV Brut Rosé**
❗ |

This very fresh, elegant, easy-drinking rosé has all the finesse it showed when first released and none of the inelegant, green aromas found in last year's releases. Drink now-2002.
ⓔⓔ Local Price **165FF**

90 | **Moët & Chandon Les Champs**
❗ | **de Romont NV Sillery Grand Cru**

This is the class wine of the trio, with its restrained richness, creamy fruit and a velvety mousse demonstrating a degree of finesse the other two wines will never achieve. The sheer length and strawberry aftertaste are indeed the essence of Aÿ Pinot Noir. Drink now-2004.
ⓔⓔⓔⓔ Local Price **500FF**

85 | **Moët & Chandon Les Sarments**
❗ | **d'Aÿ NV Aÿ Grand Cru**

I was initially less impressed with this than I was with the Chouilly, essentially because of an element of underripe fruit, but I knew this

would turn toasty and having tasted all three wines after being resealed and refrigerated for 24 hours, I picked up a greater concentration of flavour in the Sillery. However, Meunier is intrinsically less expressive than either Chardonnay or Pinot Noir and to get more Meunier oomph they should have made more effort. Such as? Well, how about concentrating the varietal character by late-harvesting, say, 20% and fermenting this minor element in barrique? Drink now-2003.
ⓔⓔⓔⓔ Local Price **500FF**

85 | **Moët & Chandon Les Vignes**
❗ | **de Saran NV Chouilly Grand Cru**

Chouilly is a bit of an odd choice for an expressive Chardonnay. Although there are top-rate Champagnes produced in this village (Vazart-Coquart's Grand Bouquet springs to mind), they are few and far between. This is in general the least expressive of Champagne's Chardonnay grands crus, but it does have significant historical ties to this house, initially belonging to Jean-Rémy Moët, who passed it on to his son Victor and his son-in-law Pierre Gabriel Chandon, from whence Moët & Chandon was born. This is good citrussy blanc de blancs that will pick up some complexity and a touch more finesse over the next year or two. Drink now-2003.
ⓔⓔⓔⓔ Local Price **500FF**

84 | **Moët & Chandon**
❗ | **NV Nectar Impérial**

Not as outstanding as last year (less finesse on the nose, less freshness of fruit on the palate), but still very good in its class. Drink now-2004.
ⓔⓔ Local Price **150FF**

88 Moët & Chandon
❢ 1995 Brut Impérial
A shade deeper in colour than most other 1995s, this is, however, extremely fresh and beautifully balanced. Drink now-2006.
ⒺⒺ Local Price **190FF**

86 Moët & Chandon
❢ 1995 Brut Impérial Rosé
Much fresher and fruitier than either last year's 1993 or the year before's 1992, with plenty of cherry-strawberry fruit.
Drink now-2002.
ⒺⒺⒺ Local Price **210FF**

96 Cuvée Dom Pérignon Brut
❢ 1993 Moët & Chandon
This vintage of DP is so seductive it is all too easy to drink that you can forget this is a great quality Champagne, but the citrus and floral notes on the nose are pure class, as is the light, elegant, creamy-textured fruit on the palate. Drink now-2011.
ⒺⒺⒺ Local Price **500FF**

89 Cuvée Dom Pérignon Brut
▬ 1992 Moët & Chandon
All the greenness has now gone from all the disgorgements of this cuvée I have been able to retaste this year. It has, however, dropped into a fairly anonymous phase of its development, so you would be wasting an excellent, possibly great, Champagne if you do not give it at least another year, preferably three before drinking it. This part of its evolution reminds me of the 1970, which went through a 'so what?' period before turning into a great DP (the magnums were particularly fine at 20 years of age).
Drink 2002-2011.
ⒺⒺⒺⒺ Local Price **500FF**

91 Cuvée Dom Pérignon Rosé
❢ Brut 1990 Moët & Chandon
The Pinot aroma is still quite strong, but moving away from the pungent smell of raspberries reducing prior to becoming jam, as not last year. On the palate the fruit is soft, with redcurrants and a hint of orange peel. This wine has crept up one percentile point, although I must confess that it was pretty obvious to me what I was tasting, blind or not.
Drink now-2005.
ⒺⒺⒺⒺ Local Price **1200FF**

95 Cuvée Dom Pérignon
❢ Brut 1985 Moët & Chandon
Disgorged October 1999 as part of the Dom Pérignon Oenotheque, this vintage now seems so complete and satisfying, with such an ultra-smooth, velvety mousse to add to its already great finesse that you could easily be fooled into thinking it is at its peak. In is indeed at a peak, but take your time to roll the wine around your mouth and to study the depth of aftertaste and you will soon realise there are more peaks to come. Drink now-2016.
ⒺⒺⒺⒺ Local Price **1250FF**

91 Cuvée Dom Pérignon
❢ Brut 1973 Moët & Chandon
Disgorged October 1999 as part of the Dom Pérignon Oenotheque, this wine has been slightly over-dosaged in my estimation. Although this has blunted the knife-edge acidity that gave this vintage of DP so much vitality at one point, it is still excellent and five or 10 years down the line, it could well outshine earlier disgorgements. Drink now-2011.
ⒺⒺⒺⒺ Local Price **3750FF**

98 Cuvée Dom Pérignon
❦ Brut 1964 Moët & Chandon
Disgorged October 1999 as part
of the Dom Pérignon Oenotheque,
this vintage is showing better than
ever before. With such richness,
great length and profound
complexity, it is surprising just
how elegant the fruit dancing on
the tongue is. A classic
demonstration of impeccable
balance. Drink now-2011.
ⓔⓔⓔⓔ Local Price **4000FF**

Moli Coloma

Barrio el Rebato
08739 Subirats
Spain
Phone (93) 891 1092
Fax (93) 891 1092

---

77 Sumarroca 1998
❦ Cava Brut Reserva
Although there is merely 7%
Chardonnay in this wine, it is
obviously from vineyards suitable
for the variety (so much
Chardonnay used in Cavas comes
from unsuitable vineyards and
is worse than the poorest quality
Parellada) and well-blended
because it fills so nicely the
hollow left by Cava's three
traditional varieties.
Drink now-2002.
ⓔ Local Price **1,090 Ptas**

70 Sumarroca 1997
❦ Cava Brut Nature Gran Reserva
Very soft raspberry jam aftertaste!
Drink upon purchase
ⓔ Local Price **1,350 Ptas**

Attention!

*To submit samples for review
see page 52*

Moncuit

Champagne Pierre Moncuit
11 rue Persault-Maheu
51190 Le Mesnil-sur-Oger
France
Phone (326) 57.52.65
Fax (326) 57.97.89

---

87 Pierre Moncuit NV Brut Réserve
❦ A combination of fruit, power
and youth. Should go toasty.
Drink now-2004.
ⓔ Local Price **91FF**

84 Pierre Moncuit 1995
❦ Blanc de Blancs
Quite fat for Moncuit with
buttery-malo aromas frankly
too dominant, but should develop
quite nicely for a few years.
Drink now-2004.
ⓔⓔ Local Price **134FF**

Monogram

See Castel Faglia

Mont-Ferrant

Córcega 73
08029 Barcelona
Spain
Phone (93) 4191000
Fax (93) 4193170

*The oldest, surviving
Cava house.*

---

76 Mont-Ferrant Blanes Nature
❦ 1997 Cava Extra Brut
This crisp, fluffy fizz is much
preferred to Mont-Ferrant's
Augusti Vilaret, which sells for
almost twice the price.
Drink now-2002.
ⓔ Local Price **1,200 Ptas**

Montana

Montana Marlborough Winery
Main Road South
State Highway 1
Riverlands
Blenheim
New Zealand
Phone (3) 578 2099
Fax (3) 578 0463

78 Lindauer NV Rosé
Fresh and crisp with pure
strawberry fruit.
Drink upon purchase.
ⓔ Local Price **NZ$13**

75 Lindauer NV Brut
Good, but not the lemon-pie fluffy
fruit this cuvée has when it is at
its freshest best.
Drink upon purchase.
ⓔ Local Price **NZ$13**

83 Lindauer NV Special Reserve
Lovely Pinot Noir richness. Since
this has crept up one point on last
year's tasting and, at that time,
the magnum was significantly
better, it's a pity that I was not
shown the magnum this year.
Drink now-2002.
ⓔ Local Price **NZ$16**

75 Lindauer NV Grandeur
Nice, but prefer the Special
Reserve. Although a good wine,
nothing grabs me particularly
about this wine except the
bottle, which is reminiscent
of Duval-Leroy's La Femme.
Drink upon purchase.
ⓔⓔ Local Price **NZ$40**

80 Montana Deutz NV
Marlborough Cuvée
Nicely tart fruit supported by a
pin-cushion mousse, which adds
to the finesse. Drink now-2002.
ⓔ Local Price **NZ$26**

78 Montana Deutz 1996
Blanc de Blancs
A fresh and frothy Blanc de Blancs
that should be kept at least one
year. Drink 2002-2003.
ⓔⓔ Local Price **NZ$38**

Monte Rossa

Monte Rossa di Paola Rovetta
Via L. Marenzio
14 – 25040 Bornato
Italy
Phone (30) 725066
Fax (30) 7750061

72 Monte Rossa NV Franciacorta Sec
Attractive fresh, sweet fruit on
the palate, with bell-pepper and
broad-bean aroma on the nose.
Drink upon purchase.
ⓔ Local Price **30,000 Lira**

74 Monte Rossa NV
Franciacorta Brut Satèn
A touch of bell-pepper lifts
the aroma on the very rich fruit.
Drink now-2002.
ⓔⓔ Local Price **37,000 Lira**

80 Monte Rossa 1995 Cabochon,
Franciacorta Rosé Brut
Just as pale as the basic Monte
Rossa rosé, with even more acidity
and elegance of fruit.
Drink now-2003.
ⓔ Local Price **30,000 Lira**

Montgueret

Château de Montgueret
25 rue de la Mairie
49560 Neuil-sur-Layon
France
Phone (241) 59.26.26
Fax (241) 59.01.94

72 Château de Montgueret 1997
Tête de Cuvée, Saumur Brut
Fullish fizz with apricot-jam fruit.

Drink upon purchase.
ⓔ Local Price **45FF**

Montina

La Montina
Via Baiana
17 – 25040 Monticelli Brusati
Italy
Phone (30) 653278
Fax (30) 6850209

78 La Montina 1996
Ⲩ Franciacorta Brut
Soft and fruity with a pleasing
mix of freshness and complexity.
Drink now-2003.
ⓔⓔ Local Price **42,000 Lira**

Montorfano de Filippo

Via Vittorio Veneto
3 – 25030 Coccaglio
Italy
Phone (30) 7721541
Fax (30) 7721504

75 Montorfano de Filippo NV
Ⲩ Franciacorta Brut
Crisp, almondy fruit starting
to pick up biscuity aromas.
Drink now-2002.
ⓔ Local Price **18,000 Lira**

Montvermeil

La Cheteau SA
ZI Saulaie 49700
Doue la Fontaine
France
Phone 02 41.59.26 26
Fax 02 41.59.01 94

72 Montvermeil NV
Ⲩ Crémant de Loire, Brut
Enough greengage fruit for even
the most ardent Chenin lover.
Drink upon purchase.
ⓔ Local Price **35FF**

Monzio

Monzio Campagnoni
C.da Barone Monti della Corte
25040 Nigoline di Cortefranca
Italy
Phone (35) 940311
Fax (30) 9884158

76 Monzio Campagnoni NV
Ⲩ Franciacorta Extra Brut
Although this wine should be nice
and toasty by Christmas 2001,
it will retain its delightfully fresh,
crisp fruit on the palate.
Pin-cushion mousse of delicately
minuscule bubbles.
Drink now-2002.
ⓔ Local Price **16,300 Lira**

75 Monzio Compagnoni NV
➡ Franciacorta Brut
Very fruity with toasty aromas on
the finish, but the nose needs until
Christmas 2001 to come into
balance with the rest of this wine.
Drink 2002-2003.
ⓔ Local Price **15,700**

75 Monzio Compagnoni NV
Ⲩ Franciacorta Satèn
Relatively deep yellowish colour,
but absolutely clear and fresh on
the nose, with rich, tangy fruit
and toasty aromas on the finish.
Drink now-2002
ⓔ Local Price **18,800 Lira**

Morgenhof

Morgenhof Wine Estate
Klapmuts Road
Stellenbosch 7599
South Africa
Phone (21) 889 5510
Fax (21) 889 5266

80 Morgenhof 1997 Brut,
Ⲩ Cap Classique
I can see why this very oaky fizz
with big citrussy fruit scored well

at Veritas 2000 and if you love oak that much you should perhaps add another three or four points to my score. Drink upon purchase.
Ⓔ Local Price **R43**

Morton

State Highway 2
RD2 Katikati
Bay of Plenty
New Zealand
Phone (7) 552 0795
Fax (7) 552 0651

78 Morton Estate NV
Ⓣ **Premium Brut, Marlborough**
Clean-cut fruit, appley, some stone fruits, crisp acidity.
Drink now-2003.
Ⓔ Local Price **NZ$19**

89 Morton Estate 1995 RD,
Ⓣ **Marlborough**
This wine and hence this tasting note is totally at odds with last year, when it notched up just 72 points and its toasty bottle aromas suggested that it was not at all RD (recently disgorged). This year's sample is deliciously pure and fresh, with plenty of fruit and finesse. Drink now-2002.
Ⓔ Local Price **NZ$25**

Mosnel

Il Mosnel di E. Barboglio
Via Barboglio
14 – 25050 Camignone
Italy
Phone (30) 653117
Fax (30) 654236

75 Il Mosnel NV Franciacorta Brut
Ⓣ Very fresh, light and fruity.
Drink now-2002.
Ⓔ Local Price **18,000 Lira**

74 Il Mosnel NV
Ⓣ **Franciacorta Extra Brut**
Toasty aromas followed by high-acid fruit.
Drink upon purchase.
Ⓔ Local Price **20,500 Lira**

77 Il Mosnel 1997
Ⓣ **Franciacorta Brut Satèn**
Toasty-rich fruit with a smooth, ultra-satèn-like mousse.
Drink now-2002.
Ⓔ Local Price **26,500 Lira**

Mountain Dome

Mountain Dome Winery
16315 E. Temple Road
Spokane
WA 99217
USA
Phone (509) 928 2788
Fax (509) 922 8078

78 Mountain Dome NV Brut
Ⓣ Excellent tangy fruit-driven style. Best served not too cold.
Drink now-2002.
Ⓔ Local Price **$12**

85 Mountain Dome NV Cuvée Forté
Ⓣ Quite full, as the name suggests, but filled with lush fruit supported by a soft and silky mousse. Maybe I did not look hard enough, but I could not find any vintage on this cuvée, although I know it is pure 1995. Drink now-2003.
ⒺⒺⒺ Local Price **$30**

83 Mountain Dome 1995 Brut
Ⓣ Deep, rich and satisfying.
Drink now-2003.
ⒺⒺ Local Price **$21**

Attention!

To submit samples for review see page 52

Moutard

Champagne Moutard
Buxeuil
10110 Bar-sur-Seine
France
Phone (25) 38.50.73
Fax (25) 38.57.72

82 **Moutard NV Brut Réserve**
This lemony fizz reminds me of
last year's Grande Réserve, but of
course it cannot be because of the
different shape of the bottle.
Drink now-2002.
€€ Local Price **85FF**

84 **Moutard NV Brut Grande Cuvée**
A light and elegant style that is
absolutely clean, with fresh, floral
fruit and a nice crisp finish.
Drink upon purchase.
€ Local Price **95FF**

Moutardier

Champagne Jean Moutardier
51210 Le Breuil
France
Phone (326) 59.21.09
Fax (326) 59.21.25

83 **Jean Moutardier NV**
Carte d'Or Brut
Extremely fruity style with
excellent acidity and lifted fruit
aromas on the finish. The next
release (due in September 2001) is
finer and not overtly lifted, but
not quite so good acidity.
Drink upon purchase
€ Local Price **79FF**

84 **Jean Moutardier NV Rosé Brut**
Bags of cherry-flavoured fruit.
Drink upon purchase.
€ Local Price **88FF**

? **Jean Moutardier NV**
La Centenaire Brut
The malo-dominated nose with

caramel on the palate is more
reminiscent of Moutardier's 1991
than it is of any previous release
of Centenaire I have ever tasted.
Judgement reserved. Wait and see.
€ Local Price **99FF**

84 **Jean Moutardier 1993**
Brut Millésime
A serious attempt at a complex
style of Champagne that could do
with more finesse, although it will
gain in complexity.
Drink now-2004.
€ Local Price **85FF**

Mumm

Champagne G.H. Mumm
29 rue du Champ-de-Mars
51053 Reims
France
Phone (326) 49.59.69
Fax (326) 40.46.13

85 **Mumm Cordon Rouge NV Brut**
I've tasted past, present and future
blends of this cuvée a number
of times and it is evident that
a stylistic change for the better
occurred in the 1995-based blend
(marketed in 1998) and that it has
steadily improved ever since. My
favourite so far is the 1998-based
blend, which came onto the
market in February 2001. This
classic quality non-vintage
Champagne almost comes up
to elegance of Mumm Cordon
Rouge in its heyday, albeit in more
authentically brut style than it
was back then. Drink now-2004.
€€ Local Price **160FF**

87 **Mumm Cordon Vert NV**
Demi-Sec
A big mouthful of clean, good
quality fruit, with oodles of
extract demonstrating its excellent
potential. This beats Clicquot's
demi-sec in every aspect except

the mousse, which is very good, but not silky-special.
Drink now-2006.
ⒺⒺ Local Price **130FF**

87 **Mumm de Cramant NV**
❗ **Chardonnay, Brut Grand Cru**
Very fresh with a hint almost green, early-picked fruit, which will go toasty, although currently dominated by lemon and lime flavours (L0609904922).
Drink now-2003.
ⒺⒺ Local Price **180FF**

87 **Mumm Grand Cru NV Brut**
The preview sample of Mumm's new non-vintage prestige cuvée (there's a new vintage prestige cuvée in the pipeline) was dominated by malolactic. This might be more overt than I like to see, even in a preview sample, but it is absolutely clean with not the slightest hint of choucroute stink that the Mumm winemaker before last was so fond of. I can see this going biscuity-creamy with delicate toasty notes floating through the fruit, but as this is the first of its kind, such predictions should be taken with a pinch of salt. Drink 2002-2004
ⒺⒺ Local Price **150FF**

87 **Mumm Cordon Rouge**
❗ **1998 Brut Millésime**
Chardonnay dominates the nose at the moment. Very elegant fruit on the palate, beautifully focused and gently supported by a feathery mousse. I believe that this will be an earlier developer compared to the 1997, although Dominic Demarville thinks it will be the reverse. Both are, however, far more forward than the 1996. Not likely to be released until mid-2003. Drink now-2004.
ⒺⒺ Local Price **160FF**

87 **Mumm Cordon Rouge**
1997 Brut Millésime
Fresh, light, feathery fruit that dances on the tongue. Slightly firmer structure and acidity than the 1998. Not likely to be released until mid-2002. Drink 2002-2005.
ⒺⒺ Local Price **160FF**

89 **Mumm Cordon Rouge**
1996 Brut Millésime
I've tasted this vintage several times and I know that the potential is there. The problem is that it has been released too early. Both the 1997 and 1998 vintages are more forward than this Champagne. It is debatable which order they should be released, strictly chronological or 1998 followed by 1997, but the 1996 deserves another two years on its lees and should have been the last Drink 2003-2007.
ⒺⒺ Local Price **160FF**

Mumm Napa Valley

8445 Silverado Trail
Rutherford
CA 94573
USA
Phone (800) 686 6272
Fax (707) 942 3470

---

80 **Mumm Cuvée Napa**
❗ **NV Brut Prestige**
Very fresh, elegant fruit with a lovely creaminess at the back of the palate. Excellent mousse. Surprising length.
Drink upon purchase.
ⒺⒺ Local Price **$18**

78 **Mumm Cuvée Napa**
❗ **NV Blanc de Noirs**
Lovely, sherbety-fresh pin-cushion fruit. Drink now-2002.
ⒺⒺ Local Price **$19**

77 Mumm Cuvée Napa
➤   NV Blanc de Blancs
Very fresh, tangy fruit. Needs a
year post-disgorgement ageing.
Drink 2002-2003.
€€ Local Price $22

85 Mumm Cuvée Napa
❗   NV Sparkling Pinot Noir
Mumm's typically over-the-top
sparkling red Pinot Noir is a wine
you will love or hate. Limited
availability. Drink upon purchase.
€€ Local Price $22

85 Mumm Cuvée Napa
➤   1996 DVX Brut
Needs one year ageing after
purchase to achieve potential
complexity. High acids. Delicious,
smooth. Drink 2002-2004.
€€€ Local Price $43

75 Mumm Cuvée Napa 1995 Brut
❗   Good, but not special. At least,
not yet. Drink now-2002.
€

85 Mumm Cuvée Napa
❗   1994 Winery Lake
Lovely sherbety pin-cushion
mousse with deep, fresh, fleshy
fruit. Drink now-2004.
€€

Muré

René Muré
RN 83
68250 Rouffach
France
Phone (389) 78.58.00
Fax (389) 78.58.01

73 René Muré NV
❗   Crémant d'Alsace Brut
Very fruity and easy to drink.
Drink upon purchase.
€ Local Price **54FF**

75 René Muré 1997
❗   Crémant d'Alsace Brut
Exotic, creamy aromas, even
more exotic fruits on palate.
Would have liked more acidity,
but special as it is anyway.
Drink now-2002.
€ Local Price **85FF**

Nägelsförst

Gut Nägelsförst
Nägelsförst 1
76534 Baden.-Baden
Germany
Phone (7221) 35550
Fax (7221) 355556

74 Gut Nägelsförst 1998
❗   Blanc de Blanc Brut
This Pinot Noir and Meunier
blend offers plenty of richness
and flavour. (50% Weißburgunder,
50% Chardonnay; bottle-
fermented, Baden)
Drink now-2002.
€ Local Price **DM25**

Naveran

Sadeve SA
Can Parellada
St. Martín Sadevesa
08775 Torrelavit
Spain
Phone (93) 8988274
Fax (93) 8989027

77 Naveran 1998 Cava Brut Reserva
❗   The fruit swells out in the mouth
thanks to the lovely, soft, fluffy
mousse, while nice acidity gives
length. Drink now-2002.
€ Local Price **900 Ptas**

Nero

See Conti

Nostalgie

See Beaumont des Crayères

Nyetimber

Nyetimber Vineyard
Gay Street
West Chiltington
Pulborough
Sussex
RH20 2HH
Great Britain
Phone (1798) 813989
Fax (1798) 815511

There is a rumour that in early 2000 the captain of the yet to be launched P&O cruise liner Aurora came across a magnum of this wine in a shop near Nyetimber, purchasing it on impulse. At the ceremony, the Champagne bottle selected to christen the vessel refused stubbornly to break. As every sailor knows this is bad luck, so it came as no surprise when the Aurora broke down on its maiden voyage and had to be towed back to the UK. Back at the launch, however, everyone shrugged off omen and the Captain served Nyetimber's wine to Princess Anne during lunch. Apparently. Being an author rather than a journalist by nature, I have the habit of letting the truth get in the way of a good story. The Champagne did not break, that was true, as indeed was the Aurora's breakdown on its maiden voyage, but Nyetimber was never served to Princess Anne (although her mother did drink it on her Golden Anniversary). I tracked down the Aurora's Captain Bourgoine and via P&O pestered the man whilst he was on leave. He

Nyetimber (cont.)

states that Nyetimber was not served on the day although there was talk about getting a few bottles to sell during the maiden season, but this never happened. Maybe they should have used the English-produced Aurora Cuvée to launch the English-made Aurora? It would have been more appropriate and, who knows, it might have been luckier.

87 **Nyetimber 1994**
➤ **Classic Cuvée, Brut**
The yeast-complexed, pineapply Chardonnay fruit is beginning to assert itself, jumping up three percentile points, but it needs at least another year.
Drink 2002-2005.
ⓔⓔ Local Price £17

88 **Nyetimber 1994 Première Cuvée,**
➤ **Chardonnay Blanc de Blancs, Brut**
The pre-release sample had beautifully matured, mellow Chardonnay fruit, but it needs at least one year post-disgorgement ageing to bring the nose into balance with the palate. Should go toasty-biscuity.
Drink 2002-2004.
ⓔⓔ Local Price £17

89 **Nyetimber 1994 Aurora Cuvée,**
➤ **Chardonnay Blanc de Blancs, Brut**
(*magnum*)
The magnum has worked its magical effect on Nyetimber's 1994 blanc de blancs, integrating fruit and mousse to a sumptuous degree. Drink 2002-2004.
ⓔⓔ Local Price £40

? **Nyetimber 1993 Première Cuvée,**
Chardonnay Blanc de Blancs, Brut
The sample received this year was disconcertingly dull on nose, yet

excellent on palate, with a typical richness, complexity and finesse of fruit. Wait and see.
ⓔⓔ Local Price £17

Odyssey

Odyssey Wines
322 Henderson Valley Road
799 Henderson
New Zealand
Phone (6) 437 5410
Fax (6) 437 5409

?   **Odyssey 1998 Blanc de Blancs**
An oaky Chardonnay with bubbles. Not my sort of thing, but technically correct and will improve for those who like the style. Drink now-2002.

Offensee

See Ribeauvillé

Omni

See BRL Hardy

Orlando Wyndham

Orlando Wyndham Group
33 Exeter Terrace
Devon Park
SA 5008
Australia
Phone (8) 8208 2444
Fax (8) 8208 2403

79   **Jacob's Creek Chardonnay Pinot Noir NV Special Cuvée, Selected Reserve**
Creamy-biscuity fruit gives this particular blend a classy, more mature character than previous releases. Drink now-2002.

ⓔ Local Price A$10

Orschwiller

CV de Orschwiller
Route du Vin
67600 Orschwiller
France
Phone (388) 92.09.87
Fax (388) 82.30.92

73   **CV d'Orschwiller 1998 Moenchberner, Crémant d'Alsace**
Very fresh and crisp.
Drink now-2003.
ⓔ Local Price 34FF

70   **CV d'Orschwiller 1998 Chardonnay, Crémant d'Alsace**
Some perfumed Chardonnay on nose, heaps of acidity, but needed a cruder first fermentation, no filtering and longer on lees, with (then) higher dosage to work.
Drink now-2003.
ⓔ Local Price 47FF

Pacific Echo

Scharffenberger Winery
8501 Highway 128
Philo
CA 95466
USA
Phone (707) 895 2065
Fax (707) 895 2758

75   **Pacific Echo NV Brut, Mendocino County**
Creamy-malo aroma followed by creamy green-apple fruit on the palate, with a nice fresh finish.
Drink upon purchase.
ⓔⓔ Local Price $16

Attention!

To submit samples for review see page 52

Paillard, Bruno

Champagne Bruno Paillard
avenue du Champagne
51100 Reims
France
Phone (326) 36.20.22
Fax (326) 36.57.72

*Owner Bruno Paillard is also
the chairman of and largest
shareholder in the BCC group
(Boizel, Alexandre Bonnet,
Chanoine, Abel Lepitre,
Philipponnat and De Venoge).*

87 Bruno Paillard NV
❗ **Brut Première Cuvée**
If it's not a contradiction in terms,
each new blend of this wine just
gets better and better, yet it
is one of the most consistent
non-vintage Champagnes on
the market. The style is all about
lightness, freshness, elegance and
finesse. I loved the October 2000
disgorgement (these dates can
be found at the base of the back
label), yet the January 2001 was
even better. Same style, just more
finesse and complexity, with a
mousse that just gets smoother.
The amount of barrique-aged
wines that get into this blend has
almost doubled in recent years,
but there is never any awareness
of oak, just a certain je ne sais
quoi. Don't over-chill, especially if
serving with food, when this cuvée
shows best at around 12 Celsius.
Drink now-2004.
ⒺⒺ Local Price **140FF**

87 Bruno Paillard NV
❗ **Rosé Brut Première Cuvée**
This is the one wine from Bruno
Paillard that does not always grab
me. Not that there is anything
wrong with it, just that this rosé
is sometimes merely correct but
uninteresting. The current release
(disgorged October 2000) is

interesting and does grab me.
Classic Pinot aromas are followed
by fresh, cherry-Pinot fruit on
the palate, fine acidity and is
supported by a lovely pin-cushion
mousse. Drink now-2003.
ⒺⒺ Local Price **165FF**

85 Bruno Paillard NV
❗ **Chardonnay Réserve Privée, Brut**
Lovely lemony-creamy fruit.
Sometimes this cuvée matures
very well, other times not so,
but it is always attractive to drink
when young. This release
(disgorged February 2000 – see
back label) promises to be one
that ages, albeit for the mid-term.
Drink now-2003.
ⒺⒺ Local Price **185FF**

88 Bruno Paillard 1995
❗ **Brut Millésime**
Good concentration of fruit, very
accessible, yet with the potential
of more complexity and finesse
(Disgorged June 2000).
Drink now-2005.
ⒺⒺⒺ Local Price **205FF**

85 Bruno Paillard 1990
➤ **N.P.U., Nec Plus Ultra, Brut**
The barrique aromas have
increased, but last year's score
remains. Last year I reckoned
that this cuvée should have been
disgorged in 1996 rather than 1999
and this year's sample was
disgorged one year later than that.
If Bruno has an older disgorged
sample I hope to taste it before
the next edition. Drink 2002-2005.
ⒺⒺⒺⒺ Local Price **540FF**

Attention!

*To submit samples for review
see page 52*

Paillard, Pierre

Champagne Pierre Paillard
2 Rue du XXe Siècle – B.P.9
51150 Bouzy
France
Phone 326 57.08.04
Fax 326 57.83.03

90 Pierre Paillard NV
❗ Bouzy Grand Cru Brut
Very young, succulent, pineapply
fruit aromas, with very clean and
crisp fruit on the palate, a touch
creamy in the middle. Excellent
acidity giving lovely length.
Drink now-2004.
ⓔⓔ

Palliser Estate

Kitchener Street
Martinborough
New Zealand
Phone (6) 306 9019
Fax (6) 306 9946

77 Palliser Estate 1997
❗ Martinborough
Lightly rich and tasty.
Drink now-2003.
ⓔ Local Price **NZ$32**

Palmer

Champagne Palmer
67 rue Jacquart
51100 Reims
France
Phone (326) 07.35.07
Fax (326) 07.45.24

89 Palmer 1991 Blanc de Blancs Brut
❗ An excellent 1991 for current
drinking, this will also improve
considerably over the coming
years. Drink now-2006.
ⓔⓔ Local Price **133FF**

Pannier

Champagne Pannier
23 rue Roger Catillon
02400 Château-Thierry
France
Phone (323) 69.13.10
Fax (323) 69.18.18

85 Pannier NV Brut Rosé
❗ Very pale but true pink rosé with
a fresh, cherry-flavoured fruit in a
crisp aperitif style.
Drink upon purchase.
ⓔⓔ Local Price **129FF**

85 Pannier NV Cuvée
❗ Louis Eugène, Brut
A mature non-vintage with true
brut dryness. Drink now-2003.
ⓔⓔ Local Price **163FF**

86 Pannier NV Cuvée
❗ Louis Eugène, Rosé Brut
Pale peach with apricot hues.
Very Pinot on the nose and
palate, rich in red-fruits laced
with strawberry and cherry
liqueur. Not to everyone's taste,
but a WOW wine for some.
Drink upon purchase.
ⓔⓔ Local Price **166FF**

84 Egérie de Pannier 1996 Brut
▸ The malo aroma seems to
contradict the very high, ripe
acids on the palate, even though
the latter is the hallmark of 1996.
I think I will want to taste this
again next year and a couple of
times after that to get a firm grip
on how this will develop, but I
will score it as it appears now.
Drink 2003-2007.
ⓔⓔ Local Price **194FF**

? Pannier 1996 Brut Vintage
Both samples submitted literally
stank, yet this wine at the Annual
Champagne Tasting in March
2001 was not only absolutely clean
and fresh, it boasted seriously

good, crisp, sherbety fruit that would rate 88 points and should improve for up to seven years. Caveat emptor! Wait and see.
ⒺⒺ Local Price **144FF**

88 Egérie de Pannier 1995 Brut
➤ The nose needs some time to fall in line with the palate, which has nicely focused fruit and an immaculate, soft, cushiony mousse. Drink 2002-2005.
ⒺⒺ Local Price **194FF**

Parató

Can Respall de Renardes
08733 El Pla del Penedès
Spain
Phone (93) 8988182
Fax (93) 8988510

? Elias i Terns 1997
Cava Brut Nature Gran Reserva
American oak on the nose and terpenes on the palate. This will appeal greatly to a small few. Wait and see.
ⒺⒺ Local Price **2,900 Ptas**

Parxet

Mas Parxet
08391 Tiana
Spain
Phone (93) 3950811
Fax (93) 3955500

---

75 Cuvée 21 de Parxet NV Cava Brut
❗ Fresh, soft and fluffy (1999-based). Drink now-2002.
Ⓔ Local Price **1,650 Ptas**

77 Titiana de Parxet NV
❗ **Cava Brut Nature**
Titiana is Parxet's homage to Tiana, where the firm has been making wine since 1920 and where wines have been made since Roman times, when the village

was known as Titiana. A pure Chardonnay Cava with barrel-ferment aromas dominating the nose and chewy-creamy fruit on the palate. There's evidence also of malolactic, which I respectfully suggest they drop next time. Not because the malo is too prominent, but because a lack of acidity is the only thing stopping this wine from being one of best Cavas I've tasted. It's probably dropped ten points as a result (1998-based).
Drink upon purchase.
Ⓔ Local Price **2,000 Ptas**

Pelorus

See Cloudy Bay

Penley Estate

McLeans Road
Coonawarra
SA 5263
Australia
Phone (8) 8736 3211
Fax (8) 8736 3124

---

80 Penley 1994 Coonawarra
❗ **Pinot Noir Chardonnay**
Fresh and classy for its age. Drink now-2002.
ⒺⒺ Local Price **A$33**

Perelada

Cavas del Castillo de Perelada
Plaza del Carmen 1
17491 Perelada
Spain
Phone (34) 972.538011
Fax (93) 2231370

---

70 Castillo de Perelada
❗ **NV Cava Brut Reserva**
Soft, clean and easy, with a

creamy aftertaste.
Drink upon purchase.
ⓔ Local Price **800 Ptas**

80 **Gran Claustro 1998 Cava Brut**
! **Nature**
With 30% (good) Chardonnay
adding to the mouth-feel of this
Cava, it achieves a relatively high
score, but will not gain much with
age. Drink upon purchase
ⓔ Local Price **2,500 Ptas**

Perrier

Champagne Joseph Perrier
69 avenue de Paris
51016 Châlons-en-Champagne
France
Phone (326) 68.29.51
Fax (326) 70.57.16

Part of the Thienot group.

---

85 **Joseph Perrier**
▰ **NV Cuvée Royale Brut**
Good fruit is immediately
noticeable, but there is a tightness
from mid-palate to finish that
needs to mellow. Drink 2002-2004.
ⓔⓔ Local Price **130FF**

85 **Joseph Perrier NV**
! **Cuvée Royale Brut Rosé**
Very pale peach colour with fresh,
floral aromas and crisp, floral-fruit
on the palate. Drink now-2003.
ⓔⓔ Local Price **140FF**

85 **Joseph Perrier NV Cuvée**
! **Royale, Blanc de Blancs Brut**
The most user-friendly,
ready-to-drink blanc de blancs
I've tasted from Joseph Perrier,
although its fresh, sherbety fruit
will improve. Drink now-2005.
ⓔⓔ Local Price **142FF**

87 **Joseph Perrier 1995**
▰ **Cuvée Royale Brut**
The flavour and attack of this

wine has really intensified since
last year. Almost as if it has a
dash of 1996 in it!
Drink 2002-2007.
ⓔⓔ Local Price **160FF**

Perrier-Jouët

Champagne Perrier-Jouët
26/28 avenue de Champagne
51200 Epernay
France
Phone (326) 55.20.53
Fax (326) 54.54.55

*Mumm and Perrier-Jouët were
part of the Seagram group for
30-odd years before being
purchased by a Texan
investment company in 2000
and sold on to Allied-Domecq
in 2001.*

---

88 **Perrier-Jouët NV Grand Brut**
▰ The UK shipment in distribution
during the first quarter of 2001
was fresh and okay, but not
special (less than 80 points),
whereas the release available on
the French market at the same
juncture (L1799902381) was just
as fresh, but much classier with a
nice weight of biscuity-rich fruit
and considerable finesse. It is the
latter wine that is scored here.
Drink 2002-2007.
ⓔⓔ Local Price **163FF**

88 **Perrier-Jouët 1996 Grand Brut**
▰ This will age gracefully and
should develop a violet-vanilla
finesse on the finish.
Drink 2002-2007.
ⓔⓔⓔ

90 **Perrier-Jouët 1995**
▰ **Belle Epoque Brut**
The barest hints of early-picked
Chardonnay is a bit of a niggle,
but the elegance and finesse shows
through. Wait three years for

the Cramant wines to start dominating and other two for the toasty aromas.
Drink 2002-2007.
ⓔⓔⓔ Local Price **470FF**

89 **Perrier-Jouët 1995**
❗ **Belle Epoque Rosé Brut**
Pale apricot without a hint of rosé colour. Lovely fruit, but so mellow and mature I would not get within five years of its age under blind conditions (that was my comment tasting it blind within a group of Champagnes known to be 1995s, but of course not knowing the identity of any individual wine). Beautiful cushiony mousse adds to the finesse. Drink now-2004.
ⓔⓔⓔⓔ Local Price **550FF**

Petaluma

Spring Gully Road
Piccadilly
SA 5151
Australia
Phone (8) 8339 4122
Fax (8) 8339 5253

---

88 **Croser 1998 Petaluma**
❗ Classy construction and fruit. Really head and shoulders above most Australian fizz.
Drink now-2005.
ⓔⓔ Local Price **A$32**

86 **Croser 1991 Petaluma**
❗ Sulphur on nose (which will go toasty), but extraordinarily fresh fruit on the palate. Very clean and crisp on the finish.
Drink now-2003.
ⓔⓔ Local Price **A$44**

Attention!

To submit samples for review see page 52

Pfaffenheim

CV de Pfaffenheim
5 rue du Chai BP 33
68250 Pfaffenheim
France
Phone (389) 78.08.08
Fax (389) 49.71.65

---

76 **Hartenberg Crémant d'Alsace**
❗ **1999 Blanc de Blancs Brut**
Elegant and easy to drink, very fruit driven, nice acidity.
Drink now-2002.
ⓔ Local Price **43FF**

77 **Hartenberg Crémant d'Alsace**
❗ **1997 Tokay Pinot Gris Brut**
Fresh, crisp, fruity with hint of spice adding finesse. Excellent, but could have been even better if it had more acidity.
Drink upon purchase.
ⓔ Local Price **58FF**

Philipponnat

Champagne Philipponnat
13 rue du Pont
51160 Mareuil-sur-Aÿ
France
Phone (326) 52.60.43
Fax (326) 52.61.49

Part of the BCC group with Boizel, Alexandre Bonnet, Chanoine, Abel Lepitre and De Venoge, this house is now under the day-to-day control of Charles Philipponnat, a descendant of the family who founded the firm and have lived in these parts since at least the 16th century.

---

86 **Philipponnat NV**
❗ **Réserve Rosé Brut**
This was released in April 2001 and has a lovely richness of cherry-flavoured fruit, long-lasting in the mouth and supported by a

pin-cushion mousse. Distinctly better than last year's release and the rather high-tone May 2000 disgorgement, which was on sale between these two releases. Drink now-2002.
ⒺⒺⒺ

87   Philipponnat NV
➤ **Royale Réserve, Brut**
The Royale Réserve did not get a recommendation in last year's edition. I remember collaring Bruno Paillard at the Annual Champagne Tasting in 2000 and telling him that it was such a shame. As chairman of BCC, Paillard has ultimate control of Philipponnat. This used to be such a distinctive and seductive cuvée, but I could not tell its amylic aromas from those of a hundred supposedly different Champagnes. Bruno was defensive, but the truth was that it takes time to make your mark on the quality of a Champagne and BCC had purchased Philipponnat as recently as November 1997. A few months later I tasted the next cuvée and was stunned by the quality. More importantly I was seduced by its character and style of the wine, with its wonderfully chewy Pinot flavours. This is what Philipponnat should be about and the September 2000 disgorgement promises to be even better, although it will take longer to develop. In fact, it will not be ready to drink when the next release comes onto the market in September 2001, and that one will take even longer again to evolve. This is my only worry.
These Champagnes are taking progressively longer to peak. Great for quality, but perhaps a problem for perception?
Drink 2002-2005.
ⒺⒺⒺ Local Price **215FF**

87   Philipponnat 1993 Réserve
➤ **Millésimée, Brut**
Extremely fresh, young and even possessing a kernel of undeveloped extract on the finish, which is quite incredible for a 1993 at any point in its development, especially this far down the line. A lovely cushiony mousse and a silky-violety finish. This vintage is pre-BCC ownership, so the previous owners (Marie-Brizard) obviously did something right! Drink 2002-2005.
ⒺⒺⒺ

?   Philipponnat 1991
Réserve Millésimée, Brut
This vintage has been trying to come good for the last 18 months, but whilst there are nice elements of fresh fruit and an interesting intensity of flavour, it still lacks finesse. However, it gives me more hope than it did last year, thus I must at least include it under the **?** sign. Wait and see.
ⒺⒺⒺ

84   Philipponnat 1991
➤ **Réserve Spéciale Brut**
White fruits, stone fruits, but rather straight and unexciting at the moment. Should open up after another year post-disgorgement ageing. Drink 2002-2005
ⒺⒺⒺ

96   Clos des Goisses
➤ **1990 Brut, Philipponnat**
Too chock-a-block with autolytic aromas to be as enjoyable as Clos des Goisses should be and how this great vintage of Clos des Goisses will be. In fact, it is the very presence of so much autolytic aroma that tells me just how fine this will be.
Drink 2005-2016.
ⒺⒺⒺⒺ Local Price **529FF**

Piper-Heidsieck

Champagne Piper-Heidsieck
51 Boulevard Henri Vasnier
51100 Reims
France
Phone (326) 84.41.94
Fax (326) 84.43.49

Pipers Brook

1216 Pipers Brook Road
Pipers Brook
Tas. 7254
Australia
Phone (3) 6332 4444
Fax (3) 6382 7226

The fastest-rising star in Australia's sparkling firmament.

87 **Piper-Heidsieck NV Brut**
This year's release is fresh and clean with an almost Charles Heidsieck style of richness on the palate including, even, a touch of vanilla on the finish.
Drink now-2005.
ⒺⒺ Local Price **125FF**

87 **Piper-Heidsieck NV Cuvée Spéciale Jean-Paul Gaultier, Brut** (*magnum*)
Only Jean-Paul Gaultier can get away with dressing a magnum of Champagne in a shiny-red lace-up basque! It is every bit as outrageous as Gauthier obviously intended it to be and I must confess that I love it. However, it is obvious that he never had to pour himself Champagne from a magnum, otherwise he would have left a hole in the base of the basque so he could stick his thumb in. On reflection, perhaps it is a good thing that he didn't know! The current release of this Champagne is from mature stocks, with plenty of fruit mellowed by toasty bottle-aromas. I have seen this only in Duty Free, but it's such fun that it should be far more widely available.
Drink now-2007.
ⒺⒺⒺ Local Price **600FF**

84 **Piper-Heidsieck 1995 Brut**
The fruit in this vintage is very young and typically Piper-Aube peppery and bright.
Drink 2002-2005.
ⒺⒺⒺ

89 **Pirie 1997 Pipers Brook**
Underlying oakiness comes out under blind tasting conditions, but is not at all obtrusive when drinking within its own context. Very classy and will gain much with bottle-age, but not quite as complete or as seductive as either the 1996 or 1995. Drink 2002-2005.
ⒺⒺ Local Price **A$45**

91 **Pirie 1996 Pipers Brook**
Wonderful vanilla undertones, not at all oaky. Very classy, stylish, crisp fruit. Even more stunning than last year. However, with such a heady score to begin with it will take a lot to earn an extra percentile point. Drink now-2006.
ⒺⒺ Local Price **A$45**

Plageoles

Robert Plageoles
Bernard et Robert Plageoles
Domaine des Très-Cantous
81140 Cahuzac-sur-Vère
France
Phone (563) 33.90.40
Fax (563) 33.95.64

75 **Robert Plageoles NV Mauzac Nature, Gaillac**
Nature in the context of this wine has nothing to do with Brut Nature. Quite the opposite in fact, for it is a méthode gaillacoise, a process that entails

bottling the wine before it has finished fermenting, thus it is absolutely natural, without any sugar added by way of either a liqueur de tirage or a dosage. Consequently there is a deposit in the bottle and a natural sweetness to the wine, which in this case must be something approaching a sec in style. Drink now-2002. €

Ployez-Jacquemart

Champagne Ployez-Jacquemart
Ludes
51500 Rilly-la-Montagne
France
Phone (326) 61.11.87
Fax (326) 61.12.20

86 **Ployez-Jacquemart 1996 Brut Vintage, Blanc de Blancs**
A whiff of SO_2 on nose was noticeable at the SAA Champagne Tasting, but this promised to go toasty and by June it was already on its way. Come Christmas there will be no sulphur detected as such on this toasty Champagne. A full bodied Champagne with bags of fruit and plenty of assertive acidity to ensure it ages fairly gracefully. Drink now-2005.
€€ Local Price **163FF**

90 **Ployez-Jacquemart 1995 Brut Vintage**
A full, firm Montagne style Pinot-dominated Champagne with a lovely, big sweet-fruit finish that has the potential to build slowly into rich, biscuity complexity. Drink now-2006.
€€ Local Price **163FF**

92 **L. d'Harbonville 1990 Brut**
This is undoubtedly a great Champagne. It has the acidity of a 1996 and tastes younger and better than many Champagnes

from that very special vintage. The complexity and finesse are fleeting images that appear just before the acidity electrifies the palate, and the nose needs at least three years to show a hint of its true potential. Drink 2004-2011.
€€€ Local Price **315FF**

Plunkett

Plunkett Wines
Lambing Gully Road
Avenel
Vic. 3664
Australia
Phone (3) 5796 2150
Fax (3) 5796 2147

77 **Strathbogie Ranges 1997 Sparkling Chardonnay Pinot Noir**
Fresh, clean, elegant and fruity wine that should age gracefully into toasty-biscuity style. Drink now-2003.
€

Pol Roger

Champagne Pol Roger
1 rue Henri Lelarge
51206 Epernay
France
Phone (326) 59.58.00
Fax (326) 55.25.70

Only a Brit would ask Pol Roger for a vertical of Champagne Rosé, but then only a Brit would discover such a sublime 20-year-old rosé as the Pol Roger 1982.

85 **Pol Roger NV Brut White Foil**
The current release of Pol Roger's White Foil is dominated by strong ripe acidity and needs at least one year before approaching. Drink 2002-2004.
€€ Local Price **159FF**

97 **Pol Roger 1996 Brut**
Tasting the preview sample of
this vintage was an extraordinary
experience. Although the yeast-
complexed fruit here was already
of profound proportions, the wine
begged for more time on its lees.
It will indeed get this, as the first
release will not be until the third
quarter of 2002, when the next
edition of this guide will be
hitting the shelves, but the mind
boggles at what the result might
be. Drink 2005-2026.
ⓔⓔⓔ Local Price **217FF**

91 **Pol Roger 1995 Brut**
Floral aromas and chewy fruit.
Drinking well now, but serious PR
drinkers will keep this vintage at
least another two years.
Drink now-2013.
ⓔⓔⓔ Local Price **217FF**

88 **Pol Roger 1993 Brut**
The very fresh, toasty fruit in
the current release of this vintage
pleads for bottle-age, whereas
the original release has already
developed a lovely mellow
toastiness. Drink 2003-2012.
ⓔⓔⓔ Local Price **217FF**

93 **Pol Roger 1996 Brut Chardonnay**
Superb acidity and a firm
structure provide the backbone for
Chardonnay fruit of great finesse.
Brilliant, even by PR's standards.
Drink now-2007.
ⓔⓔⓔ Local Price **246FF**

90 **Pol Roger 1995 Brut Chardonnay**
A deliciously soft and
easy-drinking blanc de blancs
with a silky-smooth mousse.
Luscious. Drink now-2005.
ⓔⓔⓔ Local Price **246FF**

90 **Pol Roger 1993 Cuvée
Sir Winston Churchill Brut**
Rich and yummy, with
Chardonnay currently

dominating, this wine needs a
little while to acquire more classic
Churchill Cuvée characteristics,
but it is not one of the longer-
term vin. Not to be released until
the third quarter of 2002.
Drink 2002-2009.
ⓔⓔⓔⓔ Local Price **440FF**

98 **Pol Roger 1990 Cuvée
Sir Winston Churchill Brut**
Delicately perfumed aromas,
beautifully balanced fruit and a
silky-soft mousse, with refreshing
acidity to eep this great
Champagne youthful for years
to come. Drink now-2020.
ⓔⓔⓔⓔ Local Price **440FF**

94 **Pol Roger 1996 Brut Rosé**
Pale-cherry in colour with a
hint of blue. Fabulously rich fruit,
all cherries and strawberries.
Drinking beautifully already,
although not due to be released
until the third quarter of 2002.
Drink now-2005.
ⓔⓔⓔ Local Price **237FF**

91 **Pol Roger 1995 Brut Rosé**
This peachy-salmon colour might
not have intensity or specificity
of PR's 1996 Brut Rosé, but its
melange of summer-fruit flavours
make it a truly great Champagne.
Drink now-2004.
ⓔⓔⓔ Local Price **237FF**

87 **Pol Roger 1993 Brut Rosé**
The last commercial release
(disgorged July 2000) is still
drinking well, with fine, firm fruit
and a crisp finish.
Drink now-2003.
ⓔⓔⓔ Local Price **237FF**

96 **Pol Roger 1990 Brut Rosé**
Disgorged in March 2000, this
is still beautifully fresh, with rich
cherry fruit and a long, sumptuous
finish. This has rocketed six
percentile points in the last three

to four years. Drink now-2006.
🍾🍾🍾🍾

92   **Pol Roger 1988 Brut Rosé**
🍸   Disgorged in 1998, this wine
shows extraordinarily youthful
fruit for a 12 year old rosé and
should continue to age gracefully.
Drink now-2007.
ⓔⓔⓔⓔ

96   **Pol Roger 1982 Brut Rosé**
🍸   This had been disgorged for over
eight years when I tasted it and
the lusciously rich fruit, which just
went on and on the finish, made
me question exactly how long
we must wait for a Pol Roger rosé
from a top vintage to actually
peak. Drink now-2005.
ⓔⓔⓔⓔ

Pommery

Champagne Pommery
5 Place du Général Gouraud
51053 Reims
France
Phone (326) 61.62.63
Fax (326) 61.62.99

---

83   **Pommery NV Brut Royal**
🍸   Although this is in Pommery's
typically fresh, light and elegantly
fruity vein, it is not as good as last
year's release (although I have to
admit that it was so good I almost
promised to stop campaigning for
the demise of Brut Royal).
Drink now-2002.
ⓔⓔ Local Price **142FF**

87   **Pommery NV Brut Apanage**
🍸   Stands out from the Brut Royale
by its deeper, fuller taste, yet
the balance of fruit is typically
Pommery in its almost light,
distinctly elegant style.
Drink now-2003.
ⓔⓔ Local Price **178FF**

85   **Pommery NV Summertime,**
🍸   **Blanc de Blancs Brut**
Not quite as good as last year, but
the lovely cushiony mousse puts it
above the year before.
Drink now-2003.
ⓔⓔ Local Price **189FF**

84   **Pommery NV Wintertime,**
🍸   **Blanc de Noirs Brut**
Rich, rooty Pinot fruit on the
palate, with a hint of green
enlivening the finish.
Will go toasty. Drink now-2002.
ⓔⓔ Local Price **189FF**

88   **Pommery NV Brut Rosé**
🍸   The pale apricot colour suggests
a mature cuvée, but it is definitely
a youthful Champagne, with floral
aromas, lovely young fruit on the
palate and a fresh, creamy
aftertaste. Drink now-2003.
ⓔⓔ Local Price **190FF**

90   **Pommery 1996**
🍸   **Brut Millésimé, B42**
Wow! Drink now-2006.
ⓔⓔⓔ Local Price **225FF**

88   **Pommery 1995 Brut Grand Cru**
🍸   A classic Pommery vintage, with a
soft mousse supporting a delicate
lacework of elegant fruit.
Drink now-2007.
ⓔⓔⓔ Local Price **225FF**

88   **Pommery 1992 Brut Grand Cru**
➤   This vintage was still available on
the UK market in 2001 and a very
fresh rendition too, suggesting a
more recent disgorgement than
the year before. The vanilla
building on the palate should
turn to coffee in a couple of years.
Drink 2002-2007.
ⓔⓔⓔ Local Price **225FF**

91   **Pommery 1992 Louise Rosé, Brut**
🍸   Hardly apricot yellow in colour
(although a touch more than this
year's Krug Rosé), with a lovely

floral finesse to the fruit and a wonderfully creamy-cushiony mousse. Drink now-2003.
ⓔⓔⓔⓔ Local Price **1250FF**

90 Pommery 1989 Louise, Brut
Freshness and finesse and pushed this wine up from 86 points last year, when it was quite fat and still needs time. What a transformation! Drink now-2008.
ⓔⓔⓔⓔ Local Price **650FF**

Pouillon

Champagne Roger Pouillon
3 Rue de la Couple
51160 Mareuil-sur-Aÿ
France
Fax (326) 59.49.83

---

84 Roger Pouillon & Fils,
50ème Anniversaire NV
Fleur de Mareuil, Brut Premier
I could swear that this cuvée has American oak on the nose. It even tastes like a white Rioja. I was interested to see after the tasting that I had detected barrique aromas last year, with peachy fruit from mid-palate to the finish. This suggests a much finer Champagne than I encountered this year, but unfortunately I do not have a second sample from last year to taste side-by-side, so I have no way of knowing whether it is a different disgorgement or it has evolved in an unexpected way. It certainly lack's last year's finesse, but gets its score through force of character.
Drink now-2002.
ⓔⓔ Local Price **130FF**

87 Roger Pouillon et Fils 1995
Le Millésime, Extra Brut
Chardonnay Grand Cru
The preview sample of this cuvée, which is due to be released August 2001, offers a mellowing malo

complexity to balance the truly extra-brut fruit.
Drink upon purchase.
ⓔⓔ Local Price **140FF**

Primo Estate

Old Port Wakefield Road
Virginia
SA 5120
Australia
Phone (8) 8380 9442
Fax (8) 8380 9696

---

85 Joseph NV Sparkling Red
Exquisitely rich, creamy-cedary fruit. Drink upon purchase
ⓔⓔ Local Price **A$50**

Princesse des Thunes

See Déthune

Prinz zu Salm Dalberg

See Salm Dalberg

Prüm Maximinhof

Weingut Studert Prüm
Maximinhof
Hauptstrasse 150
54470 Bernkastel-Wehlen
Germany
Phone (6531) 3920

---

78 Studert Prüm Maximinhof
1998 Maximiner Cabinet Brut
Rich and tasty Riesling supported by soft, velvety mousse. (100% Riesling, bottle-fermented, Mosel-Saar-Ruwer)
Drink now-2002.
ⓔ Local Price **DM18**

Raventós i Blanc

Plaça del Roure s/n
08770 Sant Sadurní d'Anoia
Spain
Phone (93) 8183262
Fax (93) 8912500

78 Raventós i Blanc 1998
Ⓘ Cava Brut Nature Gran Reserva
Wonderfully fresh and
attractively chewy-creamy fruit
(pre-commercialisation sample).
Drink now-2002.
Ⓔ Local Price **1,700 Ptas**

Raventós Rosell

Campanar 6
08770 Sant Sadurní d'Anoia
Spain
Phone (93) 7725251
Fax (93) 7727191

72 Joan Raventós Rosell
Ⓘ NV Cava Brut Nature
Fresh, firm, solid-style Cava has
its followers.
Drink upon purchase.
Ⓔ

Regale, Rosa

See Banfi

Reinhartshausen

Schloss Reinhartshausen
Hauptstrasse 41
65346 Eltville-Erbach
Germany
Phone (6123) 676333
Fax (6123) 4222

74 Freunde von Reinhartshausen NV
Ⓘ Hattenheimer Deutelsberg Brut
Rich and tasty with very good
acidity. (100% Riesling, bottle-
fermented, Rheingau)
Drink now-2003.
Ⓔ Local Price **DM20**

70 Freunde von Reinhartshausen
Ⓘ 1998 Schloss Reinhartshausen Brut
Elevated fruit. (100% Chardonnay,
bottle-fermented, Rheingau)
Drink upon purchase.
Ⓔ Local Price **DM29**

Reis und Luft

Weingut Reis und Luft
Am Sonnenberg 11
55459 Aspisheim
Germany
Phone (6727) 8881
Fax (6727) 8156

80 Reis und Luft 1998 Blauer
Ⓘ Spätburgunder Winzersekt
Trocken
Redcurrant Pinot Noir aroma
beautifully mirrored by red-fruits
on palate and a very crunchy,
summer-fruit pudding finish.
(100% Spätburgunder, bottle-
fermented, Rheinhessen)
Drink now-2002.
Ⓔ Local Price **DM15**

Renaudin

Champagne R. Renaudin
Domaine des Conardins
51530 Moussy
France
Phone (326) 54.03.41
Fax (326) 54.31.12

86 R. Renaudin NV Brut Réserve
Ⓘ A nice, flavoursome Champagne.
Fruit quite intense, with vanilla
building. Drink now-2004.
ⒺⒺ

Rentz

Edmond Rentz
7 route du Vin
68340 Zellenberg
France
Phone (389) 47.90.17
Fax (389) 47.97.27

Riccafana di Fratus Riccardo

Via Facchetti
91 – 25033 Cologne
Italy
Phone (30) 7721084
Fax (30) 723453

74 **Edmond Rentz 1999**
Crémant d'Alsace, Brut Prestige
Fresh citrussy-floral aromas, quite
zingy on the palate, with a lively
finish. Drink now-2002.
ⓔ Local Price **45FF**

73 **Riccafana NV Franciacorta Brut**
A very soft and smooth mousse
does its best to add finesse to the
somewhat chunky fruit.
Drink now-2002.
ⓔ

80 **Riccafana NV Franciacorta Satèn**
Fresh, crisp, crystal-clear fruit
on a soft, cushiony, authentically
satèn mousse. This is such a
delight to drink young that it
would be a shame to keep.
Drink upon purchase.
ⓔ

Ribeauvillé

CV de Ribeauvillé
2,route de Colmar
68150 Ribeauvillé
France
Phone (389) 73.61.80
Fax (389) 73.31.21

Richter

Weingut Max Ferd. Richter
Hauptstrasse 37/85
54486 Mülheim/Mosel
Germany
Phone (6534) 933003
Fax (6534) 1211

74 **Giersberger Brut 1998**
Crémant d'Alsace
Fresh, with quite a bit of finesse
mid-palate, but could do with
more on the finish.
Drink now-2002.
ⓔ Local Price **38FF**

75 **Giersberger Cuvée Prestige**
1998 Crémant d'Alsace
Fresher than most of the 99s, with
crisp, clean fruit and a good touch
of finesse on the finish.
Drink now-2003.
ⓔ Local Price **43FF**

70 **Max Ferd. Richter 1998**
Mulheimer Sonnenlay Brut
Good Riesling fruit, but needs
a slightly larger dosage if it
is to age beneficially. (100%
Riesling, bottle-fermented,
Mosel-Saar-Ruwer)
Drink now-2002.
ⓔ Local Price **DM18**

70 **Cuvée l'Offensee**
1998 Crémant d'Alsace
Sweet, talcum powder scent, fresh,
clean fruit underneath, one of the
better Chardonnay Crémant
d'Alsace. Drink now-2002.
ⓔ Local Price **47FF**

Attention!

*To submit samples for review
see page 52*

Ridgeview Estate

Fragbarrow Lane
Ditchling Common
Sussex
BN6 8TP
Great Britain
Phone (1444) 258039
Fax (1444) 230757

Ridgeview seems determined to give Nyetimber a race for its money and I for one hope that neither of these top-performing English sparkling wine producers run out of steam.

85 **Cavendish 1998 Cuvée Merret**
This is, I believe, the first Ridgeview wine I have picked up a touch of pepperiness in the fruit, but I am tasting this almost 12 months before it is due to be released in early 2002, by which time this should have disappeared. The palate is very smooth, already mellow and showing a lovely creaminess on the finish.
Drink 2002-2004.
ⓔⓔ Local Price £15

85 **Fitzrovia 1998 Cuvée Merret, Brut**
A pale, Roederer-like rosé colour, with lovely biscuity aromas intermingling with the fruit on the palate. Very classy.
Drink now-2003.
ⓔⓔ Local Price £15

84 **South Ridge 1998**
Cuvée Merret, Brut
Fruitier than the Cavendish, with none of its pepperiness and a promise to go a touch more oxidative. Drink 2002-2004.
ⓔⓔ Local Price £15

86 **Bloomsbury 1997**
Cuvée Merret, Brut
Dare I say classic English fizz? The fruit is immaculate and is ageing far more slowly than that in Ridgeview's excellent 1998 Fitzrovia rosé. Can be drunk now, but serious English fizz aficionados will want to keep it at least a year. Drink now-2005.
ⓔⓔ Local Price £15

Robert, André

Champagne André Robert
15 rue de l'Orme
51190 Le Mesnil-sur-Oger
France
Phone (326) 57.59.41
Fax (326) 57.54.90

88 **André Robert Père & Fils**
1996 Le Mesnil Blanc de Blancs
Grand Cru
Very crisp and extremely tight, this vintage promises great things, but it would be madness to open for at least three years.
Drink 2004-2011.
ⓔⓔ

Rodez

Champagne Eric Rodez
Rue de Isse
51150 Ambonnay
France
Phone (326) 57.04.93
Fax (326) 57.02.15

85 **Eric Rodez NV Cuvée des**
Crayères, Brut Grand Cru
Very fruity, albeit a touch lifted, with hints of strawberry on the finish. Drink now-2002.
ⓔⓔ

88 **Eric Rodez NV Blanc de Blancs,**
Brut Grand Cru
Another Champagne for oak-lovers, this cuvée is, however, finer, fresher and more elegant than most its ilk. It's also interesting to taste a pure Chardonnay Champagne from

a grand cru best-known for its Pinot Noir. Drink now-2005.
ⓔⓔ

86 **Eric Rodez NV Cuvée des Grands Vintages, Brut Grand Cru**
! A barrique character dominates the lifted fruit aroma in this rich tasting Champagne. An excellent level of ripe acids is balanced by a well judged dosage. Nicely present in a special dark-glass bottle. Oak-lovers should probably add another three points to the score. Drink now-2003.
ⓔⓔ

Roederer Estate

4501 Highway 128
Philo
CA 95466
USA
Phone (707) 895 2288
Fax (707) 895 2120

Without doubt one of the top six sparkling wine producers outside of Champagne itself.

80 **Roederer Estate NV Brut**
! The release that was the shelf in California in April 2001 had a tendency to go oxidatively nutty rather than biscuity, hence its drop in score, albeit to a very respectable 80 points.
Drink now-2003.
Local Price **$18**

85 **Roederer Estate NV Rosé Brut**
! A lean rosé of some class.
Drink now-2003.
ⓔⓔ Local Price **$23**

90 **Roederer Estate**
! **L'Ermitage 1996 Brut**
Beautiful fruit, wonderfully deep, slow evolving complexity, great length. Drink now-2006.
ⓔⓔⓔ Local Price **$40**

91 **Roederer Estate**
! **L'Ermitage 1994 Brut**
Fresh, zippy, deep, potentially complex, fatter than the 1996 yet fresher, crisper and even slower-evolving. Fresh, zippy, deep, potentially complex, fatter than the 1996 yet fresher, crisper and even slower-evolving.
Drink now-2006.
ⓔⓔⓔ Local Price **$40**

Roederer, Louis

Champagne Louis Roederer
21 Boulevard Lundy
51053 Reims
France
Phone (326) 40.42.11
Fax (326) 47.66.51

? **Louis Roederer NV Brut Premier**
This cuvée at the Annual Champagne Tasting was as excellent as ever. Exquisitely rich and concentrated, it Will go biscuity, but you will need to keep it a good two years for this style to develop. The Roederer-owned British importers are to be congratulated for maintaining consistency (88 points) despite the youthfulness, but Millennium sales must have made a significant dent in home stocks because the sample submitted to the Guide's tastings direct from France had a green, Chablis-like aroma followed by rounded Chablis-like fruit on the palate, with none of the biscuity-richness expected and much difficulty in discerning how much finesse there will finally be. Wait and see.
ⓔⓔ Local Price **165FF**

87 **Louis Roederer NV Rich Sec**
! For 20 years I have witnessed this cuvée getting less sweet. Drink now it appears to be getting younger. Sweeter styles of

Champagne age extraordinarily well, but younger is better as far as Roederer Rich is concerned, since it was often so old it was decrepit! With the youth comes lovely fruit – oranges and nectarines – and a beautifully balanced sweetness. Drink now-2006.
ⓔⓔ Local Price **180FF**

85   Louis Roederer NV Brut Premier (*magnum*)
Very young and fresh, but softer and more Roederer-like on the palate. Drink 2003-2007.
ⓔⓔ Local Price **350FF**

89   Louis Roederer 1995 Brut Vintage
Very rich and biscuity succulent. Absolute Roederer and a million miles from the disappointing 1994 (although the 1994 Cristal earned a superb 92 points). Promises great finesse. Drink now-2006.
ⓔⓔⓔ Local Price **290FF**

85   Louis Roederer 1995 Blanc de Blancs Brut
Chablis-like fruit on nose and palate. Should go toasty, but hopefully will have some biscuitiness. Drink 2002-2005.
ⓔⓔⓔ Local Price **300FF**

90   Louis Roederer 1995 Vintage Rosé Brut
Roederer has a reputation for producing rosés with very little colour, but if this is a rosé then I'm a Dutchman's uncle! However, we Dutchmen like the richness of fruit, the exquisiteness, the complexity, the finesse and the perfect cushiony mousse of a Champagne such as this. Drink now-2006.
ⓔⓔⓔ Local Price **300FF**

92   Louis Roederer 1995 Cristal Brut
Blending a Champagne with such a great intensity of fruit plus impeccable wonderful finesse and elegance is exceedingly difficult to pull off. Drink now-2006.
ⓔⓔⓔⓔ Local Price **300FF**

93   Louis Roederer 1995 Cristal Brut Rosé
Softer than the 1995 Cristal Brut with a touch less intensity, but a touch more depth and finesse. Drink now-2005.
ⓔⓔⓔ Local Price **1700FF**

82   Louis Roederer 1994 Brut Vintage
There is nothing wrong with this wine. It is absolutely clean and has a superb, cushiony mousse, but on retasting last year's release, my score of 82 points still stands. It is not in the same class as the Roederer 1994 Rosé (87 points) or, of course, the Cristal 1994 (92 points). Drink now-2003.
ⓔⓔⓔ Local Price **280FF**

Ronchetti, I

See Martelletti

Ronco Calino

See Calino

Rosa Regale

See Banfi

Roux

The House of J.C. Le Roux
Devon Valley Road
Devon Valley
Stellenbosch 7599
South Africa
Phone (21) 882 2590
Fax (21) 882 2585

78 J.C. Le Roux 1996
Chardonnay, Cap Classique
Classic biscuity aroma followed
by biscuity fruit with hints of
coconut. The acidity is sufficient,
quite good even, but this wine
would have scored much higher
with if it had been higher.
Drink upon purchase.
Ⓔ Local Price **R45**

? J.C. Le Roux 1989
Pinot Noir, Cap Classique
It would be unfair to score this
in pure qualitative terms because
its relative youthfulness is truly
remarkable for a Cap Classique
of this age. I hope curiosity gets
the better of some of my readers!
Drink upon purchase.
Ⓔ Local Price **R45**

Ruff

Domaine Daniel Ruff
64 route du Vin
67140 Heiligenstein
France
Phone (388) 08.10.81
Fax (388) 08.43.61

76 Domaine Daniel Ruff 1999 Blanc
de Noirs, Crémant d'Alsace
Expressive of Pinot Noir, quite fat
and silky mid-palate with good
acidity on finish. Might develop
well over short term.
Drink now-2003
Ⓔ Local Price **45FF**

Ruhlmann

Gilbert Ruhlmann Fils
31 rue de l'Ortenbourg
67750 Scherwiller
France
Phone (388) 92.03.21
Fax (388) 82.30.19

74 Gilbert Ruhlmann 1997 Cuvée
Prestige, Crémant d'Alsace
Really quite fat with vanilla
underneath, but very fresh and
not lacking finesse, although
could do with more acidity.
Drink upon purchase.
Ⓔ Local Price **44FF**

Ruinart

Champagne Ruinart
4 rue des Crayères
51100 Reims
France
Phone (326) 85.40.29
Fax (326) 82.88.43

86 R de Ruinart NV Brut
Really fresh and sherbety. Keep
two years for typical Ruinart
toasty aromas to develop.
Drink 2002-2005.
ⒺⒺⒺ Local Price **245FF**

89 R de Ruinart 1995 Brut
This did not show very well at
the Annual Champagne Tasting
in March 2001, when there was a
touch of green fruit showing and
would not have rated a
recommendation. However, the
samples submitted to my Guide
tastings had no green, were
broader than most 1995s (often
the case for Ruinart) and should
go toasty quite quickly.
Drink 2002-2007.
ⒺⒺⒺ Local Price **235FF**

90 Dom Ruinart 1993
Blanc de Blancs
Sherbety fresh with a crisp finish,
this disgorgement (LKAPIE) is
unbelievably youthful for a 1993,
but it has every indication of
going typically Ruinart-toasty in
a year or two. It would be nice to
serve this as an aperitif before a
special dinner, then follow on to
the more mellow 1990 with the

first course. Drink now-2006.
ⒺⒺⒺⒺ Local Price 525FF

93 Dom Ruinart 1990
❚ **Blanc de Blancs**
The current release of this oldie
is extraordinarily fresh, but as
anyone who is used to the
development of Dom Ruinart
will recognise, this wine is itching
to go toasty, in addition to which
there is a nice smack of vanilla
on the finish. Drink now-2006.
ⒺⒺⒺⒺ Local Price **525FF**

90 Dom Ruinart 1988 Rosé
❚ Big, rich, toasty aromas followed
by sweet, juicy-ripe Pinot fruit on
the palate. This is behaving more
like Dom Ruinart Brut than Dom
Ruinart Rosé, particularly on the
nose. Drink now-2004.
ⒺⒺⒺⒺ Local Price **550FF**

Rumpel

Riesling-Weingut C. Rumpel &
Cie.
Am Bahnhof 20
56841 Traben-Trarbach
Germany
Phone (6541) 5666

---

70 C. Rumpel & Cie.
❚ **1998 Trabener Gaispfad Brut**
Rich, almondy-Riesling fruit,
with a touch of vanilla sweetness
on the finish. (100% Riesling,
bottle-fermented,
Mosel-Saar-Ruwer)
Drink now-2002.
Ⓔ Local Price **DM16**

Runner

François Runner et Fils
1 rue de la Liberté
68250 Pfaffenheim
France
Phone (389) 49.62.89
Fax (389) 49.62.89

---

77 François Runner et Fils 1999
❚ **Runner, Crémant d'Alsace**
Will go toasty with creamy-lemony
fruit, touch exotic on finish.
Drink now-2002.
Ⓔ Local Price **38FF**

Saar-Mosel-Winzersekt

Gilbertstrasse 34
54290 Trier
Germany
Phone (6519) 752914
Fax (6519) 752920

---

72 Saar-Mosel-Winzersekt 1999
❚ **Mosel Riesling Sekt Brut**
A clean, fresh, entry-level Riesling
Sekt with a cordon rouge on the
label, which I would have thought
might upset Mumm a bit!
(100% Riesling, bottle-fermented,
Mosel-Saar-Ruwer)
Drink now-2002.
Ⓔ Local Price **DM20**

Sacred Hill

See Bortoli

Sacy

Champagne Louis de Sacy
6 rue de Verzenay
51380 Verzy
France
Phone (326) 97.91.13
Fax (326) 97.94.25

---

88 Louis de Sacy NV Brut Tradition
❚ Light, fresh, fruity and delightful,
with elegant citrussy-rich fruit,
a fine mousse and truly great
acidity. It was my belief that Louis
de Sacy Tradition is a vintaged
Champagne, yet it was listed
as a non-vintage at the SAA
Champagne Tasting. Perhaps

it was because the vintage in question was less than three years old and could not legally be labelled as such.
Drink now-2005.
ⓔⓔ

84 **Louis de Sacy NV Brut Grand Cru**
The clean fruit and its lean structure is consistent with last year's style, although it dropped a point in the blind tasting.
Drink now-2003.
ⓔ Local Price **98FF**

84 **Louis de Sacy**
NV Brut Rosé, Grand Cru
Very fresh, attractive, floral, red-fruit nose with rich fruit on the palate and firm, red-fruit finish. Drink now-2003.
ⓔⓔ Local Price **112FF**

85 **Louis de Sacy 1985**
Cuvée Tentation, Demi-Sec
A strange one this. Strong toasty aromas immediately announce a mature Champagne and mellow-toasty, sweet-peachy fruit on the palate confirms this. The dosage is sweet, but not that sweet and does not appear to have aged at the same rate as the rest of the Champagne. Could be interesting to play with at the table, accompanying it with a savoury dish that has fruity ingredients.
Drink now-2004.
ⓔⓔ Local Price **109FF**

Salm Dalberg

Prinz zu Salm Dalberg'sches Weingut
Schloss Wallhausen
55595 Wallhausen
Germany
Phone (6706) 94440
Fax (6706) 944418

75 **Prinz zu Salm Dalberg'sches**
Weingut 1998 Rheingraf
Riesling Sekt Brut
Tart Riesling fruit, not unripe, but certainly verging on green-zesty. Immaculate mousse of minuscule bubbles. (100% Riesling, bottle-fermented, Nahe)
Drink now-2002.
ⓔ Local Price **DM19**

Salon

Champagne Salon
Le Mesnil-sur-Oger
51190 Avize
France
Phone (326) 57.51.65
Fax (326) 57.79.29

Owned by Laurent-Perrier, Delamotte is the sister company of the great Champagne Salon, which is literally next door.

92 **Salon 1990 Blanc de Blancs Brut**
I've tasted this numerous times prior to its launch, all of which led me to believe that it would be one of Salon's very greatest vintages, but on no occasion have I noted the pepperiness found in the pre-release sample tasted this year. Salon always needs post-disgorgement ageing and this one possibly requires as much as the 1982. Start tasting in three years time, but do not expect this wine to show its full potential for at least five or six years. Knowing what it is, I suspect that I have under-marked this wine, but I have to go with my blind tasting score for now at least.
Drink 2004-2016.
ⓔⓔⓔⓔ Local Price **800FF**

San Cristoforo

San Cristoforo di Dotti Bruno
Via Villa Nuova
25030 Villa d'Erbusco
Italy
Phone (30) 7760268
Fax (30) 7760116

80 San Cristoforo
! NV Franciacorta Brut
Very clean and crisp, with fruit of
some finesse and an immaculate,
soft, cushiony mousse.
Drink now-2003
Ⓔ Local Price **17,500 Lira**

Santero

Via Cesare Pavese 28
12058 Santo Stefano Belbo
Italy
Phone (141) 841212
Fax (141) 841222

75 Santero NV Asti Dolce
! Very fresh, pale and grapy,
but let down by a sugary finish.
Drink upon purchase.
Ⓔ

Saumur, CV de

CV de Saumur
Route de Saumoussay
49260 Saint-Cyr-en-Bourg
France
Phone (241) 53.06.08
Fax (241) 51.69.13

75 CV de Saumur, Crémant de Loire
! Cuvée de la Chevalerie NV, Brut
Clean, fresh and light-bodied with
elegant fruit. Drink upon purchase.
Ⓔ

78 Cuvée de la Chevalier NV,
! Cabernet Demi-Sec
Attractive currant bush fruit with
smoky undertones and a slightly

tannic raspberry finish.
Drink now-2002.
Ⓔ

74 Crémant de Loire 1998
! Les Médaillés, Brut
Serious style Saumur, rather full,
but not heavy.
Drink upon purchase.
Ⓔ

Schaeffer Woerly

3 Place du Marché
67650 Dambach/ville
France
Phone (388) 92.40.81
Fax (388) 92.49.87

74 Schaeffer Woerly 1998
! Crémant d'Alsace Brut
Firm mousse, creamy fresh fruit.
Drink now-2004.
Ⓔ Local Price **41FF**

Schales

Weingut Schales
Alzeyerstrasse 160
67592 Flörsheim-Dalsheim
Germany
Phone (6243) 7003
Fax (6243) 5230

75 Schales 1997 Weisser Burgunder
! Sekt Extra Trocken
Elegant Pinot Blanc fruit,
nice acidity, good ripeness. (100%
Weißburgunder, bottle-fermented,
Rheinhessen) Drink now-2002.
Ⓔ Local Price **DM24**

74 Schales 1991 Riesling Sekt Brut
! A very youthful 10 year old Sekt
with good, clean, fruit. Although
mature, this Sekt will benefit from
further ageing. (100% Riesling,
bottle-fermented, Rheinhessen)
Drink now-2005.

ⒺLocal Price **DM22**

Scharsch

Domaine Joseph Scharsch
12 rue de l'Eglise
67120 Wolxheim
France
Phone (388) 38.30.61
Fax (388) 38.01.13

80 **Domaine Joseph Scharsch 1998**
Ⓨ **Cuvée Prestige, Crémant d'Alsace**
Real Champagne lookalike! Very
rich and complex with bags of
acidity. Should go biscuity.
Drink now-2004.
ⒺLocal Price **39FF**

Schlegel Boeglin

Domaine Schlegel Boeglin
22 rue d'Orschwihr
68250 Westhalten
France
Phone (389) 47.00.93
Fax (389) 47.65.32

78 **Domaine Schlegel Boeglin**
Ⓨ **1998 Crémant d'Alsace Brut**
Creamy-biscuity, richly flavoured
with very good acidity. Very much
in the Champagne style rather
than Alsace per se.
Drink now-2003.
ⒺLocal Price **35FF**

70 **Domaine Schlegel Boeglin**
Ⓨ **1996 Réserve de la Vallée Noble,**
Crémant d'Alsace
High acidity, firm fruit, fine
mousse. Will go toasty. Need more
finesse to score higher.
Drink now-2003.
ⒺLocal Price **50FF**

Schleinitz

Weingut Freiherr von Schleinitz
Kirchstrasse 17
56330 Kobern-Gondorf
Germany
Phone (2607) 972020

72 **Freiherr von Schleinitz**
Ⓨ **1999 Riesling Sekt Brut**
Fresh, creamy Riesling with zippy
finish. (100% Riesling, bottle-
fermented, Mosel-Saar-Ruwer)
Drink now-2002.
ⒺLocal Price **DM19**

Schloss Affaltrach

See Baumann

Schloss Castell

See Castell'sches Domänenamt

Schloss Schönborn

Domänenweingut Schloss
Schönborn
Hauptstrasse 53
65347 Hattenheim
Germany
Phone (6723) 91810
Fax (6723) 918191

75 **Schloss Schönborn 1994**
Ⓨ **Assmannshäuser Höllenberg Brut**
Exquisite Pinot Noir perfume, but
this is exaggerated on the palate
to the point of highly perfumed
strawberry jam. Interesting
nonetheless. (100% Spätburgunder,
bottle-fermented, Rheingau)
Drink upon purchase.
ⒺLocal Price **DM30**

Schmitges

Weingut Heinrich Schmitges
Im Unterdorf 12
54492 Erden
Germany
Phone (6532) 3934

71 Heinrich Schmitges
1999 Riesling Sekt Brut
Clean and fresh with perfumed
Riesling aromas beginning to
build. (100% Riesling, bottle-
fermented, Mosel-Saar-Ruwer)
Drink now-2003.
ⓔ Local Price **DM22**

71 Schmitges 1999
Riesling Sekt Trocken
Clean, correct and sherbety.
(100% Riesling, bottle-fermented,
Mosel-Saar-Ruwer)
Drink upon purchase.
ⓔ Local Price **DM25**

Schmitt-Peitz

Weingut-Sektkellerei Schmitt-
Peitz
Hauptstrasse 35
55595 Wallhausen
Germany
Phone (6706) 6346

74 Schmitt-Peitz 1999
Wallhäuser Pfarrgarten Trocken
Very fresh with a sherbety finish
providing some finesse. (100%
Riesling, tank-fermented, Nahe)
Drink now-2002.
ⓔ Local Price **DM20**

Schoenheitz

Henri Schoenheitz
1 rue de Walbach
68230 Wihr Au Val
France
Phone (389) 71.03.96
Fax (389) 71.14.33

75 Henri Schoenheitz
1998 Crémant d'Alsace Brut
Fruity nose, with plenty of
easy-going fruit on the palate.
Very fine mousse.
Drink upon purchase.
ⓔ Local Price **41FF**

Schönhals

Weingut Eugen Schönhals
Hauptstrasse 23
55234 Biebelnheim
Germany
Phone (6733) 960052

70 Eugen Schönhals
1999 Pinot Blanc de Noir Brut
Sweetish, easy-drinking. (100%
Spätburgunder, bottle-fermented,
Rheinhessen)
Drink upon purchase.
ⓔ Local Price **DM19**

Schramsberg

1400 Schramsberg Road
Calistoga
CA 94515
USA
Phone (707) 942 2414
Fax (707) 942 5943

76 Mirabelle NV Brut, Schramsberg
Fresh, clean, easy drinking with a
crisp finish. Elegant for the price.
Drink upon purchase.
ⓔⓔ Local Price **$13**

82 Schramsberg 1997 Blanc de Blancs
Very fine mousse, minuscule
bubbles, with fruit that is so clean
and creamy-fresh.
Drink now-2003.
ⓔⓔ Local Price **$27**

Schubert'sche Gutsverwaltung Grünhaus

54318 Mertesdorf
Germany
Phone (6515) 111
Fax (6515) 2122

74 **Schubert'sche Gutsverwaltung**
   Grünhaus 1998 Maximin
Grünhäuser Riesling Sekt Brut
Fresh, sherbety Riesling fruit
supported by a very good,
cushiony mousse.
(100% Riesling, transfer-method,
Mosel-Saar-Ruwer)
Drink now-2003.
ⓔ Local Price **DM30**

Schwach

Bernard Schwach
25 route de Ste Marie aux
Mines
68150 Ribeauvillé
France
Phone (389) 73.72.18
Fax (389) 73.30.34

75 **Bernard Schwach 1999 Brut**
   Réserve, Crémant d'Alsace
Fresh fruit and custard!
Drink now-2002
ⓔ Local Price **53FF**

Schweinhardt Nachf.

Weingut Bürgermeister W.
Schweinhardt Nachf.
Heddesheimerstrasse 1
55450 Langenlohnsheim
Germany
Phone (6704) 93100
Fax (6704) 931050

75 **Bürgermeister W. Schweinhardt**
   Nachf. 1998 Chardonnay Brut
Clean Chardonnay fruit aromas
with very fresh fruit supported by
lovely pin-cushion mousse. (100%

Chardonnay, bottle-fermented,
Nahe)
Drink now-2003.
ⓔ Local Price **DM25**

Seaview

Edwards & Chaffey Winery
Chaffeys Road
McLaren Vale
SA 5171
Australia
Phone (8) 8323 8250
Fax (8) 8323 9308

75 **Seaview 1996 Chardonnay Blanc**
   de Blancs, Vintage Research Brut
Fresh and light yet firm mousse.
This wine is usually for ready
drinking, but the current release
needs a good year in bottle.
Drink 2002-2003.
ⓔ Local Price **A$18**

Secondé

Champagne François Secondé
6 rue des Galipes
51500 Sillery
France
Phone (326) 49.17.67
Fax (326) 49.11.55

85 **François Secondé**
   NV Brut Grand Cru
Overtly fruity with a soft, fluffy
mousse. Drink now-2003.
ⓔ Local Price **82FF**

90 **François Secondé**
   NV Brut Rosé, Grand Cru
This is gorgeous! If this was not
a rosé it would be taken far more
seriously. Close your eyes and
imagine you're drinking a (white)
brut non-vintage and ask yourself
what you think of all that fruit.
Drink now-2002.
ⓔ Local Price **87FF**

85 François Secondé 1996 Blanc de
Blancs, Brut Millésime Grand Cru
Needs a year of post-disgorgement
ageing for the nose to come
together, but the fruit on the
palate with its typically high ripe
1996 acids is lovely now.
Drink 2002-2004.
ⓔⓔ Local Price **115FF**

Segura Viudas

Segura Viudas SA (Grupo
Freixenet)
Sant Antoni 11
08770 Sant Sadurní d'Anoia
Spain
Phone (93) 8997227
Fax (93) 8996006

---

85 Torre Galimany 1998
Cava Brut Nature
Beautifully understated
presentation, this cuvée is
obviously an attempt to produce
the best possible Cava from
traditional Cava grapes (with
an emphasis on Xarel.lo), using
cold-maceration on the skins
prior to fermentation (to enhance
the aromatics) and barriques for
the first fermentation (for
complexity). Has it worked? A
resounding yes! I gave Freixenet
extra marks for trying when it
introduced its revolutionary
Monastrell-Xarel.lo, but it's first
release was disappointing and
progress embarrassingly slow,
as indeed I fear its Trépat rosado
will be. However, Freixenet's
subsidiary, albeit upmarket, brand
Segura Viudas has not only tried
but succeeded with the first
vintage of what is a truly radical
wine in traditional Cava terms.
For me to award 85 points to
a Cava made exclusively from
Xarel.lo, Macabéo and Parellada
grapes is in itself revolutionary
because this score equates not

only to the quality of
Champagne, but to the quality a
Champagne must be to warrant a
place in my own cellar. I could
make constructive criticisms about
how it could be tweaked here and
there, but that would only detract
from the fact that this is a superb
sparkling wine, with real fruit
beautifully balanced by good
acidity. Not only should Cava
drinkers buy it, but Cava sceptics
too. Drink now-2003.
ⓔ Local Price **2,600 Ptas**

Selbach-Oster

Weingut Selbach-Oster
Uferallee 23
54492 Zeltingen
Germany
Phone (6532) 2081
Fax (6532) 4014

---

78 Selbach-Oster 1997
Zeltinger Himmelreich Brut
Bright, clear, Riesling bottle-
aromas followed by very crisp
fruit on the palate, which would
have benefited from an additional
2-3 grams sugar in the dosage,
although it is still very good
as it is. (100% Riesling, bottle-
fermented, Mosel-Saar-Ruwer)
Drink now-2003.
ⓔ Local Price **DM19**

Selosse

Champagne Jacques Selosse
22 rue Ernest Vallée
51190 Avize
France
Phone (326) 57.53.56
Fax (326) 57.78.22

---

87 Jacques Selosse NV Extra Brut,
Grand Cru Blanc de Blancs
Floral youthful oak aromas on the
palate and crisp fruit, but the oak

paints broader strokes on the finish when compared to Gimonnet's cuvée Oenophile. Drink upon purchase.
ⒺⒺ Local Price **170FF**

Senez

Champagne Senez
6 Grande Rue
10360 Fontette
France
Phone (326) 29.60.62

84 **Cristian Senez NV Brut**

This producer occupies a strange place in my affections; on the one hand its 1981 was so good that I drank myself through a case so quickly that I wanted another and could not get one, whilst on the other the 1982 was very disappointing and I have enjoyed very little from Senez since. The current release of this cuvée strikes me that he has gone back to basics, getting as much freshness as possible out of cool fermentation without straying into the bland amylic aromas. Not top stuff, but there is a nice vanilla-finesse about the fruit, which I hope points to a brighter future. Drink now-2002.
ⒺⒺ

Serafino

Enrico Serafino
12043 Canale
Italy
Phone (173) 98131
Fax (173) 98253

73 **Enrico Serafino 1995 Cuvée Speciale per il Millennio, Brut Millesimato**
Very fresh, clean fruit supported by a smooth, cushiony mouse. Drink upon purchase.

ⒺLocal Price **15,600 Lira**

Serra

Jaume Serra SA (Grupo J. Garcia Carrion)
Finca el Padruell
08800 Vilanova i la Geltrú
Spain
Phone (93) 8936404
Fax (93) 8142262

72 **Cristalino NV Cava Brut**
Fresh fruit riding on a nice fluffy mousse. Drink upon purchase.
Ⓔ

Shadow Creek

See Chandon (California)

Signat

Escultor Llimona s/n
08328 Alella
Spain
Phone (93) 5403400
Fax (93) 5401471

78 **Signat 1999 Cava Brut Nature**
Excellent fruit and just enough acidity to please me! Drink upon purchase.
ⒺLocal Price **1,300 Ptas**

Sigolsheim

La Cave de Sigolsheim
11-15, rue St. Jacques
68240 Sigolsheim
France
Phone (389) 78.10.10
Fax (389) 78.21.93

76 **La Cave de Sigolsheim 1995 Brut Rosé, Crémant d'Alsace**
Salmon-coloured, cherry-flavoured

fizz from Alsace. Nice acidity.
Perfectly dosaged.
Drink now-2002.
Ⓔ Local Price **47FF**

Sipp

Louis Sipp
5 Grand'Rue
68150 Ribeauvillé
Frances
Phone (389) 73.60.01
Fax (389) 73.31.46

74   Louis Sipp 1999
🍷 **Crémant d'Alsace Brut**
Fresh, crisp, clean and dry to the
bottom of the glass.
Drink now-2002.
Ⓔ Local Price **45FF**

Sipp Mack

Domaine Sipp Mack
1 rue des Vosges
68150 Hunawihr
France
Phone (389) 73.61.88
Fax (389) 73.36.70

70   Domaine Sipp Mack 1998
🍷 **Crémant d'Alsace Brut**
Amylic nose, everything
technically correct, but the fruit
could be from anywhere!
Drink upon purchase.
Ⓔ Local Price **46FF**

Sir James

See BRL Hardy

Attention!

*To submit samples for review
see page 52*

Smith

Samuel Smith & Son
Yalumba Winery
Eden Valley Road
Angaston
SA 5353
Australia
Phone (8) 8561 3200
Fax (8) 8561 3393

74   Jansz of Tasmania NV
🍷 Hazelnutty Chardonnay.
Drink upon purchase.
Ⓔ Local Price **A$21**

**?   Jansz of Tasmania 1996 Brut
Pipers River Cuvée**
Is this Pipers River Cuvée different
from the Jansz 1996 Tasmania
Brut Cuvée tasted last year
(83 points)? If it's not, then this
was either a duff bottle or it has
gone downhill rapidly. Whatever
the answer, I have to put a **?** sign
on this until I retaste it.
Wait and see.
ⒺⒺ Local Price **A$32**

Soljans

Soljans Wines
263 Lincoln Road
Henderson
New Zealand
Phone (6) 438 8365
Fax (6) 438 8366

80   Soljans Estate 1998
🍷 **Sparkling Pinotage**
This experimental cuvée is
decidedly drier than the classic
Aussie Sparkling reds, but there
is plenty of fruit, it's better than
most non-fizzy Cape Pinotage,
and it has a good tannin
grip, making it an ideal
accompaniment for roast
pork. Drink now-2003.
ⒺⒺ

? **Soljans Estate 1997 Legacy**
An exotic, oaky fizz for those
who like a walk on the wild side.
Drink upon purchase.
ⓔ Local Price **NZ$22**

Sorg

Domaine Bruno Sorg
8 rue Mgr Stumpf
68420 Eguisheim
France
Phone (389) 41.80.85
Fax (389) 41.22.64

*Sorg might be a master of
Muscat, but he needs a helping
hand with his bubbles.*

70 **Domaine Bruno Sorg**
1998 Crémant d'Alsace Brut
Some greenness, but quite strong
flavour backing it up. Will go
toasty. Drink now-2002.
ⓔ Local Price **39FF**

Sousa

Champagne de Sousa & Fils
12 place Léon-Bourgoise
51190 Avize
France
Phone (326) 57.53.29
Fax (326) 52.30.64

80 **De Sousa NV Brut Réserve**
Quite fat with sulphur evident on
nose, but this should blow off and
help turn the fruit toasty.
Drink now-2004.
ⓔⓔ

South Ridge

See Ridgeview Estate

Sparr

Pierre Sparr
2 rue de la 1ère Armée
68240 Sigolsheim
France
Phone (389) 78.24.22
Fax (389) 47.32.62

78 **Pierre Sparr 1999**
Brut Réserve, Crémant d'Alsace
Love fruit and acidity balance.
Not a complex wine, but a
delightful, fruity wine to drink,
with vanilla sugar on finish.
Drink now-2002.
ⓔ Local Price **47FF**

74 **Pierre Sparr 1995**
Brut Dynastie, Crémant d'Alsace
Very fresh and youthful for age,
crisp finish. Drink now-2003.
ⓔ Local Price **57FF**

74 **Pierre Sparr 1995**
Glorius 2000, Crémant d'Alsace
Has finesse on nose, very crisp
fruit with a tart finish.
Drink now-2002.
ⓔ Local Price **60FF**

Sparviere

Lo Sparviere
Gusalli Beretta di Poncelet M.
Via Costa
2 – 25040 Monticelli Brusati
Italy
Phone (30) 652382
Fax (30) 652382

74 **Lo Sparviere NV**
Franciacorta Extra Brut
Not as special as last year's cuvée,
but should also go biscuity.
Drink 2002-2004.
ⓔ Local Price **18,000 Lira**

Spitz et Fils

2/4, route des Vins
67650 Blienschwiller
France
Phone (388) 92.61.20
Fax (388) 92.61.26

70 Spitz 1998 Brut
Blanc de Noirs, Crémant d'Alsace
Good tasty Pinot Noir fruit,
just let down by the nose lacking
finesse and the finish a touch
sweet, but the latter does make
it user-friendly.
Drink upon purchase.
ⓔ Local Price **43FF**

75 Spitz 1997 Brut
Blanc de Noirs, Crémant d'Alsace
Rich and tasty with just enough
acidity to keep it fresh.
Drink now-2002.
ⓔ Local Price **41FF**

St. Laurentius Sektgut

Laurentiusstrasse 4
54340 Leiwen
Germany
Phone (6507) 3836
Fax (6507) 3896

75 St. Laurentius Sektgut
1998 Riesling Brut
Smooth and complete Riesling
fruit supported by a soft, velvety
mousse. (100% Riesling, bottle-
fermented, Mosel-Saar-Ruwer)
Drink now-2002.
ⓔ Local Price **DM20**

75 St. Laurentius Sektgut
1998 Chardonnay Brut
A fresh, elegant, fruit-driven fizz
with light, sweet, ripe fruit on the
finish. (100% Chardonnay, bottle-
fermented, Mosel-Saar-Ruwer)
Drink now-2002.
ⓔ Local Price **DM22**

St. Urbans-Hof

Weingut St. Urbans-Hof
Urbanusstrasse 16
54340 Leiwen
Germany
Phone (6507) 93770
Fax (6507) 937730

75 St. Urbans-Hof 1998 Brut
Clean focused Riesling fruit
with a creamy-leesy, fuller, almost
Champagne-like stamp on it.
Theoretically these two styles
should conflict, but where it
matters – in the mouth – they
don't. (100% Riesling, bottle-
fermented, Mosel-Saar-Ruwer)
Drink now-2002.
ⓔ Local Price **DM18**

Staatsweingut Meersburg

Seminarstrasse 10
88709 Meersburg
Germany
Phone (7532) 357
Fax (7532) 358

73 Staatsweingut Meersburg
1999 Pinot Brut
French grapes (Pinot Gris and
Pinot Blanc) with Germanic fruit,
acidity and freshness floating on a
fine mousse of tiny bubbles. (50%
Grauburgunder, 50%
Weißburgunder; transfer-method,
Baden) Drink now-2002.
ⓔ Local Price **DM24**

Stefano

I Vignaioli di S. Stefano
Fr. Marini 13
12058 S. Stefano Belbo
Italy
Phone 141840419
Fax 141840419

85 **Vignaioli di S. Stefano**
Ⱦ **2000 Asti Spumante**
Whatever this bottle should be
used for, wine it is not the first
thing to spring to mind.
Extremely fresh as might be
expected from last year's wine,
but somehow more winey and
tastes less sweet than most Asti.
Why is this producer still using
'Spumante' on its label?
Drink upon purchase.
Ⓕ Local Price **20,000 Lira**

Stein

Sektkellerei Edith Stein
Auf dem Stiel 5
55585 Oberhausen
Germany

72 **Edith Stein 1999 Riesling**
Ⱦ **Gewürztraminer Trocken**
An entry-level Sekt with 15%
Gewürztraminer providing the
spice of life. (85% Riesling, 15%
Gewürztraminer; tank-fermented,
Nahe) Drink upon purchase.
Ⓕ Local Price **DM12**

Stentz Buecher

Domaine Stentz Buecher
21 rue Kleb
68920 Wettolsheim
France
Phone (389) 80.68.09
Fax (389) 79.60.53

74 **Domaine Stentz Buecher 1998**
Ⱦ **Crémant d'Alsace Brut**
Creamy-tangy fruit of some
complexity, good acidity.
Drink now-2003.
Ⓕ Local Price **38FF**

70 **Stentz Buecher 1997**
Ⱦ **Chardonnay, Crémant d'Alsace**
Fresh, easy, clean.
Drink upon purchase.

Ⓕ Local Price **43FF**

Stoffel

Antoine Stoffel
21 rue de Colmar
68420 Eguisheim
France
Phone (389) 41.32.03
Fax (389) 24.92.07

73 **Antoine Stoffel 1998**
Ⱦ **Crémant d'Alsace Brut**
Lovely fine fruity aromas. Mousse
clings to the inside of the glass.
Easy-drinking style.
Drink now-2002.
Ⓕ Local Price **38FF**

Strathbogie Ranges

See Plunkett

Sumarroca

See Moli Coloma

Suss

Champagne Jean-Paul Suss
10110 Buxeuil
France
Phone (325) 38.56.22
Fax (325) 38.58.58

82 **Jean-Paul Suss NV Brut Réserve**
Ⱦ The fruit here is fresh, crisp and
easy to drink as an aperitif, but
promises to go oxidative, so
unless you particularly like that
style, don't bother keeping it.
Drink upon purchase.
Ⓕ Local Price **65FF**

Taittinger

Champagne Taittinger
9 Place Saint-Nicaise
51061 Reims
France
Phone (326) 85.45.35
Fax (326) 85.84.65

84 Taittinger NV Brut Réserve
At the Annual Champagne
Tasting, this cuvée was atypically
fat and not too brut, while the
sample submitted had a touch of
pepperiness. Both were extremely
fresh, with excellent acidity and
scored the same.
Drink now-2004.
ⒺⒺ Local Price **160FF**

90 Taittinger 1996 Brut Millésimé
The wonderful autolytic finesse
on the nose pervades every corner
of this wine, which has obviously
undergone malolactic because of
its relative softness for a 1996, yet
has no malo character whatsoever.
That is the perfect application
of so-called malolactic: to reduce
acidity without declaring its
presence. Given time, the lactic
acid produced will contribute to
creamy-biscuitiness of a mature
Champagne, as will happen to
this, but it should never leave a
tell-tale trace of its presence.
Taittinger have everything right
here. And what a beautiful,
breezy, fluffy mousse!
Drink now-2004.
ⒺⒺⒺ Local Price **200FF**

**92 Taittinger Comtes de Champagne
1996 Rosé Brut**
Attractive, pale peach in colour
with fresh floral aromas and very
rich fruit on the palate. There is a
deepness and intensity of fruit
that is undeniably 1996, but not
that year's electrifying acidity,
although the acidity is indeed
excellent. One of the few Comtes

de Champagne Rosé to drink
well on release, this vintage also
offers a great chance to age well.
Drink now-2006.
ⒺⒺⒺⒺ Local Price **750FF**

90 Taittinger 1995 Brut Millésimé
Excellent! Beautifully focused,
crisp aromas indicating future
biscuity complexity. Creamy
biscuity fruit already on the
palate, yet there is so much
potential development. One of
the very best examples of this
vintage. Drink now-2011.
ⒺⒺⒺ Local Price **200FF**

**95 Taittinger Comtes de Champagne
1995 Blanc de Blancs Brut**
This has started to drink one year
earlier than anticipated, with its
big, toasty aroma and fresh,
peachy fruit supported by bags of
ripe acid on the palate.
Drink now-2010.
ⒺⒺⒺⒺ Local Price **660FF**

**90 Taittinger Comtes de Champagne
1995 Rosé Brut**
Fresh, perfumed aroma, lovely
cherry fruits. Drink 2002-2004
ⒺⒺⒺⒺ Local Price **750FF**

Tarlant

Champagne Tarlant
51480 Oeuilly
France
Phone (326) 58.30.60
Fax (326) 58.37.31

85 Tarlant NV Cuvée Louis, Brut
Yet another barrique Champagne,
but at least the producer is
completely open about this on
the back label, advising potential
buyers that this wine underwent
its first fermentation in wood,
20% of which was new, and there
was no malolactic. So there's no
question what the style is. Indeed,

if I gave scores for back labels, Tarlant would receive a perfect 100 for the information shown here. We are told that this is a 1994-based blend, with reserve wines from 1993 and that it is composed of 50% Chardonnay and 50% Pinot Noir. But what really impresses me is that we are informed that the wine was bottled in June 1995 and disgorged in October 2000. Oak-lovers should probably add a couple of points. Drink now-2002.
Ⓔ Ⓔ Local Price **163FF**

85 **Tarlant 1995 Rosé, Brut Prestige**
❢ A food Champagne rosé with full-bodied, intense fruit.
Drink now-2004.
Ⓔ Ⓔ Local Price **112FF**

84 **Tarlant 1995 Brut**
━ Good concentration of fruit, but needs a couple of years at least.
Drink 2003-2004
Ⓔ Ⓔ Local Price **112FF**

Tatachilla

151 Main Road
McLaren Vale
SA 5171
Australia
Phone (8) 8323 8656
Fax (8) 8323 9096

75 **Tatachilla NV Sparkling Malbec**
❢ Very violety let down by toffee-fruit on the finish.
Drink upon purchase
Ⓔ Ⓔ

Tauberfränkische Wg. Beckstein

Weinstrasse 30
97922 Lauda-Königshofen
Germany
Phone (9343) 50031
Fax (9343) 50060

73 **Tauberfränkische Wg. Beckstein**
❢ **1998 Becksteiner Kirchberg Riesling Sekt Trocken**
A good display of ripeness, freshness and acidity. (100% Riesling, bottle-fermented, Baden)
Drink now-2003.
Ⓔ Local Price **DM19**

Tenuta Castellino

See Castellino

Thienot

Champagne Alain Thienot
14 rue des Moissons
51100 Reims
France
Phone (326) 77.50.10
Fax (326) 77.50.19

83 **Alain Thienot NV Brut**
❢ Fresh, clean and elegant fruit.
Drink now-2002.
Ⓔ Ⓔ Local Price **122FF**

85 **Alain Thienot 1996 Brut Rosé**
❢ A very pale apricot with almost no pink or peach colour, suggesting a mature cuvée and that is confirmed on the nose, but mature in a ripe-fruit sense, without any hint of oxidativeness. Those who like a nicely aged Champagne will find this really quite lush. Surprisingly soft for the vintage. Drink now-2002.
Ⓔ Ⓔ Local Price **146FF**

88 **Alain Thienot**
━ **1995 Brut Millésime**
Fine, keen, clean Champagne aromas backed up by intense fruit and acidity, with lots of extract on the finish and a true brut dosage. Could mistake this for a 1996! Drink 2002-2007.
Ⓔ Ⓔ Local Price **142FF**

89   Alain Thienot
1995 Grande Cuvée, Brut
Youthfully-complex aromas.
Crafted for elegance and finesse.
Drink 2002-2007.
ⒺⒺⒺ Local Price **300FF**

Thornton

Thornton Winery
32575 Rancho California Road
Temecula
CA 92591
USA
Phone (909) 699 0099
Fax (909) 699 5536

---

70   Thornton NV
Natural Brut Reserve
This wine lacks fruit, not the least
because it would benefit from a
dosage, but it has a clean and
fresh flavour that builds in mouth.
Nice soft mousse and a crisp
finish. Drink now-2002.
ⒺⒺ Local Price **$22**

77   Thornton NV Millennium Cuvée
Toasty-rich aroma with a soft
mousse enhancing the silkiness of
the fruit on the finish.
Drink now-2003.
ⒺⒺ Local Price **$22**

76   Thornton NV Brut Rosé
All red fruits on the palate
and luminous-pink on the eye!
Drink upon purchase.
ⒺⒺ Local Price **$22**

?   Thornton NV Cuvée Rouge
Raspberry jam on the nose,
blackcurrant jam on the palate.
All that's needed now is for the
fruit to get creamy and toasty and
this will be a complete afternoon
tea in a bottle!
Drink upon purchase.
ⒺⒺ Local Price **$22**

79   Thornton NV
Cuvée de Frontignan
California's answer to Asti.
Drink upon purchase.
ⒺⒺ Local Price **$22**

Thunes

See Déthune

Titchfield Vineyard

Misty Haze
Brownwich Lane
Titchfield
Hampshire
PO14 4NZ
Phone (1329) 845531

---

72   Southern Shore NV Brut
A touch green with almondy
fruit. Try keeping it for up to
one year, but keeping an eye on
its development at least every
three months. Drink now-2002.
Ⓔ

Torre Galimany

See Segura Viudas

Torre Oria

Ctra. Pontón-Utiel
46390 Derramador-Requena
Spain
Phone (96) 2320289
Fax (96) 2320311

---

75   Torre Oria NV Cava Brut Reserva
Soft perfumed fruit with a very
fresh, crisp finish (1997-based).
Drink upon purchase.
Ⓔ Local Price **850 Ptas**

Torreblanca

Finca Masía Torreblanca s/n
08734 Sant Miquel d'Olerdola
Spain
Phone (93) 8915066
Fax (93) 8900102

76 **Masblanc NV Cava Extra Brut**
Hints of green fruit, but there's
enough satisfyingly rich and ripe
fruit backing it up (1998-based).
Drink now-2002.
ⓔ Local Price **1,055 Ptas**

75 **Torreblanca NV Cava Extra Seco**
Sherbety fizz (1997-based).
Drink now-2002.
ⓔ Local Price **700 Ptas**

80 **Torreblanca NV Cava Brut**
Excellent acidity gives this crisp,
elegant Cava a leg up over much
of the rest (1997-based).
Drink now-2002.
ⓔ Local Price **800 Ptas**

80 **Torreblanca 1999**
Cava Extra Brut Reserva
Excellent, fresh, mouth-filling
fruit. Drink upon purchase.
ⓔ

? **Torreblanca 1998**
Cava Extra Brut Reserva
The Chardonnay is a little bit too
exaggerated, but some will like it!
Wait and see.
ⓔ

Torelló

Augusti Torelló SA
La Serra s/n
08770 Sant Sadurní d'Anoia
Spain
Phone (93) 8911173
Fax (93) 8912616

76 **Agustí Torelló Mata 1998**
Cava Brut Reserva
Very soft and so clean, I
recommend this particularly
for well-established Cava-lovers.
Drink upon purchase.
ⓔ Local Price **1,200 Ptas**

Toso

Loc. San Bovo 4
12054 Cossano Belbo
Phone (141) 83789
Fax (141) 88588

85 **Toso NV Asti Dolce**
Beautifully fresh and floral,
with very rich, sweet Moscato
fruit. Just so fresh that I tended
to use this wine as a yardstick
when blind-tasting other Asti.
Drink upon purchase.
ⓔ

? **Toso NV Brachetto d'Acqui Dolce**
Most red-winey aromas and
flavours. Regular Brachetto
drinkers might find this odd,
but others trying to get a grip
on the red, grapy fizz might well
appreciate it.
Drink upon purchase.
ⓔ

Tosti

Bosca Giovanni Tosti
Regione Secco 30
14053 Canelli
Italy
Phone (141) 822011
Fax (141) 823773

81 **Tosti NV Brachetto d'Acqui**
Certainly one of the sweetest
Brachetti. Drink upon purchase.
ⓔ

85 **Tosti NV Asti Dolce**
Extraordinarily rich, sweet,

grapy Moscato aroma and fruit.
Drink upon purchase.
ⓔ

Tribaut, G.

Champagne G. Tribaut
88 rue d'Eguisheim – BP5
51160 Hautvillers
France
Phone (326) 59.40.57
Fax (326) 59.43.74

88   **G. Tribaut NV Brut Rosé**
Young and fresh on the nose,
but super-rich, ultra-fresh,
yummy-creamy fruit on the
palate, with excellent acidity
to finish. Drink now-2002.
ⓔ Local Price **89FF**

83   **G. Tribaut NV Grande Cuvée**
Spéciale, Brut
I could not get Tribaut's Cuvée de
Réserve or Premier Cru past my
nose and into my mouth, but the
Grande Cuvée Spéciale has
a satisfying richness of fruit.
Drink 2002-2003.
ⓔⓔ Local Price **108FF**

Tsarine

See Chanoine

Turckheim

CV de Turckheim
16 rue des Tuilerie BP 6
68230 Turckheim
France
Phone (389) 30.23.60
Fax (389) 27.35.33

76   **Mayerling Brut 1999**
Crémant d'Alsace
Elegant, fruity. Best drunk as
young as possible.

Drink upon purchase.
ⓔ Local Price **39FF**

Twee Jonge Gezellen

Tulbagh 6820
South Africa
Phone (23) 230 0680
Fax (23) 230 0686

74   **Krone Borealis 1998 Brut,**
Cap Classique
This was the first unsulphured
Cap Classique. A bit high-toned
with hints of oak in its rich fruity
and much preferred to the 1997,
which was unpleasant on the nose.
Drink now-2002
ⓔ Local Price **R45**

85   **Private Vintners Limited Release**
1995 Pinot Noir, Cap Classique
Big nose of autolysis,
terpenes and toast followed by
extraordinarily fresh fruit on the
palate, with excellent acidity giving
a very crisp finish.
Drink now-2002.
ⓔ

83   **Krone Borealis 1994 Brut,**
Cap Classique
The peachy fruit is excellent, very
fresh and far better than I
remembered it to be, whereas the
1993 (one of Nicky Krone's two
best-ever vintages) was either
totally over the hill or a bad bottle
(it was so malty that it reminded
me of a brewery in full ferment).
Drink upon purchase.
ⓔ Local Price **R54**

Attention!

*To submit samples for review
see page 52*

Uberti

Uberti G. & G.A.
Via Enrico Fermi
2- -25030 Erbusco
Italy
Phone (30) 7267476
Fax (30) 7760455

75 **Uberti NV Magnificentia,**
Franciacorta Satèn
Fresh, sweet fruit with a lively
mousse that adds crispness to
the finish. Drink now-2002.
ⓔⓔ Local Price **38,000 Lira**

82 **Uberti NV Francesco I,**
Franciacorta Extra Brut
The best by far of this year's
Franciacorta Extra Brut, this
cuvée has a nicely understated
toasted fruit aroma, well-focused
fruit and a vanilla-biscuit finish.
Drink upon purchase.
ⓔⓔ Local Price **48,000 Lira**

Union Champagne

7 rue Pasteur
51190 Avize
France
Phone (326) 57.94.22
Fax (326) 57.57.98

89 **De Saint Gall NV Brut Sélection**
I deliberately avoid references to
any visual aspects of the mousse
because the effect is always
dependent of the physical
qualities of each individual glass.
The cordon on the Champagne
was, however, so creamy and
clingy that I tried it in numerous
different glasses and in each and
every one it was the same. Despite
this, the aggressiveness of the
mousse needs some taming down.
Electric fruit acidity.
Drink now-2004.
ⓔⓔ

Vallformosa

Vilafranca del Penedès
08735 Vilobí del Penedès
Spain
Phone (93) 897 82 86
Fax (93) 897 83 55

79 **Vallformosa NV Cava Brut**
Fresh and flowery with crisp,
elegant fruit and plenty of ripe
acidity. The 1998-based blend of
this cuvée is almost as good as
traditional Cava gets without
resorting to elaborate winemaking
processes. Drink now-2002.
ⓔ

78 **Gala de Vallformosa**
1998 Cava Brut
Crisp lemony Cava with lots of
acidity. Drink now-2002.
ⓔ

Vazart-Coquart

Champagne Vazart-Coquart
6 rue des Partelaines
51530 Chouilly
France
Phone (326) 55.40.04
Fax (326) 55.15.94

87 **Vazart-Coquart NV Brut Réserve**
Fresh and youthful with a
lovely cushiony mousse giving
a fluffiness to the fruit. Excellent
depth and length.
Drink now-2004.
ⓔⓔ

Velut

Champagne Jean Velut
9 rue du Moulin
10300 Montgueux
France
Phone (325) 74.83.31
Fax (325) 74.17.25

80   Jean Velut NV Brut
Lifted fruit aroma following through onto the palate. Drink upon purchase.
ⓔ Local Price **70FF**

84   Jean Velut 1995 Cuvée Millésimée, Brut
Creamy-biscuity fruit with a kernel of undeveloped extract on the finish. Drink 2002-2004.
ⓔ Local Price **87FF**

Venoge

Champagne de Venoge
46 avenue de Champagne
51204 Epernay
France
Phone (326) 53.34.34
Fax (326) 53.34.35

Part of the BCC group, which also includes Boizel, Alexandre Bonnet, Chanoine and Philipponnat.

---

85   De Venoge NV Demi-Sec, Cordon Bleu
Back in the frame after a dismal year in the wilderness, the exuberant fruitiness of this year's cuvée puts its a full five percentile points ahead of its last score in this guide. Drink now-2004.
ⓔⓔ

81   De Venoge NV Brut Sélect, Cordon Bleu
This cuvée is fresh and clean, but not special, although certainly very acceptable as the pouring Champagne at a reception.
Drink now-2002.
ⓔⓔ

83   De Venoge NV Brut Rosé
Soft, fresh, cherry-like fruit.
Drink now-2002.
ⓔⓔ

88   De Venoge 1995 Brut Millésimé
The first sample of this vintage was cloudy and obviously out of condition. I think this is the first time that I have had a cloudy Champagne. This is because most faults that create a cloudy wine are ones that occur before disgorgement and the turbidity clears as the sediment drops out. Quite why and how this Champagne survived in a cloudy condition I have no idea, but if there are any in distribution, take them back and demand a refund. This vintage is, or should be, absolutely clear and bright with a fine, fresh nose of some autolytic finesse and complexity, not too mention an almost 1996-like balance of fruit and acidity.
Drink 2002-2007.
ⓔⓔ

87   De Venoge 1993 Grand Vin des Princes Brut
Typical Grand Vin des Princes complexity with a touch of almost coconutty oakiness. Very crisp and dry, with excellent acidity and a soft, cushiony mousse.
Drink now-2004.
ⓔⓔⓔⓔ Local Price **405FF**

Vesselle

Champagne Georges Vesselle
16 rue des Postes
51150 Bouzy
France
Phone (326) 57.00.15
Fax (326) 57.09.20

---

85   Georges Vesselle NV Bouzy Grand Cru Brut
Fresh, easy, delightful drinking Champagne that you can serve to Champagne drinkers and non Champagne drinkers alike.
Drink now-2004.
ⓔⓔ

Vesselle

Champagne Maurice Vesselle
2 rue Yvonnet
51150 Bouzy
France
Phone (326) 57.00.81
Fax (326) 57.83.08

Veuve Clicquot

Champagne Veuve Clicquot-
Ponsardin
12 rue du Temple
51100 Reims
France
Phone (326) 40.25.42
Fax (326) 40.60.17

? **Maurice Vesselle NV**
Brut Rosé, Grand Cru
Creamy-toffee redcurrants
dusted with vanilla-sugar on the
mid-palate. Is this a good wine
that could have been better if
had the sort of delicate charm
associated with a fine rosé, or is
it a malo-complexed Champagne
that will develop finesse with age?
If it's the former it would rate 84
points, but I'm reserving my
opinion. Wait and see.
ⒺⒺ Local Price **115FF**

87 **Maurice Vesselle 1995**
Brut Millésime, Grand Cru
There were buttery-malo hints
on the nose of this wine at the
SAA Champagne Tasting and this
let it down, despite the brilliantly
racy fruit on the palate. However,
the sample submitted to my Guide
tastings (L2530) had no buttery
character whatsoever. As
malolactic is part of the production
process and in Champagne they
go out of their way to avoid
butteriness, by using a low-diacetyl
malolactic cocktail, I can only
assume that the SAA sample was
out of condition. This is a firm,
fine 1995 with excellent acidity
and a true brut dosage that
currently has an almost metallic
edge, although this should fall
away as the wine matures.
Drink 2002-2004.
ⒺⒺ Local Price **115FF**

85 **Veuve Clicquot Ponsardin**
NV Brut
Atypically light in weight and
style in the early part of 2001,
this had developed a perfumed
aroma and very fine fruit by June,
although whether it is the same
wine it is impossible to tell. The
palate is more fruit-driven than
one expects for VCP's orange-
coloured Yellow Label and if this
cuvées typical biscuitiness does
develop, it will be a long time in
coming. I would not have drunk
this label at the beginning of the
year, but although Clicquot
devotees might be disappointed
with the current rendition, it is a
very good Champagne in its own
right. Drink now-2005.
ⒺⒺ Local Price **175FF**

85 **Veuve Clicquot Ponsardin**
NV Demi-Sec
This is very good. The core wine
does not have the potential class
of Clicquot's 1995 Rich, but there
are no malo-aromas dominating.
More has been made of the
intrinsically lesser (not low)
quality raw products. It is rich and
full in the mouth, yet has a lovely
light balance, with vanilla-sugar
dusting the fruit on the finish.
Drink now-2006.
ⒺⒺ Local Price **175FF**

85 **Veuve Clicquot Ponsardin 1995**
Rich Réserve
Too malo-dominated on the nose,
but exquisite fruit on the palate.
What a pity this cuvée missed out

from being a 90-pointer because of a deliberate winemaking decision. Drink now-2006.
ⓔⓔⓔ Local Price **255FF**

87 **Veuve Clicquot Ponsardin**
🍷 **1995 Brut Vintage Réserve**
This vintage has distinctive buttery-malo aromas, which will go biscuity in three or four years. The richness of fruit is already approachable, and will lengthen. Drink now-2007.
ⓔⓔⓔ Local Price **255FF**

85 **Veuve Clicquot Ponsardin**
🍷 **1995 Rosé Réserve, Brut**
A rich and biscuity food wine. Drink now-2003.
ⓔⓔⓔ Local Price **270FF**

92 **Veuve Clicquot Ponsardin**
🍷 **1990 La Grande Dame Rosé, Brut**
Some malo-mellowness on the nose balanced by amazingly youthful fruit, hinting of cherries. Drink now-2006.
ⓔⓔⓔⓔ Local Price **1100FF**

Vezzoli Attilio

Via Costa Sopra
22 – 25030 Erbusco
Italy
Phone (30) 7267601
Fax (30) 7267601

85 **Vezzoli 1997 Franciacorta Brut**
🍷 Delicate, elegant fruit, so pure and fresh. Drink now-2004.
ⓔ

Attention!

To submit samples for review see page 52

Vigna Dorata

Vigna Dorata di Luciana Mingotti
Via Sala
80 – 25040 Calino di Cazzago S.M.
Italy
Phone (30) 7254275
Fax (30) 7254275

77 **Vigna Dorata NV**
🍷 **Franciacorta Brut**
Bags of fruit and a soft, cushiony mousse. Drink upon purchase.
ⓔ Local Price **18,000 Lira**

Vignaioli di S. Stefano

See Stefano

Vigne Regali

Via Vittorio Veneto 22
15019 Strevi Al
Italy
Phone 144363485
Fax 144363777

85 **Vigne Regali NV Asti,**
🍷 **Spumante Dolce**
More piquant nose than most Asti, also fuller-bodied with soft, amazingly rich, succulently sweet Moscato fruit.
Drink upon purchase.
ⓔ

Vilarnau

Castell de Vilarnau
Vilarnau 34-36
08770 Sant Sadurní d'Anoia
Spain
Phone (93) 8912361
Fax (93) 8912913

70 Castell de Vilarnau NV Cava Brut
❗ Little green tinges to the fruit,
but these are balanced by dosage
(1998-based).
Drink upon purchase.
ⓔ Local Price **900 Ptas**

74 Castell de Vilarnau 1997 Cava
❗ **Brut Gran Reserva**
Very fresh and fruity with
a particularly round finish.
Drink upon purchase.
ⓔ Local Price **1,600 Ptas**

Villa

Villa di A. Bianchi
Via Villa
12 – 25040 Monticelli Brusati
Italy
Phone (30) 652329
Fax (30) 6852305

---

82 Villa 1995 Franciacorta
❗ **Brut Selezione**
The oodles of upfront peachy-
plummy-apricot fruit in this fresh,
seductively fruity reserve bottling
reminds me of the sweep of 1996s
tasted last year and is precisely the
element missing from Villa's
1997s, only one of which qualified
for recommendation this year.
Drink now-2002.
ⓔⓔ Local Price **33,300 Lira**

Villiera

Koelenhof 7605
South Africa
Phone (21) 8822002
Fax (21) 8822314

---

75 Villiera NV Tradition Brut,
❗ **Cap Classique**
This wine turned up twice, several
months apart. The first release
had a good weight of fruit, but
could have done with more ripe
acidity, rather than what appears

to be an attempt at correcting the
balance with some early-picked
grapes (74 points). The second
release was after a year in bottle.
The wine was drinking.
Drink upon purchase.
ⓔ Local Price **R40**

72 Villiera NV Brut Rosé,
❗ **Cap Classique**
Very pale salmon colour, with
amylic aromas dominating.
Obviously very fresh, so amylic
character should recede, but does
not have the structure or acidity
of Villiera's Tradition Brut.
Bit sweetish on the finish.
Drink upon purchase.
ⓔ Local Price **4R45**

76 Villiera 1998 Brut Natural
❗ **Chardonnay, Cap Classique**
I like the elegant, quietly complex
aroma and the front-to-mid
palate, where the fruit is delightful
and there are very subtle
undertones of oak, but the finish
and aftertaste lack the finesse that
a dosage would, I am sure, have
brought to this wine. It is the only
Villiera fizz that claims to be
'made from grapes cultivated in
ecologically friendly vineyards'.
It also has no added sulphur.
A pity to score this wine just 76,
when it had the potential to break
the 85-point barrier.
Drink upon purchase.
ⓔ

Attention!

*To submit samples for review
see page 52*

Vilmart

Champagne Vilmart & Cie
4 rue de la République
51500 Rilly-la-Montagne
France
Phone (326) 03.40.01
Fax (326) 03.46.57

*The 1996 illustrates how
Vilmart has at long last reduced
the domination of new oak
over fresh fruit.*

**84 Vilmart & Cie NV
Grande Réserve, Brut Premier Cru**
A good, rich-flavoured
Champagne, with plenty of
fruit, but not as good as Grande
Réserve used to be and sweeter
on the finish. It is, however, a
darn sight better than the sweet-
amylic release encountered at the
SAA Champagne Tasting.
Drink now-2004.
Ⓔ Local Price **92FF**

**90 Vilmart & Cie NV
Grand Cellier, Brut Premier Cru**
Does this tastes younger than the
cuvée Cellier because it is younger
or because it is a better quality
Champagne that is taking
longer to develop? These are the
questions that cannot be asked in
a blind tasting, but I loved the
freshness of the fruit and the
velvety mousse enough to put it
ahead. It is certain, however,
that this particular release
(Lot number L249) is different
from the one at the SAA Tasting,
which although it had a seductive
aroma, was disappointing on the
palate, with quite a sweet dosage.
Drink now-2005.
ⒺⒺ Local Price **116FF**

**88 Vilmart & Cie NV
Cuvée Cellier, Brut**
Rich, classy, complex fruit in a
cuvée that used to be second from

top in the range, but is now
theoretically second from the
bottom. For me, however, it's
classic Champagne.
Drink now-2004.
ⒺⒺ Local Price **130FF**

**98 Vilmart & Cie 1996 Coeur de
Cuvée, Brut Premiers Crus**
The oak has been reined back
and the fruit propelled to the
front and since this is 1996 we're
discussing, that fruit is incredibly
intense with an almost excruciating
level of ripe acidity. Due to be
released in March 2002.
Drink now-2011.
ⒺⒺⒺ Local Price **205FF**

**90 Vilmart & Cie 1993
Coeur de Cuvée, Brut Premier Crus**
Ripe, oaky fruit with a sweet
finish. I think we will have to wait
for the vintages of the mid-to-late
1990s before we see the Vilmart
toning down the oaky dominance
of these Champagnes, but there
are plenty out there who like a bit
of 4x3 between. Drink now-2004.
ⒺⒺⒺ Local Price **205FF**

**95 Vilmart & Cie 1991 Coeur de
Cuvée, Brut** (*magnum*)
The oak in this magnum is more
assertive than last year, but the
fruit has gone up several notches
too. Purists might be worried by
the oak on the nose of this cuvée,
but they will forget all about that
once its succulent fruit hits the
palate. The finish is so fresh and
sherbety. Drink now-2006
ⒺⒺⒺ Local Price **410FF**

**? Vilmart & Cie 1990
Grand Cellier d'Or, Brut**
Rather sweet on the palate and
the nose needs some ageing.
Wait and see.
ⒺⒺⒺ Local Price

Vins El Cep

Can Llopart de les Alzines s/n
08770 Sant Sadurní d'Anoia
Spain
Phone (93) 8912353
Fax (93) 8183956

76 Marques de Gelida NV
Cava Brut Reserva
Fresh and creamy with good
acidity and a touch of vanilla
on the finish(1997-based).
Drink upon purchase.
ⓔ Local Price **900 Ptas**

73 Marques de Gelida NV
Cava Brut Nature
Interesting undertone of
pepperiness to the soft, chewy
fruit (1995-based).
Drink upon purchase.
ⓔ Local Price **1,700 Ptas**

Virginie

See Brun Family Estate, Le

Vollereaux

Champagne Vollereaux
48 rue Léon-Bourgeois
51200 Pierry
France
Phone (326) 54.03.05
Fax (326) 55.06.37

83 Vollereaux NV Extra Dry
Clean and tangy with a sweet,
creamy finish. Drink now-2002.
ⓔ Local Price **74FF**

82 Vollereaux NV Brut
A clean, fresh and easy drinking
style with mellow fruit. Drink
now-2002.
ⓔ Local Price **78FF**

86 Vollereaux NV
Blanc de Blancs Brut
Very fresh, elegant sherbety-lemon
fruit with floral aromas. The best
Vollereaux Champagne I've tasted
to date. Drink now-2003.
ⓔ Local Price **82FF**

Vranken-Monopole

Champagne Demoiselle
42 avenue de Champagne
51200 Epernay
France
Phone (326) 53.33.20
Fax (326) 51.87.07

The Vranken group includes
Charles Lafitte, Demoiselle,
Heidsieck Monopole,
Barancourt, Collin, Charbaut
and Germain.

85 Demoiselle 1995
Grande Cuvée Brut
This really is quite good. Okay,
that may sound like I'm damning
with faint praise, but so few
Vranken products grab me and yet
this does. Fresh, clean and elegant,
with plenty of crisp, sherbety
fruit. Drink now-2003.
ⓔ Local Price **95FF**

Wantz, André

André Wantz
41 rue des Vosges
67140 Mittelbergheim
France
Phone (388) 08.44.52
Fax (388) 08.46.32

70 André Wantz 1996 Crémant
d'Alsace Brut
Oxidative Bollinger Special Cuvée
style, but without the depth and
extract. Drink upon purchase.
ⓔ Local Price **41FF**

Wantz, Domaine

Domaine Wantz
3 rue des Vosges
67140 Mittelbergheim
France
Phone (388) 08.91.43
Fax (388) 08.58.74

77 **Domaine Wantz 1999**
❗ **Crémant d'Alsace Brut**
Yeasty-mellow, fuller more
Champagny style of some
complexity, but this complexity is
showing very early, so not one to
keep very long. Enjoy now.
Drink now-2002.
ⓔ Local Price **41FF**

Waris-Larmandier

Champagne Waris-Larmandier
608 Rempart du Nord
51190 Avize
France
Phone (326) 57.79.05
Fax (326) 52.79.52

83 **Waris-Larmandier NV Tradition,**
❗ **Brut Blanc de Blancs Grand Cru**
Very fresh, clean and correct.
Drink now-2003.
ⓔ Local Price **79FF**

84 **Waris-Larmandier NV Collection,**
❗ **Brut Blanc de Blancs Grand Cru**
Clean, fresh and fruity. This is the
one in the flower-adorned bottle.
Should get deeper in flavour and
adopt some complexity with
finesse. Very smooth mousse.
Drink now-2004.
ⓔⓔ Local Price **110FF**

? **Waris-Larmandier NV Empreinte**
2000, Brut Blanc de Blancs
Grand Cru
The fruitiest and most easy-going
of Waris-Larmandier's three
non-vintage blanc de blancs,
but I was confused under blind

conditions by a hole in the
mid palate and the sneaking
feeling I was missing something!
Wait and see.
ⓔⓔ Local Price **125FF**

Weck

Clément Weck
2 Place de la Mairie
68420 Gueberschwihr
France
Phone (389) 49.31.89
Fax (389) 49.34.81

75 **Clément Weck 1999**
❗ **Crémant d'Alsace Brut**
Fresh, floral, tasty, clean.
Drink now-2002.
ⓔ Local Price **38FF**

White Quartz

See Glenara

Wilhelmshof

Wein-und Sektgut Wilhelmshof
76833 Siebeldingen
Germany
Phone (6345) 919147
Fax (6345) 919148

73 **Wilhelmshof 1999 Siebeldinger**
❗ **Königsgarten Blanc de Noir Brut**
A copper tinge was noticed when
pouring out this blanc de noirs,
which boasts very fresh, crisp fruit.
(100% Spätburgunder, bottle-
fermented, Pfalz)
Drink now-2002.
ⓔ Local Price **DM30**

78 **Wilhelmshof 1998 Siebeldinger**
❗ **Königsgarten Blanc de Noir Brut**
Elegant Pinot fruit, excellent
acidity and freshness. A classy
classic-style fizz from Germany.

(100% Spätburgunder, bottle-
fermented, Pfalz) Drink now-2003.
ⓔ Local Price **DM30**

Willm

Alsace Willm
32 rue du Dr Sultzer BP 13
67140 Barr
France
Phone (388) 08.19.11
Fax (388) 08.56.21

74 **Willm NV Crémant d'Alsace Brut**
❢ Satisfying mouthful.
Drink upon purchase.
ⓔ Local Price **44FF**

79 **Willm 1998 Blanc de Noirs,**
❢ **Crémant d'Alsace**
Lovely deep-flavoured Pinot
fruit with a wonderful mousse
of the finest bubbles in over 200
Crémant d'Alsace tasted this year.
Drink now-2002.
ⓔ

74 **Willm 1997 Prestige Cuvée Emile**
❢ **Willm, Crémant d'Alsace**
Exotic fruity fizz.
Drink now-2002.
ⓔ Local Price **60FF**

Willows Vineyard

The Willows
Location Light Pass Road
Light Pass
SA 5355
Australia
Phone (88562) 1080
Fax (88562) 3447

77 **Willows Vineyard, The Doctor NV**
❢ **Sparkling Red, Shiraz/Pinot Noir**
A dry tannic finish balances the
sweetness on this fizzy red in
which you can't see the Pinot
for the Shiraz! Drink now-2003.
ⓔⓔ

Winzersekt

Winzersekt Sprendlingen
Michel-Mort-strasse
55576 Sprendlingen
Germany
Phone (6701) 93200
Fax (6701) 932050

*Every year this cooperative
puts itself out to host my
nationwide Sekt tastings, yet its
wines have never scored higher
than 74 and in some years no
wines have been recommended.
That Winzersekt continues
to host me is a tribute to the
honesty and industry of its
management, but I do wish
that I could find an exciting
Sekt here to wax lyrical about.
I think that it is possible. When
I first visited Winzersekt in the
mid-1980s, just a few years after
it was established, I was struck
by its range of pure varietal
Sekte. At that time Deutscher
Sekt did not have to contain a
single German grape and most
did not. More than 98% was
industrialised garbage
produced from the unwanted
dregs of the Loire and Italy.
There were barely a handful
of wines produced exclusively
from German Riesling and no
one had considered any other
pure varietal. The wines were
clean, but not as exciting as the
concept, and the quality is
about the same. I think that
Winzersekt could climb several
quality levels, but to do so
would need the eye and
expertise of an international
consultant. I know such a
person if Winzersekt is
interested (and it's not me!).*

70 Winzersekt 1999 Rheinhessen
Spätburgunder Weißherbst Extra
Trocken
Clean, fresh, almondy fruit.
(100% Spätburgunder, bottle-
fermented, Rheinhessen)
Drink upon purchase.
Ⓔ Local Price **DM15**

Winzerverein Deidesheim

Prinz-Rupprecht-Strasse 8
67146 Deidesheim
Germany
Phone (6326) 968842

74 Winzerverein Deidesheim 1999
Spätburgunder Trocken Rotsekt
Excellent varietal Pinot Noir fruit
on nose, with sweet, vanilla-sugar
dusted red-fruits on palate. (100%
Spätburgunder, bottle-fermented,
Pfalz)
Drink now-2002.
Ⓔ Local Price **DM15**

70 Winzerverein Deidesheim 1998
Deidesheimer Paradiesgarten
Extra Brut
Fresh sherbety Riesling aroma
melting into honeyed richness
on palate, with a perfumed finish.
It is, however, extremely soft and
would need more acidity to score
any higher. (100% Riesling,
bottle-fermented, Pfalz)
Drink upon purchase.
Ⓔ Local Price **DM20**

Wirra Wirra

McMurtrie Road
McLaren Vale
SA 5171
Australia
Phone (8) 8323 8414
Fax (8) 8329 4777

78 Wirra Wirra 1997 The Cousins,
Pinot Noir Chardonnay
Very fresh and clean, with
richness and elegance of fruit.
Drink now-2003.
ⒺⒺ Local Price **A$30**

Wolf

Weingut Dr. Bürklin Wolf
Weinstrasse 65
67157 Wachenheim
Germany
Phone (6322) 953330

80 Dr. Bürklin Wolf 1997
Chardonnay Brut
Fresh, German 'champagne'!
Made from a Champagne grape
in a full'ish yeast-complexed
Champagne style, with a creamy-
rich finish. So obviously aiming at
a Champagne style and succeeding
very well, yet manages to express
its German origins. (100%
Chardonnay, bottle-fermented,
Pfalz) Drink now-2003.
Ⓔ Local Price **DM27**

Wolfberger

CV de Eguisheim
Grand'Rue
68420 Eguisheim
France
Phone (389) 22.20.20
Fax (389) 23.47.09

*There has been a marked
improvement in freshness,
acidity, depth and finesse since
this cooperative stopped
putting their wines through
malolactic as a matter of rote.*

70 Wolfberger 1999
Crémant d'Alsace Brut
Very fresh, but a touch cloying on
the finish. This wine would have
scored 80-plus if it had more

acidity. Drink now-2002.
Ⓔ
Local Price **40FF**

79 **Wolfberger 1999 Chardonnay,**
Crémant d'Alsace
Good Chardonnay varietal
character on nose, nice and tasty
fruit, very easy to drink.
Drink now-2003.
Ⓔ Local Price **43FF**

73 **Wolfberger 1999 Riesling,**
Crémant d'Alsace
No aromatic varietal character
on the nose of this pure Riesling
Crémant d'Alsace, but plenty of
zippy-zingy fruit. Not Riesling per
se, but a nice tangy fizz all the
same. Drink now-2002.
Ⓔ Local Price **45FF**

75 **Wolfberger 1997 Prestige Cuvée**
An 2000, Crémant d'Alsace Brut
Ripe and creamy with some exotic
spice and lots of creamy fruit.
Drink now-2002.
Ⓔ Local Price **54FF**

Wunsch & Mann

2 rue des Clefs
68920 Wettolsheim
France
Phone (389) 22.91.25
Fax (389) 80.05.21

73 **Wunsch Mann 1998**
Crémant d'Alsace Brut
Clean, fresh and fruity aroma,
crisp, easy-drinking fruit.
Nice acidity. Refreshing finish.
Drink upon purchase.
Ⓔ Local Price **37FF**

Attention!

To submit samples for review
see page 52

Yellowglen

Whites Road
Smythesdale
Vic. 3351
Australia
Phone (35342) 8617
Fax (35333) 7102

76 **Yellowglen NV Pinot Noir**
Chardonnay Grande Cuvée
Fresher, crisper, more elegant style
than the basic Pinot Noir
Chardonnay, but potentially less
complex. Drink now-2002.
Ⓔ

77 **Yellowglen NV**
Brut Pinot Noir Chardonnay
Good varietal flavours. Should
go biscuity.
Drink now-2003.
Ⓔ Local Price **A\$17**

80 **Yellowglen 1997 Brut Pinot Noir**
Chardonnay Pinot Meunier
Very fresh, clean, nicely
structured yeast-complexed fruit
that should go biscuity with
toasty after-aromas.
Drink now-2003.
ⒺⒺ Local Price **A\$31**

Zink

Pierre Paul Zink
27 rue de la Lauch
68250 Pfaffenheim
France
Phone (389) 49.60.87
Fax (389) 49.75.03

74 **Pierre Paul Zink 1999**
Crémant d'Alsace Brut
Fresh, clean, tasty fruit.
Drink now-2002.
Ⓔ Local Price **44FF**

77 **Pierre Paul Zink 1998**
Crémant d'Alsace Brut
Upfront fruity aroma with Alsace

purity of fruit on the palate.
Good acidity. Drink now-2002.
ⓔ Local Price **44FF**

Zoeller

Maison Zoeller
14 rue de l'Eglise
67120 Wolxheim
France
Phone (388) 38.15.90
Fax (388) 38.15.90

---

73 **Maison Zoeller 1998**
🍷 **Crémant d'Alsace Brut**
Very fruity. Drink now-2002.
ⓔ Local Price **39FF**

Zusslin

Domaine Valentin Zusslin et
Fils
57 Grand'Rue
68500 Orschwihr
France
Phone (389) 76.82.84
Fax (389) 76.64.36

---

73 **Domaine Valentin Zusslin NV**
🍷 **Saint Valentin, Crémant d'Alsace**
Strong stone-fruits, assertive
mousse. Drink upon purchase.
ⓔ Local Price **42FF**

Attention!

*To submit samples for review
see page 52*

see page 52

Annual Crémant Competition

Every year there is a competition specifically for all Crémant appellation (Alsace, Bordeaux, Bourgogne, Die, Jura, Limoux, Loire and Luxembourg). The following is a complete list of medal-winners from the Concours des Crémants held in Bordeaux in June 2001.

Crémant d'Alsace

Gold medal winners
Bestheim NV Lot 4
Cave de Sigolsheim NV Comte de Sigold 2
Cave d'Ingersheim Jean Geiler NV Brut Prestige
Cave Vinicole de Beblenheim NV 'Au Château' No2
Cave Vinicole de Wuenheim NV Lot 14
Clément Klur NV Brut
Denis Meyer 1996 Prestige Domaine Kehren
Dopff & Irion NV Lot 1
Lucien Albrecht NV Lot 3
Lucien Albrecht NV Rosé Brut
Maison Heim NV Lot 2
René Mure NV Brut
René Mure 1997 Brut

Silver medal winners
Cave Coop Daubachlaville NV Lot 10
Cave Coop Daubachlaville NV Riesling Lot 11
Cave Coop Daubachlaville NV Tokay Pinot Gris Lot 12
Cave de Kientzheim-Kaysersberg NV Anne Boecklin Rosé Brut
Cave de Turckheim NV Ame du Terroir
Cave d'Ingersheim Jean Geiler NV Riesling
Cave Vinicole de Beblenheim NV 'Au Château' No4
Cave Vinicole de Cleebourg 1998 Clérotstein Tokay Pinot Gris
Cave Vinicole d'Obernai NV Fritz Kobus Rosé Brut
Cave Vinicole Eguisheim NV Lot 2
Cave Vinicole Eguisheim NV Lot 4
Chais du Tilleul NV Brut
Clément Weck NV Brut
Crémants Metz Laugel NV CR1
Domaine du Bollenberg NV Eugene
Domaine Fahrer Ackerman NV Brut
Domaine Jean-Claude Freudenreich NV Brut
Domaine Jean-Michel Welty NV Brut
Dopff & Irion NV Lot 2
Frères Cattin NV Lot 2
Frères Cattin NV Lot 4
Frey-Sohnen NV Riesling
Paul Buecher NV Prestige
Thierry Scherrer NV Cuvée Thierry

Bronze medal winners
Bestheim NV Lot 1
Bestheim NV Lot 3
Bestheim NV Prestige
Cave de Pfaffenheim & Gueberschwihr NV Lot 2
Crémants Metz Laugel NV CR5
Joseph Gruss & Fils NV Brut

Crémant de Bordeaux

Gold medal winners
Bonhur NV Crémant de Bordeaux
Brouette – Caves du Pain de Sucre NV Grande Cuvée
Cécile et Franck Lecourt NV Brut
Hervé David NV Château Garbes Cibanieu
Pierre Fourcadet NV Cuvée La Mazette Prestige
Maison Remy Brèque NV Cuvée Prestige
Vignobles Claude Modet NV Cristal de Melin
Vins de Lisennes NV Brut

Silver medal winners
Brouette – Caves du Pain de Sucre NV Bassereau Selection
Brouette – Caves du Pain de Sucre NV Tradition
Caves de la Tour du Roy NV Blanc de Blanc Lot 2001
Cordeliers NV G3
Dartigolles NV Château Picheloup St. Sauveur
Diffusion NV Crémant de Bordeaux Rosé Brut
Maison Remy Brèque NV Rosé Brut
Schuster de Ballwill NV Favory

Bronze medal winners
Ballarin NV Etiquette Bleu
Caves de la Tour du Roy NV Cuvée Prestige Lot 1704
Cordeliers NV F1
Lateyron – Château Tour Calon NV Brut
Union de Producteurs St. Pey NV Luccios

Crémant de Bourgogne

Gold medal winners
Cave Coop La Chablisienne 1995 Brut
Cave de Viré en Percheron NV Brut
Caves des Hautes Côtes NV Brut
Caves des Hautes Côtes 1997 Brut
Crémant Moingeon NV Brut
Crémant Moingeon NV Prestige
Louis Bouillot NV Perle Rosé Brut
Veuve Ambal NV Tête de Cuvée
Vignerons de Haute Bourgogne NV Les Caves du Bois de Langres

Silver medal winners
Cave Bailly Lapierre 1998 Pinot Noir
Cave Coop Bissey NV Rosé Brut
CV de Bissey NV Blanc de Blancs Brut
CV de Mancey NV Brut
Dom de la Vigne au Roy NV La Grande Chaume
Dom Gracieux Chevalier NV Brut
Louis Bouillot NV Perlede Nuit, Blanc de Noir
Vignerons de Haute Bourgogne NV Brut
Vitteaut Alberti 1998 Blanc Brut

Bronze medal winners
Cave de Lugny NV Brut
CV de Bissey NV Brut
Cave du Beau Vallon NV Brut
d'Heilly Huberdeau NV Brut
Simonnet Febvre NV Brut

Crémant de Die

Gold medal winners
Cave de Die Jaillance NV Fontailly Lot C
Cave Didier Cornillon NV Sortilège
Cave Monge et Granon NV Brut

Silver medal winners
Carod Frères 1997 Brut
Union Jeunes Viticulteurs Réunis NV Blanc de Blancs

Bronze medal winners
None

Crémant de Jura

Gold medal winners
André et Mireille Tissot NV Brut
Cie des Grds Vins du Jura 1998 Lot 2
Domaine des Grands Frères NV Brut
Domaine Richard Pierre NV Brut
Edgar Faure NV Brut
Reverchon NV Brut
Rolet Père et Fils 1997 Brut

Silver medal winners
Daniel Brocard NV Brut
Domaine Jacques Tissot NV Brut
Domaine Jacques Tissot NV Rosé Brut
Fruitière Vinicole d'Arbois NV Brut
Rolet Père et Fils 1998 Brut

Bronze medal winners
Caveau des Byards 1998 Brut
Daniel Dubois NV Brut
Domaine Désiré Petit NV Rosé Brut
Rolet Père et Fils 1998 Rosé Brut

Crémant de Limoux

Gold medal winners
Aimery Sieur d'Arques NV Prieuré Dom Neuve
Aimery Sieur d'Arques 1998 Brut
Aimery Sieur d'Arques 1997 Vanel Brut
Domaine Collin Rosier NV Château de Villelongue

Silver medal winners
Robert 1995 Domaine de Fourn

Bronze medal winners
Robert 1996 Brut

Crémant de Loire

Gold medal winners
Baumard NV Carte Turquoise
Boret NV Brut
Caves de Grenelle NV Brut
Château Langlois NV Brut
Lambert NV Brut
Vignerons de la Noëlle NV Deligeroy

Silver medal winners
Bonnigal Dom de la Prévôté NV Prestige
Caves de la Loire NV Diamant de Loire
Charier Barillot NV Brut
Domaine Dutertre NV Prestige Rosé Brut

Bronze medal winners
Cave de Vignerons de Saumur NV Chevalerie
François Pequin NV Brut
Lacheteau NV Louis Foulon

Crémant de Luxembourg

Gold medal winners
Caves de Grevenmacher NV Cuvée Brut 654
Caves de Grevenmacher NV Cuvée Brut 687
Caves Krier 1998 Brut
Caves Thill Frères 1998 Brut
Cep d'Or NV Brut

Mathes et Cie NV Brut
Poll Fabaire NV Brut 686

Silver medal winners
Caves de Stadtbredimus NV Cuvée Pinot Noir Rosé Brut
Caves Gales NV Héritage
Caves Raymond Kohll Leuck NV Brut
Caves Raymond Kohll Leuck 1998 Brut
Caves St. Remy Desom NV Brut
Domaine Clos des Rochers 1999 Brut
Domaine Gloden et Fils NV Brut
Dom Viticole Häremillen NV Brut

Bronze medal winners
None awarded

Glossary

(Fr.) French
(Ger.) German
(It.) Italian
(Port.) Portuguese
(Sp.) Spanish

Abboccato (It.) *See* Demi-Sec

Accessible Easy to drink.

Acetic acid The most important volatile acid found in wine (apart from carbonic acid), small amounts of acetic acid contribute positively to the attractive flavour of a wine, but too much gives an artificially high fruitiness that will eventually smell like vinegar.

Acidic Some people confuse this term with bitter. Think of lemon juice as acidic, lemon peel as bitter. A relatively high level of ripe acidity is vital for sparkling wine.

Aftertaste The flavour and aroma left in the mouth after the wine has been swallowed.

Ages gracefully A wine that retains finesse as it matures.

Aggressive The opposite of soft and smooth.

Agrafe (Fr.) An inverted U-shaped metal clip once used to secure the first corks during prise de mousse, but it is rarely encountered since the advent of crown caps has seen the demise of bottles bearing bague carré.

Amino acids Proteins formed by a combination of fruit esters, amino acids are formed during autolysis and are essential precursors to the complexity and finesse of a sparkling wine. *See* Autolysis, Autolytic, Reaction Maillard

Amylic The peardrop, banana or bubble-gum aromas of amyl or isoamyl acetate, excessive amounts of which can be produced if the first fermentation is conducted at a temperature that is too low. An amylic preponderance is not ideal for classic sparkling wine as it overshadows the subtle aromas of autolysis, and may prevent the development of post-disgorgement bottle-aromas. *See* Autolysis, Bottle-aromas

AOC (Fr.) Appellation d'Origine Contrôlée, the top rung of the French wine quality system. Champagne is unique in that it does not have to indicate that it is an AOC wine on the label: the name Champagne is considered sufficient guarantee.

Aperitif Originally a beverage taken as a laxative, aperitif now refers to any drink before a meal. It is refers to a relatively light, fresh, easy-drinking style of Champagne.

Appellation Literally a 'name', this usually refers to an official geographically-based designation for a wine.

Aroma Some people use the word aroma for grape-derived fragrance, and bouquet for more winey odours especially when developed in bottle; however the two are synonymous in this book.

Aromatic grape varieties Grapes such as Gewürztraminer, Muscat, and Riesling overwhelm the subtle effects of autolysis, and are thus too aromatic for classic brut sparkling wines, yet this character often make then ideal for sweet styles of sparkling wine.

Assemblage (Fr.) Blend of base wines that creates the final cuvée.

Asti (It.) A town in Northern Italy that gives its name to the world's finest sweet sparkling wine.

Atmosphere
A measurement of atmospheric pressure, one atmosphere is 15lbs per square inch (psi), which is the pressure our bodies are subjected to at sea-level. A sparkling wine can be anything up to six atmospheres, which is 90lbs psi – the equivalent to the pressure of a double-decker bus tyre. The actual pressure at serving temperature, however, is much lower, so although care must always be taken when opening a bottle, it is not like pulling the plug from a bus tyre. A fully sparkling wine of six atmospheres will, for example, be just 2.5 atmospheres at 6°C.

Austere A wine that lacks fruit or has insufficient dosage.

Autolysis The breakdown of yeast cells after the second fermentation. It is the amino acids created by autolysis that are the precursors to the complex aromas we call the inimitable 'champagny' character. In my experience, it is the amount of autolysis found in a young sparkling wine that is directly responsible for the degree of finesse that builds with age.

Autolytic The smell of a freshly disgorged brut-style sparkling wine, which is not 'yeasty' at all, but has an acacia-like flowery freshness.

Bague Carré (Fr.) A squared-off glass rim around the neck of a Champagne bottle onto that the agrafe is fixed.

Bague Couronne (Fr.) An exaggerated lip on the neck of a Champagne bottle is necessary if a crown-cap is to be used for the prise de mousse.

Balance Refers to the harmonious and therefore pleasing relationship between acids, alcohol, fruit, tannin (not often found in fizz, except for sparkling Shiraz) and other natural elements.

Balthazar Large bottle equivalent to 16 normal-sized 75cl bottles.

Barrel-fermented A few Champagnes like Krug still ferment in oak barrels that traditionally are well-used (averaging 40 years old) and do not contribute overt oakiness, although the oakiness does stand out against other Champagnes under blind conditions. However, an increasing number of producers are following the lead set by growers such as Selosse and Vilmart, who deliberately use new oak, and this fashion has been picked up by many New World producers.

Barrique (Fr.) Literally means barrel, but generically used in English-speaking countries for any small oak cask and often denotes the use of new oak. *See* Pièce

Base wines The fully-fermented dry wines that when blended together form the basis of a sparkling wine cuvée.

Biscuity A desirable aspect of bouquet found in some sparkling wines, particularly a well-matured Pinot Noir dominated Champagne. Some top-quality Chardonnay dominated Champagnes can slowly acquire a creamy-biscuitiness.

Bitterness Can be good or bad:
[1] An unpleasant aspect of a poorly

made wine. [2] An expected characteristic of an as yet undeveloped concentration of flavours that should, with maturity, become rich and delicious. *See* acidic

Blanc de Blancs (Fr.) A white wine made from white grapes.

Blanc de Noirs (Fr.) A white wine made from black grapes. In Champagne and throughout the rest of France, the art of the winemaker is to produce as colourless a wine as possible from black-skinned grapes, whereas in the New World a certain copper tinge is expected and there is often no difference between a genuine rosé and blanc de noirs.

Blind, blind tasting An objective tasting where the identity of wines is unknown to the taster until after he or she has made notes and given scores. All competitive tastings are blind.

Blowzy Overblown and exaggerated.

Blush wine Synonymous with rosé.

BOB An acronym for 'Buyer's Own Brand', under which numerous retailers and restaurants sell wine.

Body The extract of fruit and alcoholic strength together give an impression of weight in the mouth.

Bottle-age The length of time a wine spends in bottle before it is consumed. A wine that has good bottle-age is one that has sufficient time to mature properly. Bottle-ageing has a mellowing effect.

Bottle-aromas Mellowing aromas created after disgorgement.

Bottle-fermented I use this without discrimination for any sparkling wine that has undergone a second fermentation in bottle, but when seen on a label, it invariably means the wine has been made by transfer method.

Bottle sizes *See* Large-format bottles

Bouquet *See* Aroma

Breed The finesse of a wine that is due to the intrinsic quality of grape and terroir combined with the irrefutable skill and experience of a great winemaker.

Brut (Fr.) Literally means raw or bone dry, but in practice there is always some sweetness and so can at the most only be termed dry. Technically relates to wines with between 0 and 15 grams per litre of residual sugar.

Brut de Brut (Fr.) Synonymous with Brut Natural.

Brut Intégral (Fr.) Synonymous with Brut Natural.

Brut Natur (Sp.) *See* Brut Natural

Brut Nature (Fr. & Sp.) Relatively recent category at the very driest end of the sweetness scale, between 0 and 3 grams per litre of residual sugar, thus infers no dosage whatsoever. Such wines do not age well after disgorgement, therefore if it is not ready for drinking, don't buy it.

Brut Non-Dosé (Fr.) Synonymous with Brut Natural.

Brut Sauvage (Fr.) Synonymous with Brut Natural.

Brut Zéro (Fr.) Synonymous with Brut Natural.

Bruto (Port. & Sp.) *See* Brut

Buttery Normally caused by diacetyl, which is a natural byproduct of malolactic. The food industry uses diacetyl to make margarine taste like more like butter. Although a certain butteriness is fine in still Chardonnay, the slightest hint detracts from the finesse of a sparkling wines. This is why the Champagne producers use a special cocktail malolactic bacteria designed to create the least amount of diacetyl as possible.

Cap Classique South African equivalent of Spain's Cava appellation.

Caramel An extreme version of buttery.

Cava (Sp.) The generic appellation for méthode champenoise wines produced in various delimited areas of Spain.

Cave, caves (Fr.) Literally cellar, cellars.

Champagne (Fr.) Specifically a sparkling wine produced in a delimited area of northern France, the Champagne appellation is protected within the EU, and elsewhere. It is, however, abused by certain other countries, especially in the USA, where it is perfectly legal to sell domestically-produced 'champagne'. Even worse, the Champagne appellation is exploited in South America by the champenois themselves.

Champaña (Sp.) The appellation for sparkling wine made in Champagne is protected within the EU, whatever language it is translated into, but is sometimes used loosely elsewhere, especially in the USA, where it is legal to sell domestically produced 'Champagne'. It has also been exploited shamelessly by the champenois themselves, who have marketed their South American fizz as Champaña for more than 30 years.

Champenois (Fr.) The people of Champagne.

Chaptalisation (Fr.) Sugar added to grape must to raise a wine's alcoholic potential. Named after Jean-Antoine Chaptal, a brilliant chemist and technocrat who served Napoleon as minister of the interior and instructed vignerons on the advantages of adding sugar to grape juice.

Chardonnay One of the two greatest sparkling wine grapes for the classic brut style.

Charmat (Fr.) *See* Cuve close

Chef de caves (Fr.) Literally the 'cellar manager', but also the winemaker, to a lesser or greater extent according to the traditions of the house.

Chocolaty Chocolate in Champagne is part of the complexity of a well-aged Chardonnay cuvée.

Citrus Citrussy indicates aromas and flavours of far greater complexity than mere lemony can suggest. Usually confined in Champagne to a blanc de blancs.

CIVC (Fr.) *See* Comité Interprofessionnel du Vin de Champagne.

Classic, classy Both subjective words to convey an obvious impression of quality. These terms are applied to wines that not only portray the correct characteristics for their type and origin, but possess the finesse and style indicative of only the most top-quality wines.

Clean A straightforward term applied to any wine devoid of any unwanted or unnatural undertones of aroma and flavour.

Clos (Fr.) A plot of land that was once enclosed by walls. However, only those that still are enclosed by walls are considered true clos, since it is the physical effect of these walls that cut off the vines from the surrounding area, creating its own, superior terroir.

Closed Refers to the nose or palate of a wine that fails to open or show much character. It also implies that the wine has some qualities, even if they are 'hidden' – these should open up as the wine develops in bottle.

Cloying Applies to the sickly and sticky character of a poor sweet wine, where the finish is heavy and often unclean.

Coarse A term that can be applied to a 'rough and ready' wine, which may not necessarily unpleasant, but is certainly not fine. In still wines it is more often than not associated with younger product, but in Champagne it occurs more often than not in more mature examples. Champagnes with too little dosage or none at all have a tendency to go coarse as they age.

Cold Duck A cheap, sweet, carbonated wine first made by the Bronte Winery in Detroit from the 'foxy' Concord, Cold Duck enjoyed an extraordinary vogue in the USA throughout the 1960s. The name comes from 'Kalte Ente' (Cold Duck), a fizzy concoction made on the fly by German bar staff from the dregs of red and white wine, which they livened up with Sekt.

Comité Interprofessionnel du Vin de Champagne or CIVC (Fr.) The semi-governmental interprofessional body that regulates the Champagne industry.

Commercial A diplomatic way for experts to say 'I don't like this, but I expect the masses will', a commercial wine is blended to a widely acceptable formula, which at worst may be bland and inoffensive.

Complete Refers to a wine has everything (fruit, tannin, acidity, depth, length, etc) and thus feels satisfying in the mouth.

Complexity An overworked word that refers to many different nuances of smell or taste. Great wines in their youth may have a certain complexity, but it is only with maturity in bottle that a wine will eventually achieve full potential in terms of complexity.

Cool-fermented An obviously cool-fermented wine is very fresh, with simple aromas of apples, pears and bananas, at best, but could be blighted by more oppressive aromas of peardrops, bubblegum or nail-varnish. *See* Amylic

Corked Nothing inherently wrong with the wine, the term corked applies to a penicillin infection inside the cork, which gives an unpleasant musty character, spoiling an otherwise good wine. Not too long ago it was highly improbable to have two consecutive corked bottles of the same wine, but every day scientists are discovering 'corky' smelling compounds that have nothing to do with the cork, so it is quite possible for entire batches of wine to smell or taste corked. Furthermore, the most common of these (*see* TCA) affects casks as much as cork, and the spores are highly volatile, thus one affected cork siting in a plastic bag with thousands of other can infect the entire batch. However, no wine buyer should purchase such wines, let alone put them on the shelf.

Correct All the correct characteristics for its type and origin, but not necessarily an exciting wine.

Courtier en vins (Fr.) A wine broker who acts as the go between growers and producers.

Crayères (Fr.) Chalk-pits dug out in Gallo-Roman times.

Creamy Dr Tony Jordan believes that creaminess in a sparkling wine is probably a combination of the finesse of the mousse (created by the most minuscule of bubbles and their slow release) and an understated malolactic influence, the combined effect of which is picked up at the back of the throat on the finish of the wine, and this is most apparent in Chardonnay-based wines.

Creamy-biscuity *See* Biscuity

Creamy-caramel malo A lesser, more acceptable version of caramel.

Crémant (Fr.) Originally a Champagne with a gentler mousse than normal, this term is now reserved in the EU for various sparkling wine appellations, such as Crémant d'Alsace, Crémant de Loire, etc.

Crisp A clean sparkling wine with good acidity backing up the effervescence on the finish.

Cross A vine that has been propagated by crossing two or more varieties within the same species (Vitis vinifera for example), while a hybrid is a cross between two or more varieties from more than one species.

Crown-cap The common beer-bottle cap now widely used as the temporary closure while a sparkling wine undergoes its second fermentation.

Cru (Fr.) Literally a growth, a cru normally refers to a vineyard site, although in Champagne it is used for an entire village. *See* Premier Cru, Grand Cru

Cushiony A beautifully soft, ultra-fine sensation caused by the minuscule bubbles of a first rate mousse.

Cuve close (Fr.) A method invented by Eugène Charmat of producing sparkling wine through a second fermentation in a sealed vat or tank. Synonymous with Charmat method or tank method.

Cuvée (Fr.) Originally the wine of one cuve or vat, this now refers to a precise blend or specific product that could well be blended from several vats.

CV (Fr.) Abbreviation for Caves Vinicole and variations on this theme.

Débourbage (Fr.) The settling process that removes bits of skin, pips and other flotsam and jetsam from the freshly pressed grape juice.

Definition A wine with good definition is one that is not just clean with a correct balance, but also has a positive expression of its grape variety and/or origin.

Dégorgement (Fr.) *See* Disgorgement

Delicate Describes the quieter characteristics of quality that give a wine charm.

Demi-Sec (Fr.) Literally semi-dry, but

semi-sweet for all practical purposes, a Demi-Sec may contain between 35 and 50 grams per litre of residual sugar.

Depth Refers first to a wine's depth of flavour and secondly to its depth of interest.

Deutscher Qualitätsschaumwein (Ger.) Same as Deutscher Sekt.
Deutscher Qualitätsschaumwein BA (Ger.) Same as Deutscher Sekt BA.

Deutscher Qualitätsschaumwein Bestimmter Anbaugebiete (Ger.) Same as Deutscher Sekt BA.
Deutscher Sekt (Ger.) A sparkling wine made by any method (though probably cuve close), exclusively comprising of wine from German-grown grapes. It may indicate a maximum of two grape names and should be at least 10 months old when sold.

Deutscher Sekt BA (Ger.) A sparkling wine made by any method (though probably cuve close), exclusively comprising of wine made from grapes grown in one of Germany's 13 specified regions, although it may indicate an even smaller denomination if 85 per cent of the grapes come from the named area.

Deutscher Sekt Bestimmter Anbaugebiete (Ger.) Same as Deutscher Sekt BA.

Disgorgement The removal of sediment after the second fermentation.

Distinctive A wine with a positive character. All fine wines are distinctive to one degree or another, but not all distinctive wines are necessarily fine.

DOC/DOCG (It.) Denominazione di Origine Controllata/e Garantita. Italian wine quality system based on grape variety and origin. 'Garantita' denotes an extra rung of quality.

Doce (Port.) *See* Doux

Dolce (It.) *See* Doux

Dosage (Fr.) The amount of sugar solution added to a sparkling wine after disgorgement.

Doux (Fr.) Sweet. In excess of 50 grams per litre of residual sugar.

Dry straw *See* Straw

Dulce (Sp.) *See* Doux

Easy-drinking Probably not a complex wine, but it slips down easily.

Echelle des Crus (Fr.) All the wine-producing villages of Champagne are classified on a percentage basis known as the échelle des crus. Those considered to be grands crus receive the maximum échelle of 100%, whereas those at the bottom of the scale are classified at the minimum of 80%. Villages with vineyards rated between 90 and 99% inclusive are considered to be premiers crus. At one time the minimum échelle was just 22.55%, but due to various ad hoc re-classifications this has gradually increased over the years and many villages have been 'promoted' in the process. There used to be 12 grands crus and 32 premiers crus – now there are 17 and 43 respectively.

Elegant A subjective term applied to wines that may be described as stylish and possessing some finesse.

Elevated fruit Synonymous with VA fruitiness.

English aroma A very fresh herbaceous character.

Esters, Estery A prickly, ethereal-minerally impression. Esters are essential components of any wine and contribute to its fruitiness, but when estery aromas dominate a wine it is unready and has probably been disgorged too soon.

Expansive A wine that is big, but open and accessible.

Expressive A wine that is expressive is true to its grape variety and area of origin.

Extract The term covers everything all the solid in a wine and literally gives the wine its body.

Explosive A sparkling wine can be explosive in the bottle, which is to say it can gush all over the place even when chilled and opened skilfully. This will either be due to a poor quality inner-surface of the bottle, where deformities in the glass act as nuclei for the release of gas before the wine gets out of the bottle, or to microscopic elements acting as nuclei in the wine in itself. Sparkling wine can also be explosive in the mouth, which can also be the result of nuclei in the wine, but may also be due to an excess of carbonic gas that is free (ie., not bound to the wine). The subject of free and bound carbonic gas is far less researched and understood than that of free and sulphur, but it is known that the longer a sparkling wine is kept at cooler temperatures, the more carbonic gas that is bound. We also know that free carbonic gas is the first to be released in the glass, while it is the bound carbonic that keeps a sparkling wine fizzy in the long-term.

Extra-Brut In theory between 0 and 6 grams per litre of residual sugar, thus drier than most bruts. Possibly no dosage, but probably a very light one only, since wines without dosage can now utilise the Brut Nature designation.

Extra Herb (Ger.) *See* Extra-Brut

Extra-Sec (Fr.) Literally 'extra-dry', but merely dry in most cases, since such wines may contain between 12 and 20 grams per litre of residual sugar.

Extra Trocken (Ger.) *See* Extra-Sec

Fat A wine full in body and extract. It is good for any wine to have some fat, but fat in an unqualified sense can be derogatory and no wine should be too fat, as it will be flabby or too blowzy.

Feminine Subjective term used to describe a wine with a preponderance of delicately attractive qualities, rather than weight or strength. A wine of striking beauty, grace and finesse with a silky texture and exquisite style.

Fermentation The biochemical process by which enzymes secreted by yeast cells convert sugar molecules into almost equal parts of alcohol and carbonic gas.

Fermentación en botella (Sp.) Literally 'bottle-fermented', thus actually transfer method.

Fermentazione naturale (It.) Literally 'naturally fermented', which should apply to every wine ever made – even a carbonated fizz must have been naturally fermented in the first place. What it is supposed to infer, however, is that a wine has been rendered sparkling by natural refermentation in a tank or bottle (usually the former).

Finesse That elusive, indescribable quality that separates a fine wine from those of lesser quality.

Fixed Sulphur added to wine primarily to prevent oxidation, which it does by fixing itself to the oxygen on a molecular basis. Once a molecule of sulphur is fixed, it stays fixed. It continues to do its job, keeping the oxygen prisoner, but it is no longer free to protect the wine against other molecules of oxygen: only free sulphur can do that. Sulphur can fix to all sorts of molecules in a wine, mostly harmless, but a few things are potentially hazardous in a smelly way. When sulphur fixes with hydrogen, for example, hydrogen sulphide (stink bombs, bad eggs) is formed. These are called fixed-sulphur faults. On the other hand, we are just beginning to understand that the toasty bottle-aroma most Champagne aficionados adores is in fact a fixed-sulphur fault!

Flaschengärung nach dem Traditionellen Verfahren (Ger.) *See* Méthode champenoise

Fleshy Refers to a wine with plenty of fruit and extract and infers a certain underlying firmness.

Flowery Floral aromas are found in young sparkling wines, and are the precursors to fuller, deeper, fruitier aromas of maturity. Specific acacia aromas are found in recently disgorged wines of any age.

Foamy A less acute degree of explosive.

Foudre (Fr.) A large wooden cask or vat.

Foxy The very distinctive, highly perfumed character of certain indigenous American grape varieties that can be sickly sweet and cloying to unconditioned European and Antipodean palates.

Free Sulphur The acrid odour of sulphur in a wine should, if detected, be akin to the smell of a recently extinguished match, and will go away with time in bottle, or a swirl of the glass.

Frizzante (It.) Semi-sparkling or slightly fizzy, the equivalent of pétillant.

Frizzantino (It.) Very lightly sparkling, the equivalent of perlant.

Fruity Although wine is made from grapes, it will not have a fruity flavour unless the grapes used have the correct combination of ripeness and acidity.

Full Usually refers to body, eg., full-bodied. But a wine can be light in body yet full in flavour.

Fully fermented A wine that is allowed to complete its natural course of fermentation and so yield a totally dry wine.

Fully sparkling A wine with a pressure of 5-6 atmospheres.

Fut (Fr.) An empty pièce.

Gasificado (Sp.) Artificially carbonated wine.

Generic A wine, usually blended, of a general appellation.

Generous A generous wine gives its fruit freely on the palate, while an ungenerous wine is likely to have little or no fruit and, probably, an excess of tannin. All wines should have some degree of generosity.

Gluggy Easy to guzzle.

Goût américain (Fr.) From the 19th century through to the 1920s, there was not an established regime of dosage for Champagne as there is today. Instead of brut, sec, demi-sec etc., the different market determined the dosage of Champagne. The American market was the third sweetest, and we know from the observation of Henry Vizetelly that in 1882 Champagnes labelled gout américain contained between 110 and 165 grams per litre of residual sugar.

Goût anglais (Fr.) Although the English market was demanded the driest Champagne, and the first Champagnes ever to be labelled brut were shipped to London sometime after 1876, at 10-30 grams per litre of residual sugar, the concept of brut was obviously relative to its times. Vizetelly recorded that the gout anglais varied between 22 and 66 grams, which was considered dry in its day, but would now be though very sweet indeed.

Goût français (Fr.) In the late-19th century, goût français, a style that was popular in both France and Germany, carried a dosage of between 165 and 200 grams, making it second only in sweetness to Champagnes destined for Russian market (which did not have a designated 'goût', but according to Vizetelly contained between 200 and 300 grams, which is two to three times as sweet as Château d'Yquem).

Grand cru (Fr.) Literally 'great growth', in regions such as Burgundy, where its use is strictly controlled, this term has real meaning, but in other winemaking areas where are no controls exist, it will mean very little. Between these two extremes is Champagne, where the grands crus are strictly controlled on the one hand (there are only 17), but applicable to entire villages – rather than specific, superior vineyards – on the other, thus encompasses vineyards of varying intrinsic quality. *See* Echelle des Crus

Grande marque (Fr.) Literally a 'great brand' or 'famous brand', in the world of wine the term grande marque is specific to Champagne and until 1997 applied to members of a 'club' called the Syndicat de Grandes Marques, but this was disbanded when they could not agree on quality criteria for continued membership. The term will continue to be used, particularly in English-speaking countries, for the most famous brands.

Granvas (Sp.) Same as cuve close.

Grapey Can be applied to an aroma or flavour that is reminiscent of grapes rather than wine, a particular characteristic of German wines and wines made from various Muscat or Muscat-like grapes.

Green Young and tart, as in Vinho Verde. It can be either a derogatory term, or simply an indication of youthful wine that might well improve.

Halbsüss (Austrian) *See* Demi-Sec

Halbtrocken (Ger.) *See* Demi-Sec

Handgerüttelt (Ger.) Hand-riddled (manual remuage), thus the wine has been bottle-fermented and not transferred, therefore this term can be taken to mean méthode champenoise.

Harsh A more derogatory form of coarse.

Herb (Ger.) *See* Brut

Herbaceous A green-leaf or white-currant characteristic that is usually associated with under-ripeness, particularly with aromatic grape varieties.

High-tone A term used in this book to describe aromas of bouquet that aspire to elegance, but that can become too exaggerated and be slightly reminiscent of vermouth.

Hollow A wine that appears to lack any real flavour in the mouth compared to the promise shown on the nose. Usually due to a lack of body, fruit or acidity.

Honeyed Many Champagnes develop a honeyed character through bottle-age, as indeed can Riesling Sekte.

Horizontal tasting This is a tasting of different wines of the same style or vintage, as opposed to a vertical tasting, which consists of different vintages of the same wine.

Jahrgangssekt (Ger.) Literally 'vintage Sekt', this merely means a sparkling wine from a single year and does not infer any special connotation of quality.

Jammy Commonly used to describe a fat and eminently drinkable red wine rich in fruit, if perhaps a bit contrived and lacking a certain elegance.

Jeroboam Large bottle equivalent to four normal-sized 75cl bottles.

Kabinett The first rung of predication in Germany's QmP range, one below Spätlese and often drier than a QbA.

Klassische Flaschengärung (Ger.) *See* Méthode champenoise

Lactic acid The acid that develops in sour milk, which is also created in wine during the malolactic fermentation.

Large-format bottles Large-format bottles are confusingly different according to the region. The most famous oversized bottles are found in Champagne and Bordeaux. However, a Jeroboam in Champagne is the equivalent of four normal-sized 75cl bottles, whereas in Bordeaux it is six bottles. Furthermore, there is no such thing as a Rehoboam in Bordeaux, where this size is known as an Imperiale. An Imperiale is in fact the largest Bordeaux bottle, whereas in Champagne the Salmanazar, Balthazar and Nebuchadnezzar are all very much larger formats. The full list of classic large-format Champagne bottles is as follows:

Magnum
= 2 normal-sized 75cl bottles
Jeroboam
= 4 normal-sized 75cl bottles
Rehoboam
= 6 normal-sized 75cl bottles
Methuselah
= 8 normal-sized 75cl bottles
Salmanazar
= 12 normal-sized 75cl bottles
Balthazar
= 16 normal-sized 75cl bottles
Nebuchadnezzar
= 20 normal-sized 75cl bottles

The larger the bottle, the longer the wine should last, but this theory cannot be applied with any certainty in Champagne for sizes larger than a Jeroboam. Larger formats are theoretically superior for ageing because the air-space differs insignificantly compared to the increased volume of wine, thus the rate of oxidation should be reduced.

However, it is legally permitted fill sizes larger than the Jeroboam with finished Champagne (*see* Transvasage) and most houses that market these party-sized bottles do just that.

L.D. A sparkling wine term that stands for 'late disgorged' and paradoxically means the same as 'recently disgorged'. The use of L.D. infers that the wine in question is of a mature vintage that has been kept on its yeast deposit for an extended period. *See* R.D.

Lees The sediment that accumulates in a vat or bottle during the fermentation of a wine.

Length A wine that has length indicates that the flavour lingers in the mouth a long time after swallowing. If two wines taste the same, yet you definitely prefer one, but do not understand why, it is probably because the one you prefer has a greater length.

Lie (Fr.) The French for lees. Sur lie refers to a wine kept in contact with its lees.

Lieu-dit (Fr.) A named site within a vineyard.

Light A qualification of body.

Lime This is the classic character of Sémillon and Riesling when grown in many areas of Australia, which explains why Sémillon from the Hunter Valley used to be sold as Hunter Riesling.

Linalool Found in some grapes, particularly Muscat and Riesling varieties. It contributes to the peachy-flowery fragrance that is the varietal characteristic of wines made from Muscat grapes.

Lingering Normally applied to the finish of a wine – an aftertaste that literally lingers.

Liqueur d'expédition (Fr.) Solution of sugar and wine added to a sparkling wine after disgorgement.

Liqueur de tirage (Fr.) The bottling liqueur: wine, yeast and sugar added to still Champagne to induce the mousse.

Maceration A term that is usually applied to the period during the vinification process when the fermenting juice is in contact with its skins.

Maderized The terms maderised and oxidised are sometimes erroneously believed to be synonymous, but Madeira is reductive, while Sherry is oxidative. All Madeiras are maderized by slowly heating the wines in specially constructed ovens, then slowly cooling them. Apart from Madeira itself, this maderised character is undesirable in all but certain Mediterranean wines that are deliberately made in a rancio style (the French tend to use rancio in preference to maderisé, which they all too often confuse with oxidise).

Magnum Large bottle equivalent to two normal-sized 75cl bottles, the ideal volume for ageing Champagne.

Malic A tasting term that describes the green apple aroma and flavour found in some young wines, due to the presence of malic acid, the dominant acid found in apples.

Malic acid Although this very harsh-tasting (green apple on mild steel) acid diminishes during the ripening process, a significant quantity still persists in ripe grapes and, although reduced by fermentation, in the wine too.

Malolactic, Malo A biochemical process that transforms the hard malic acid of unripe grapes into soft lactic acid and carbonic gas.

Marque A brand or make.

Mean An extreme qualification of ungenerous.

Meio-Seco (Port.) *See* Demi-Sec

Mellow A wine that is round and nearing its peak of maturity.

Méthode champenoise (Fr.) The process that converts a fully-fermented still wine into a sparkling wine by a second fermentation in the same bottle in which it is sold. In the EU this term is forbidden on the label of any wine other than Champagne, which of course never uses it.

Méthode Classique (Fr.) Synonymous with méthode champenoise.

Méthode Traditionnelle (Fr.) Synonymous with méthode champenoise.

Methuselah Large bottle equivalent to eight normal-sized 75cl bottles. Metodo Classico (It.) *See* méthode champenoise

Metodo Tradizionale (It.) *See* méthode champenoise

Microclimate Due to a combination of shelter, exposure, proximity to mountains, water mass and other topographical features unique to a given area, a vineyard can enjoy (or be prone to) a specific microclimate.

Mid-palate [1] The centre-top of your tongue. [2] A subjective term to describe the middle of the taste sensation when taking a mouthful of wine. Could be hollow, if the wine is thin and lacking, or full, if rich and satisfying.

Mild (Ger.) *See* Doux

Mineral This is normally a positive term indicating a certain complexity and finesse, but some wines can have a minerally aftertaste that can sometimes be unpleasant.

Mono-cru Champagne made from a single cru or village.

Monopole (Fr.) Single ownership of one vineyard.

Mousse The foam produced by thousands of bubbles in a sparkling wine.

Mousseux *See* Vin Mousseux

Mouthfill Good mouthfill infers a certain satisfaction or completeness, and is the opposite of hollow.

Mushroom Not a mustiness, but the attractive aroma of freshly peeled mushroom. This is quite common in old vintages of Champagne and, curiously, for some wines it affects just a few bottles in a batch, yet not others, while for other wines this characteristic can pervade every single bottle. For the moment, no one knows its origin. At one time it was thought to be a characteristic of over-mature Meunier, but the instances where it affects only some bottles in a batch would seem to rule this out. One suggestion has been that it is a yeast-derived characteristic, the rationale being that yeasts are a form of mushroom, but this explanation strikes many oenologist as being a bit too logical. The latest idea is that it could be a reaction between the yeast and the cork, when a little wine is trapped between the lip of the bottle and the top of the cork at bottling. Although not conclusive, since hearing this explanation, I have observed an unusually large deposit of dried wine on the lip of those bottles that have a fresh mushroom aroma.

Nebuchadnezzar Large bottle equivalent to 20 normal-sized 75cl bottles.

Négociant (Fr.) Commonly used to describe larger wine producing companies, the term is derived from the traditional practice of negotiating with growers to buy grapes and wholesalers or other customers to sell the wine produced.

Négoce (Fr.) Collective form of négociant.

Neutral grape varieties The opposite of aromatic grapes, these include virtually all the minor, nondescript varieties that produce bland tasting, low-quality wines, but also encompass better known varieties such as the Melon de Bourgogne, Aligoté, Pinot blanc, Pinot meunier and even classics like Chardonnay and Sémillon. Neutral varieties are for fine sparkling wines of the brut style because their characteristics are enhanced by the subtle effects of autolysis and mellowing bottle-aromas, whereas aromatic grapes fight against these processes.

Non-dosage (Fr.) Synonymous with Brut Natural.

Non-vintage In theory a blend of at least two different years, but many producers, particularly growers in Champagne, grade their cuvées on selection, often selling a pure vintage sans année (without year).

Nose The smell or odour of a wine, encompassing both aroma and bouquet.

Oaky The aromatic qualities picked up from new oak, which usually consists of the creamy-vanilla aroma of vanillin, a natural oak aldehyde that also happens to be the principal aromatic component in vanilla pods.

Oenologist, oenology Pronounced 'enologist' and 'enology'(and spelt this way in the USA), oenology is the scientific study of wine, which is a branch of chemistry, and most winemakers today are qualified oenologists with practical, hands-on production experience and an understanding of viticulture.

Off vintage or year A year in which many poor wines are produced due to adverse climatic conditions, such as very little sunshine during the summer, which can result in unripe grapes, or rain at the harvest, which can result in rot. Generally a vintage to be avoided, but approach any opportunity to taste the wines with an open mind because there are always good wines made in every vintage.

Opulent Suggestive of a rather luxurious varietal aroma, very rich, but not quite blowzy.

Organic A generic term covering wines that are produced using the minimum amount of SO2, from grapes that have been grown without chemical fertilizers, pesticides or herbicides.

Over-oxidative Verges on oxidised, and infers aldehydic aromas such as the sherry-like acetaldehyde.

Overtone A dominating element of nose and palate and often one that is not directly attributable to the grape or wine.

Oxidation, oxidised From the moment grapes are pressed or crushed, oxidation sets in and the juice or wine will be oxidized to a certain and increasing extent. Oxidation is an unavoidable part of fermentation and an essential to the maturation process, but in order not to mislead, it is best to speak of a mature or, at the extreme, an oxidative wine because when oxidized is used, even amongst experts, it will invariably be in an extremely derogatory manner.

Oxidative A wine that openly demonstrates the character of maturation on the nose or palate, thus the longer it takes to appear in a wine, the more finesse it will have. *See* Acetaldehyde

Palate The flavour or taste of a wine.

Peak The so-called peak in the maturity of a wine is subject to the consumer's point of appreciation. Those liking fresher, crisper wines will perceive an earlier peak in the same wine than 'golden oldy' drinkers. A rule of thumb that applies to both extremes of taste is that a wine will remain at its peak for as long as it took to reach it.

Peardrop *See* Amylic.

Peppery A somewhat incongruous character in a sparkling wine, I have managed to track it down to Chardonnay, but not Chardonnay of great class, probably planted on less than suitable soil, and possibly young. If detected as just a flicker in a blend, it will eventually be subsumed by the other wines, and can even add to the future complexity of a cuvée, but be wary where it is the solitary or dominant character.

Perlant (Fr.) Lightly sparkling.

Perlwein (Ger.) Cheap, semi-sparkling wine made by carbonating

a still wine.

Pétillance, pétillant (Fr.) A wine with enough carbonic gas to create a light sparkle.

Petrol, petrolly With some bottle-age, the finest Rieslings have a vivid and zesty bouquet that some refer to as petrolly. The petrolly character has an affinity with various zesty and citrussy odours, but many lemony, citrussy, zesty smells are totally different from one another and the Riesling's petrolly character is both singular and unmistakable. As great Riesling matures, so it also develops a honeyed character, bringing a classic, honeyed-petrol richness to the wine.

Pièce (Fr.) A standard Champagne cask measure of 205 litres, the term pièce is used only when the barrel is full of wine. When it is empty it is called simply a fut.

Pinot Noir (Fr.) Black grape variety used in Champagne.

Post-disgorgement ageing The period between disgorgement and when the wine is consumed. With the sudden exposure to air after an extended period of ageing under anaerobic conditions, the development of a sparkling wine after disgorgement is very different from that before.

Pressure The pressure inside a bottle of sparkling wine is affected by temperature and altitude. Pressure increases as the temperature rises, but decreases as the altitude climbs. To be uniform when comparing the pressure of different sparkling wines, oenologists around the world refer to pressures at 20°C and sea-level.

QbA (Ger.) Germany's

Qualitätswein bestimmter Anbaugebiete is theoretically the equivalent of the French AOC.

Quaffing An unpretentious wine that is easy and enjoyable to drink.

Qualitätsschaumwein (Ger.) A so-called 'quality sparkling wine', this can be produced by any member state of the EU, but the term should be qualified by the country of origin (of the wine), thus only Deutscher Qualitätsschaumwein will necessarily be from Germany.

R.D. A sparkling wine term that stands for 'recently disgorged', the initials R.D. are the trademark of Champagne Bollinger (which often comes as something of a surprise to sparkling wine producers in other countries). *See* L.D.

Reaction Maillard An interaction between amino acids created during autolysis and residual sugar added by dosage, Reaction Maillard is responsible for many of the mellow, complex post-disgorgement aromas adored by drinkers of mature Champagne.

Récoltant-manipulant (Fr.) A grower who produces Champagne exclusively from his or her own vineyards.

Reductive The less exposure it has to air, the more reductive a wine will be. Different as they are in basic character, Champagne, Muscadet sur lie and Beaujolais Nouveau are all examples of a reductive, rather than oxidative, style. From the vividly autolytic Champagne, through Muscadet sur lie with its barest hint of autolytic character, to the amylic aroma of Beaujolais Nouveau.

Rehoboam Large bottle equivalent to six normal-sized 75cl bottles.

Remuage (Fr.) The process whereby the sediment is encouraged down to the neck of the bottle in preparation for disgorgement.

Reserve wines Older wines added to a non-vintage blend.

Reticent Suggests that the wine is holding back on its nose or palate, perhaps through youth, and may well develop with a little more maturity.

Reverse saignée In Champagne this involves a majority of Pinot Noir, commonly as much as 90%, which has undergone a light saignée, and is then blended with a small amount of Chardonnay for freshness.

Rich, richness A balanced wealth of fruit and depth on the palate and finish.

Riche (Fr.) Synonymous with Demi-Sec.

Ripe Grapes ripen, wines mature, although some of the constituents of a wine, such as fruit and even acidity, can be referred to as ripe. Tasters should however beware of mistaking a certain residual sweetness for ripeness.

Rooty Usually refers to a certain rooty richness found in Pinot Noir. Not vegetal, which is a negative term.

Rosado (Sp.) Pink.

Rosé (Fr.) Pink.

Saignée (Fr.) The process of drawing off surplus liquid from the press or vat in order to produce a rosé wine from the free-run juice. In cooler wine regions, the remaining mass of grape pulp may be used to make a darker red wine than would normally be possible because of a greater ratio of solids to liquid.

Salmanazar Large bottle equivalent to 12 normal-sized 75cl bottles.

Sassy Used to describe fruit in a wine that is lively, jaunty, breezy etc.

Satèn (It.) Literally meaning satin, this term has been coined by Franciacorta producers for a softer, crémant style of sparkling wines. The best Franciacorta Satèn are often barrique-fermented.

Schaumwein (Ger.) Literally 'sparkling wine' and with no further qualification (such as Qualitätsschaumwein), this is merely the same as Sekt.

Sboccatura (It.) Disgorged.
Sec (Fr.) Literally dry, but effectively medium to medium-sweet. A Sec may contain between 17 and 35 grams per litre of residual sugar.

Secco (It.) *See* Sec

Seco (**Port. & Sp.**) *See* Sec

Second fermentation, secondary fermentation Strictly speaking this is the fermentation that occurs in bottle during the méthode champenoise, but the malolactic is sometimes erroneously referred to as the second fermentation.

Sekt (Ger.) Sparkling wine, usually cuve close.

Semi-Dulce (Sp.) *See* Demi-Sec

Short Refers to a wine that may have a good aroma and initial flavour, but falls short on the finish, its taste quickly disappearing after the wine has been swallowed.

Sin Cosecha (Sp.) Non-vintage.
Smooth The opposite of aggressive and more extreme than round.

Soft An attractive smoothness caused when fruit has the upper-hand over acidity. This is very desirable, but a wine that is too soft will lack acidity.

Solera (Sp.) A system of continually refreshing an established blend with a small amount of new wine (equivalent in proportion to the amount extracted from the solera) to effect a wine of consistent quality and character. A few Champagne producers use this method for keeping their reserve wines, although it reduces the number of building blocks at the winemaker's disposal when blending a cuvée.

Sous marque (Fr.) Second brand. An ancillary label under which second quality wines are sold, although the standard need not necessarily inferior in any general sense.

Spätlese (Ger.) A QmP wine that is one step above Kabinett, but one below Auslese. It is fairly sweet and made from late-picked grapes.

Sprightly fruitiness I have deliberately used this expression instead of VA fruitiness because even though the latter is not a truly derogatory term, it has negative connotations, and would be taken the wrong way more times than not. Sprightly fruitiness is not even referred to under VA fruitiness, making the full explanation available only to readers curious enough to browse this far through the glossary. Hopefully those who do penetrate this triple-layered definition will appreciate that a preponderance of negative elements can sometimes create a positive effect.

Spritz, spritzig (Ger.) Synonymous with pétillant.

Spumante (It.) Literally just sparkling, but in practice spumante normally refers to a fully sparkling wine. *See* Fully sparkling

Straw Strawlike aromas often blight sparkling wines. Sometimes dry-straw, other times wet-straw, and others still are just strawlike. Producers say it is part of the complexity, but it strikes me as a very dull, ill-defined sort of complexity and one that is not completely clean. Perhaps it comes from the yeast, or maybe rotten grapes, or even the reaction of yeast-contact to wine made from a certain percentage of rotten grapes. In any case, this is not a positive attribute, although where it appears in this book the wines obviously have sufficient going for them to overcome these strawlike aromas, otherwise they would not be recommended.

Structure The structure of a wine is literally composed of its solids (tannin, acidity, sugar, and extract or density of fruit flavour) in balance with the alcohol, and how positively the form and feel in the mouth. It is interesting to speculate how much of Champagne's classic lean structure is the result of chaptalisation. Virtually all non-vintage Champagnes are chaptalised, as indeed are the majority of vintage Champagnes, and this obviously increases the amount of alcohol for the weight of fruit. *See* Chaptalisation

Stylish Wines possessing all the subjective qualities of charm, elegance and finesse. A wine might have the 'style' of a certain region or type, but a wine is either stylish or it is not. It defies definition.

Subtle Although this should mean a significant yet understated characteristic, it is often employed by wine snobs and frauds who taste a wine with a famous label and know that it should be special, but cannot detect anything exceptional and need an ambiguous word to talk their way out of the hole they have dug for themselves. The most honest use of subtle in this book refers to the effect of autolysis.

Sulphur, SO$_2$ A preservative used primarily to prevent oxidation. *See* Free Sulphur and Fixed sulphur

Supple Indicates a wine that is easy to drink, not necessarily soft, but a more graceful form of ease than the word round can manage.

Sur lie (Fr.) Refers to wines, usually Muscadets, that have been kept on the lees and have not been racked or filtered prior to bottling. Although this increases the possibility of bacterial infection, the risk is worth taking for wines made from neutral grape varieties. It also avoids aeration and retains more of the carbonic gas created during fermentation imparting a certain liveliness and freshness. In the case of sparkling wines, it is better to keep reserve wines sur lie than to rack and filter them because it reduces the production of terpenes and helps to retain the nitrogenous matter that makes the wines more susceptible to autolysis.

Sweetness designations Many countries use the French terminology and adhere to the EU technical requirements for residual sugar: Brut Nature (0-3g/l), Extra-Brut (0-6g/l), Brut (0-15g/l), Extra-Sec (12-20g/l), Sec (17-35g/l), Demi-Sec (35-50g/l) and Doux (50g/l-plus).

Talento (It.) Since March 1996, producers of Italian méthode champenoise wines may utilise the new term of 'Talento', which has been registered as a trademark by the Instituto Talento Metado Classico (formerly the Instituto Spumante Classico Italiano). Talento is almost synonymous with the Spanish term Cava, although to be fully compatible it would have to assume the mantle of a DOC.

Tank method Same as cuve close.

Tartaric acid The ripe acid of grapes that increases slightly when the grapes increase in sugar during the véraison.

Tartrates, tartrate crystals Tartaric acid deposits look like sugar crystals at the bottom of a bottle and this may have been precipitated when a wine has experienced low temperatures. It can also happen naturally deposited through the process of time, although seldom in a still or sparkling wine that has spent several months in contact with its lees, as this produces a mannoprotein called MP32, which prevents precipitation of tartrates. A fine deposit of glittering crystals can also be deposited on the base of a cork if it has been soaked in a sterilizing solution of metabisulphite prior to bottling. Both are harmless.

TCA Short for trichloroanisole, the prime but by no means only culprit responsible for corked wines, TCA is found in oak staves as well as cork. *See* Corked

Terpene Various terpenes and terpene alcohols are responsible for some of the most aromatic characteristics in wine, ranging from the floral aromas of Muscat to the petrol or kerosene character of a wonderfully mature Riesling. In sparkling wine a terpene character may indicate Riesling in the blend, but is more likely to be due to part or all of the base wine being kept unduly long in tank prior to second fermentation.

Terroir (Fr.) Literally 'soil', but in a viticultural sense terroir refers to the complete growing environment, which also includes altitude, aspect, climate and any other factors that may affect the life of a vine, and the quality of the grapes it produces.

Tête de cuvée (Fr.) The first flow of juice during the pressing, the cream of the cuvée. It is the easiest to extract and the highest in quality with the best balance of acids, sugars and minerals.

Thin A wine lacking in body, fruit and other properties.

Tight A firm wine of good extract that gives the impression of being under tension, as if a wound spring waiting to uncoil, and thus has more obvious potential than either a reticent or a closed wine.

Toast [1] A slow-developing bottle-induced aroma commonly associated with the Chardonnay, but can develop in wines made from other grapes, including red wines. Toasty bottle-aromas are initially noticeable on the aftertaste, often with no indication on the nose. [2] A fast-developing oak-induced aroma. [3] Barrels are toasted during their construction to one of three grades: light or low, medium, and heavy or high.

Traditionelle Klassische (Ger.) *See* Méthode champenoise.

Transfer method Decanting under pressure from one size bottle to another, not the ideal of méthode champenoise.

Transvasage (Fr.) *See* Transfer method

Trocken (Ger.) *See* Sec

Typical An over-used and less than honest form of honest.

Typicity A wine that shows good typicity is one that accurately reflects its grape and soil.

UC Davis Short for the University of California's enology department at Davis.

Ullage (Fr.) [1] The space between the top of the wine and the head of the bottle or cask. An old bottle of wine with an ullage beneath the shoulder of the bottle is unlikely to be any good. [2] The practice of topping up wine in a barrel to keep it full and thereby prevent excessive oxidation.

Undertone Subtle and supporting, not dominating like an overtone. In a fine wine a strong and simple overtone of youth can evolve into a delicate undertone with maturity, adding to a vast array of other nuances that give it complexity.

Ungenerous A wine that lacks generosity has little or no fruit and possibly far too much acidity for a correct and harmonious balance.

Unripe acid Malic acid, as opposed to tartaric, which is ripe acid.

Up-front Suggests an attractive, simple quality immediately recognised, which says it all. The wine may initially be interesting, but there would be no further development and the last glass would say nothing more than the first.

VA Abbreviation of volatile acidity.

VA fruitiness An ultra-fruitiness accentuated by volatile acidity, this can be a positive factor in the description of a wine, but the term VA (for volatile acidity) has such negative connotations that I have used 'sprightly fruitiness' so that the casual reader is not put off perfectly acceptable wines.

Value-for-money The difference between penny-saving and penny-pinching. In theory true value-for-money exists at any price-point, whether five or five-hundred (pounds, dollars deutschemarks or whatever), and the decision to buy will depend on how deep your pocket is.

Vanilla *See* Oaky

Vanillin The aldehyde that gives vanilla pods their characteristic aroma, vanillin is also found naturally in oak, albeit on a smaller scale.

Varietal The character of a single grape variety as expressed in the wine it produces.

Vendemia (Sp.) Harvest, often used to indicate vintage.

Vertical tasting This is a tasting of different vintages of the same wine, as opposed to an horizontal tasting, which consists of different wines of the same style or vintage.

Vigneron (Fr.) Vineyard worker.

Vignoble (Fr.) Vineyard.

Vin de cuvée (Fr.) Wine made from the first (and best) pressing only.

Vin de garde (Fr.) Wine that is capable of great improvement if left to age.

Vinifera Species covering all varieties of vines providing classic wine-making grapes.

Vinification Far more than simply fermentation, this involves the entire process of making wine, from the moment the grapes are picked to the point it is bottled.

Vin Mousseux (Fr.) Literally means sparkling wine without any connotation of quality one way or the other, but because all fine sparkling wines in France utilise other terms, for all practical purposes it infers a cheap, low quality product.

Vino de aguja (Sp.) A young, slightly sparkling or perlant wine.

Vinous Winey, characteristic of wine. When used to describe a wine, it infers basic qualities only.

Vintage The harvest or wine of a single year.

Vivid The fruit in some wines can be so fresh, ripe, clean-cut and expressive that it quickly gives a vivid impression of complete character in the mouth.

Volatile acidity This has a sweet vinegary aroma, and if clearly detectable is usually deemed a fault, but a certain amount of volatile acidity (or VA for short) is essential to the fruitiness of every wine, and occasionally even high levels can be a positive factor. *See* VA fruitiness

Weissherbst (Ger.) A single-variety rosé wine produced from black grapes only.

Wet straw *See* Straw.

Wg. (Ger.) Abbreviation of Winzergenossenschaft.

Winzersekt (Ger,.) Literally a 'grower Sekt', this can either be the product of a single grower or a cooperative of growers, but must be a Sekt bA.

Yeast A kind of fungus vital in all winemaking. Yeast cells excrete a number of enzymes, some 22 of which are necessary to complete the chain reaction known as fermentation.

Yeast enzymes Each enzyme acts as a catalyst for one activity and is specific for that task and no other in the fermentation process.

Yeasty Not a complimentary term for most wines, but a yeasty bouquet can be desirable in a good-quality sparkling wine, especially when young.

Yield There are two forms of yield: [1] the quantity of grapes produced from a given area of land, [2] how much juice is pressed from it. Wine people in Europe use hl/ha or hectolitres per hectare, which is a combination of both, literally referring to how much juice has been extracted from the grapes harvested from an area of land. This is fine when the amount of juice that can be pressed from grapes is controlled by European-type appellation systems, but in the New World, where this seldom happens, they tend to talk in tons per acre.

Zesty A lively characteristic that suggests a zippy tactile impression combined, maybe, with a hint of citrussy aroma.

Zing, zingy, zip, zippy Terms all indicative of something refreshing, lively and vital, resulting from a high balance of ripe fruit acidity.

US Retailers

A listing of major stockists of Champagne and sparkling wine in the USA, including a key to where to find selected brands.

Brand Finder

Originally compiled by Ed Masciana & Jerry Mead

Please note that not all retailers carry the full range of every brand they sell and although great care has been taken to ensure that only regularly stocked products have been included here, some retailers are bound to de-list brands from time to time.

Abelé, Henri
Ranch Acres Wine & Spirits
Acacia Hi-Time Wine Cellars
Adami J. Emerson, Inc.
Agrapart Draegers
Alain Robert Fowler's, Wine Expo
Albert le Brun
House Wines & Cheese
Albrecht, Lucien
The Wine Merchant
Alfred Gratien Arrow Wines &
Spirits, Sam's, Vieux Carré Wine &
Spirits, The Wine Merchant, Wiggy's
Anderson, S.
House Wines & Cheese
Antonin Truffer
Berman's Wine & Spirits
Argyle Gomer's Fine Wine, Hi-Time
Wine Cellars, Kahn's Fine Wines,
Vieux Carré Wine & Spirits, Wiggy's
Audoin de Dampierre
Draegers, Ranch Acres Wine &
Spirits, Sam's, Wine Cellar at the Rio
Avinyo Wine Merchants Warehouse
Ayala D&M Wine & Liquor,
Enoteca Wine Shop, House Wines &
Cheese, The Wine Merchant,
Hi-Time Wine Cellars
Baumard Fowler's
Beaumont D&M Wine & Liquor
Bellavista
Sam's, The Wine Merchant
Billecart-Salmon Enoteca Wine
Shop, J. Emerson, Inc., Wally's,
Wiggy's, Wine Merchants Warehouse
Billiot Hi-Time Wine Cellars, Wine

Exchange, Wine Expo, Wine House
Biltmore The Wine Merchant
Blue Point The Wine Merchant
Bollinger Argonaut Wine & Liquor,
Draegers, J. Emerson, Inc., Enoteca
Wine Shop, Gomer's Fine Wine,
Hi-Time Wine Cellars, Gary's Wine
& Marketplace, The Rare Wine Co.
Bouvet Wine Cellar at the Rio
Bricout Enoteca Wine Shop
Bruno Giacosa Wine Expo
Bruno Paillard Gomer's Fine Wine,
Kreston Liquor Mart, Kreston
Liquor Mart, Ranch Acres Wine &
Spirits, Wiggy's, Wine Exchange
Carneros, Domaine Ranch Acres
Wine & Spirits, Star Liquor, Wally's
Chandon, Domaine Argonaut
Wine & Liquor, Arrow Wines &
Spirits, Berman's Wine & Spirits,
Enoteca Wine Shop, Hi-Time Wine
Cellars, Kreston Liquor Mart,
Otto's Wine Cask, Vieux Carré
Wine & Spirits
Cattier Wine House
Charbaut Astor Wines & Spirits,
Gary's Wine & Marketplace
Charles de Cazanove
D&M Wine & Liquor, Hi-Time
Wine Cellars
Charles Ellner
D&M Wine & Liquor
Charles Heidsieck
House Wines & Cheese, Vieux Carré
Wine & Spirits
Chartogne-Taillet

J. Emerson, Inc., Wine Exchange

Cheval-Gatinois
The Rare Wine Co.

Chiquet, Gaston Wine Expo

Clavelin Arrow Wines & Spirits

Cristalino Wiggy's

Cruchet J. Emerson, Inc.

Dampierre Draegers, Ranch Acres Wine & Spirits, Sam's, Wine Cellar at the Rio

De Venoge Hi-Time Wine Cellars, Kreston Liquor Mart

Delamotte J. Emerson, Inc., Ranch Acres Wine & Spirits, Sam's, Wiggy's

Delbeck Draegers

Deutz Fowler's, Gomer's Fine Wine, Kahn's Fine Wines, Gary's Wine & Marketplace

Devaux Argonaut Wine & Liquor

Diebolt-Vallois Wine Exchange

Domaine Carneros Ranch Acres Wine & Spirits, Star Liquor, Wally's

Domaine Chandon
Argonaut Wine & Liquor, Arrow Wines & Spirits, Berman's Wine & Spirits, Enoteca Wine Shop, Hi-Time Wine Cellars, Kreston Liquor Mart, Otto's Wine Cask, Vieux Carré Wine & Spirits

Dom Pérignon
Argonaut Wine & Liquor, D&M Wine & Liquor, Gomer's Fine Wine, Wine Cellar at the Rio

Dom Ruinart
Wine Merchants Warehouse

Drappier
Astor Wines & Spirits, Fowler's, Kreston Liquor Mart, Otto's Wine Cask, Sam's, Wine Exchange

Drouet, Paul Astor Wines & Spirits

E. Barnaut Hi-Time Wine Cellars

Einhard Gomer's Fine Wine

Egly-Ouriet Arrow Wines & Spirits, Enoteca Wine Shop, Fowler's, Wiggy's, Wine Expo

Ellner, Charles
D&M Wine & Liquor

Eric Bordelet Draegers

Ferrari
Fowler's, Gomer's Fine Wine, Wiggy's

Feuillatte, Nicolas J. Emerson, Inc., Kahn's Fine Wines, Kreston

Liquor Mart, Sam's, Wiggy's, Wine Merchants Warehouse

Fay Drei Es Wine Expo

Flynn Gomer's Fine Wine

Gaston Chiquet Wine Expo

Gatinois Fowler's

Geoffroy, René
Argonaut Wine & Liquor, Hi-Time Wine Cellars, Wine Expo

Giacosa, Bruno Wine Expo

Gimonnet Argonaut Wine & Liquor, D&M Wine & Liquor, Kreston Liquor Mart, Sam's, Wine Exchange, Wine Expo, Wine House

Gloria Ferrer Otto's Wine Cask

Gobillard, J.M.
Berman's Wine & Spirits

Gosset Astor Wines & Spirits, D&M Wine & Liquor, The Rare Wine Co., Wally's, Wine Expo

Grande Dame
Ranch Acres Wine & Spirits

Gratien, Alfred Arrow Wines & Spirits, Sam's, Vieux Carré Wine & Spirits, The Wine Merchant, Wiggy's

Green Point
House Wines & Cheese, J. Emerson, Inc., Ranch Acres Wine & Spirits

Gruet
Arrow Wines & Spirits, Berman's Wine & Spirits, Draegers, J. Emerson, Inc., Kreston Liquor Mart, Gary's Wine & Marketplace, Otto's Wine Cask, Ranch Acres Wine & Spirits, The Wine Merchant, Wine House

Guy Larmandier
Astor Wines & Spirits

Handley Gomer's Fine Wine

Haut Villers
Berman's Wine & Spirits

Heidsieck, Charles
House Wines & Cheese, Vieux Carré Wine & Spirits

Heidsieck Monopole
Kahn's Fine Wines, Otto's Wine Cask, Sam's, The Rare Wine Co.

Henri Abelé
Ranch Acres Wine & Spirits

Henriot Fowler's

Highfield J. Emerson, Inc., Fowler's

Hunter, Robert

Arrow Wines & Spirits

Iron Horse House Wines & Cheese, Star Liquor, Wally's, Wine House, Wine Merchants Warehouse

J Arrow Wines & Spirits, Draegers, Gomer's Fine Wine, House Wines & Cheese, Gary's Wine & Marketplace, Ranch Acres Wine & Spirits, Wine House, The Wine Merchant, Wine Merchants Warehouse

J.M. Gobillard
Berman's Wine & Spirits

Jacques Selosse Draegers, Wine Expo, The Wine Merchant

Jacquesson Astor Wines & Spirits, Draegers, Fowler's, Otto's Wine Cask, Star Liquor, Star Liquor, The Rare Wine Co., Wiggy's

Jean Milan Arrow Wines & Spirits, Hi-Time Wine Cellars, Wine House

Jepson Argonaut Wine & Liquor, The Wine Merchant

Jose Michel J. Emerson, Inc.

Joseph Perrier D&M Wine & Liquor, Wine House

Jourdan, Pierre Sam's

Korbel Arrow Wines & Spirits, Kreston Liquor Mart, Gary's Wine & Marketplace, Otto's Wine Cask

Kriter Sam's

Krug Astor Wines & Spirits, D&M Wine & Liquor, Fowler's, The Rare Wine Co., Sam's, Vieux Carré Wine & Spirits, Wally's, Wine Cellar at the Rio, Wine Exchange

Kupferberg Kahn's Fine Wines

La Morandina
Berman's Wine & Spirits

Labbe Wine Expo

Laetitia Wine Exchange

Lanson Kahn's Fine Wines

Lantage Hi-Time Wine Cellars

Larmandier-Bernier Wine Expo

Larmandier, Guy
Astor Wines & Spirits

Lassalle Fowler's, Wine Exchange, The Wine Merchant

Laurent, Paul
Astor Wines & Spirits

Laurent Perrier
Vieux Carré Wine & Spirits, Wally's

Le Brun, Albert
House Wines & Cheese

Legras Wine Expo

Lenoble Hi-Time Wine Cellars

Lucien Albrecht
The Wine Merchant

Margaine Sam's, Wine Expo

Marie Stuart D&M Wine & Liquor, Hi-Time Wine Cellars

Marwood
Argonaut Wine & Liquor, Fowler's

Mathieu, Serge
D&M Wine & Liquor

Michel, Jose J. Emerson, Inc.

Michel Labbe Wine Expo

Milan, Jean Arrow Wines & Spirits, Hi-Time Wine Cellars, Wine House

Mionetto Astor Wines & Spirits

Mirabelle Otto's Wine Cask

Moët Kahn's Fine Wines, Otto's Wine Cask

Moncuit, Pierre Draegers

Montaudon
Vieux Carré Wine & Spirits

Montsarra
House Wines & Cheese, Sam's

Morandina, La
Berman's Wine & Spirits

Moscow Golden Crown Sam's

Mountadam Astor Wines & Spirits

Mumm Napa
Argonaut Wine & Liquor, Vieux Carré Wine & Spirits, Wally's

Nicolas Feuillatte J. Emerson, Inc., Kahn's Fine Wines, Kreston Liquor Mart, Sam's, Wiggy's, Wine Merchants Warehouse

Nino Franco
Vieux Carré Wine & Spirits

Orient Express
Astor Wines & Spirits

Oudinot Fowler's

Pacific Echo Wiggy's

Paillard, Bruno Gomer's Fine Wine, Kreston Liquor Mart, Kreston Liquor Mart, Ranch Acres Wine & Spirits, Wiggy's, Wine Exchange

Pannier Astor Wines & Spirits

Paul Bara Hi-Time Wine Cellars

Paul Drouet Astor Wines & Spirits

Paul Laurent Astor Wines & Spirits

Perrier, Joseph D&M Wine & Liquor, Wine House

Perrier-Jouël Kreston Liquor Mart, Wine Merchants Warehouse

Peter Rumball The Wine Merchant

Philipponnat Otto's Wine Cask, The Rare Wine Co.

Pierre Jourdan Sam's

Pierre Moncuit Draegers

Pierre Peters Argonaut Wine & Liquor, Wine Expo, Wine House

Piper Sonoma Wally's

Ployez-Jacquemart The Wine Merchant

Pol Roger Gomer's Fine Wine, Gary's Wine & Marketplace, Star Liquor, The Rare Wine Co., Wine Cellar at the Rio, Wine Merchants Warehouse

Pommery Enoteca Wine Shop, Hi-Time Wine Cellars, House Wines & Cheese, Kreston Liquor Mart, Ranch Acres Wine & Spirits, Vieux Carré Wine & Spirits, Wine House

René Geoffroy Argonaut Wine & Liquor, Hi-Time Wine Cellars, Wine Expo

Robert, Alain Fowler's, Wine Expo

Robert Hunter Arrow Wines & Spirits

Roederer Wine Cellar at the Rio

Roederer Estate D&M Wine & Liquor, Gomer's Fine Wine, House Wines & Cheese, Kahn's Fine Wines, Sam's, Star Liquor, Wally's, Wine House

Rotari Kahn's Fine Wines

Ruinart Gomer's Fine Wine, Gary's Wine & Marketplace, Ranch Acres Wine & Spirits, Vieux Carré Wine & Spirits

Salon J. Emerson, Inc., Gomer's Fine Wine, House Wines & Cheese, Gary's Wine & Marketplace, Star Liquor, Wally's, Wine Cellar at the Rio

S. Anderson House Wines & Cheese

Schlumberger Kahn's Fine Wines

Schramsberg Arrow Wines & Spirits, Berman's Wine & Spirits, Hi-Time Wine Cellars, House Wines & Cheese, Wine Cellar at the Rio

Seaview Kahn's Fine Wines, Ranch Acres Wine & Spirits, Wine House

Selosse, Jacques Draegers, Wine Expo, The Wine Merchant

Serge Mathieu D&M Wine & Liquor

Sparr J. Emerson, Inc.

Stuart, Marie D&M Wine & Liquor, Hi-Time Wine Cellars

Taillevent Berman's Wine & Spirits

Taittinger Wine Cellar at the Rio

Taltarni Sam's, Wine Expo

Tarlant Arrow Wines & Spirits, Fowler's, Kreston Liquor Mart, Star Liquor

Tribaut Kahn's Fine Wines

Trouillard J. Emerson, Inc., Gary's Wine & Marketplace, The Wine Merchant

Truffet Berman's Wine & Spirits

Turgy J. Emerson, Inc.

Venoge, De Hi-Time Wine Cellars, Kreston Liquor Mart

Veuve Ambal Wine Exchange

Veuve Clicquot Argonaut Wine & Liquor, Arrow Wines & Spirits, Astor Wines & Spirits, Gomer's Fine Wine, Hi-Time Wine Cellars, Kahn's Fine Wines, Gary's Wine & Marketplace, Otto's Wine Cask, Ranch Acres Wine & Spirits, Sam's, Star Liquor, Vieux Carré Wine & Spirits, Wally's, Wine Exchange, Wiggy's, Wine House

Vilmart Sam's, Wine Expo

Vranken Kahn's Fine Wines

Yalumba The Wine Merchant, Wine Merchants Warehouse

Zardetto Argonaut Wine & Liquor

Champagne and Sparkling Wine Stores in the USA

Originally compiled by Ed Masciana & Jerry Mead

There are very few Champagnes and sparkling wines available in the USA that cannot be found at or procured by one of the following purveyors. This list is by no means complete, but we feel that it offers a starting point and, at the very least, it consists of those who are the most passionate about bubbly in this country. If any retailer listed would like to correct or update any of the information in their profile below, or if any other retailer with a comparable range of Champagnes and sparkling wines would like to be included in a future edition, please email tom.fizz.stevenson@ntlworld.com. There is no charge for inclusion on these pages. It costs nothing other than a little time to compile and email the relevant details.

Listed alphabetically by state.

Arizona:
Soljans

House Wines & Cheese
7001 No. Scotsdale Rd. #141
Scotsdale, AZ 87053
Phone (480) 922-3470
Fax (480) 922-3269
E-mail pour@housewines.com
Web www.housewines.com

Store size 1,200 sq. ft.
Ship? N/A
Deliver? Yes
Owner K. Handal
Year opened 1997
Brands stocked 100
Bottles in stock 1,000
Best-selling Champagne Ayala
Best-selling sparkling wine
S. Anderson
Favorite Champagne
Albert le Brun
Favorite sparkling wine
Roederer Estate
Other brands carried
Salon, Pommery, Montsarra, J,
Charles Heidsieck, Iron Horse,
Schramsberg, Greenpoint
Comments Bon Appetite award
winner. Very helpful service and
exotic selection.

California:
D & M Wine & Liquor

2200 Fillmore Street
San Francisco, CA 94115
Phone (800) 637-0292
Fax (415) 346-1812
E-mail wine@dnai.com
Web www.dandm.com

Store size 6,750 sq. ft.
Ship? Yes
Deliver? Yes
Owner Joseph Politz
Employees 13
Year opened 1935
Brands stocked 300
Bottles in stock 23,000
Best-selling Champagne
Dom Pérignon
Best-selling sparkling wine
Roederer Estate Brut
Favorite Champagne Krug
Favorite sparkling wine
Roederer Estate Brut
Other brands carried Cazanove,
Beaumont, Charles Ellner, Joseph
Perrier, Marie Stuart, Gimonnet,
Ayala, Gosset, Serge Mathieu
Comments One of the top
Champagne and Sparkling wine
stores in the universe. And, they've
been in that position for longer
than anybody else.

California: Draegers

San Mateo Market
222 East Fourth Avenue
Phone (650) 685-3725
Fax (650) 685-3749

Menlo Park Market
1010 University Dr.
Menlo Park, CA 94025
Phone (650) 324-7739
Fax (650) 3247797

Los Altos Market
342 First Street
Los Altos, CA 94022
Phone (800) 650-9196

E-mail draegers@aol.com
Web www.draegers.com

Store size 30,000 sq. ft.
Ship? Yes
Deliver? Yes
Owner Anthony Draeger
Employees 10
Year opened 1925
Brands stocked 95
Bottles in stock 3,000
Best-selling Champagne Bollinger
Best-selling sparkling wine Gruet
Favorite Champagne Agrapart
Favorite sparkling wine J
Other brands carried Jacques
Selosse, Eric Bordelet, Dampierre,
Audoin de Dampierre, Jacquesson,
Pierre Moncuit, Eric Bordelet
Comments Three-store chain
offering exotic specialty foods and
a very impressive wine selection.

California: Enoteca Wine Shop

1345 Lincoln Avenue, Suite C
Calistoga, CA 94515
Phone (707) 942-1117
Fax (707) 942-1118
Web www.neteze.com/enoteca

Store size 2,000 sq. ft.
Ship? Yes
Deliver? Yes
Owner Margaux Singleton
Employees 3
Year opened 1997
Brands stocked: 35
Bottles in stock: 200
Best-selling Champagne:
Bricout Brut Prestige
Best-selling sparkling wine:
Domaine Chandon Etoile Rosé
Favorite Champagne:
Egly-Ouriet Blanc de Noir
Favourite sparkling wine
Prosecco Ex Dry
Other brands carried Bricout,
Billecart, Ayala, Pommery,
Egly-Ouriet, Pommery, Bollinger
Comments Dedicated to ferreting
out small, artisnal producers. Any
day is a great day to celebrate with
Champagne.

California: Hi-Time Wine Cellars

250 Ogle Street
Costa Mesa, CA 92627
Phone (800) 331-3005
Fax (800) 331-3005
E-mail hitimeclrs@aol.com
Web www.hitimewine.com

Store size 20,000 sq. ft.
Ship? Yes
Deliver? Yes
Owner Son-Vay Corporation
Employees 45
Year opened 1957
Brands stocked 3,500
Bottles in stock 100
Best-selling Champagne
Veuve Clicquot Brut
Best-selling sparkling wine
Domaine Chandon Brut
Favorite Champagne
Pommery Cuvée Louis Brut Rosé,
Jean Milan Brut Terres de Noel,
Bollinger R.D.
Favorite sparkling wine Domaine

Chandon Brut, Argyle Brut
Extended Triage, J Schram Napa
Brut
Other brands carried
Paul Bara, E. Barnaut, Henri
Billiot, Charles de Cazanove,
Marie Stuart, Acacia, Lantage, De
Venoge, Rene Geoffroy, Lenoble
Comments Hi-Time's
underground 3,500 square foot
climate-controlled cellar is the
ideal place to house their broad
selection of top domaines,
Récoltant-Manipulant and
boutique Champagnes and
sparkling wines as well as a huge
selection of world-class offerings.

California:
The Rare Wine Co.

21468 Eighth St East
Sonoma, CA 95476
Phone (800) 999-4342
Fax (800) 893-1501
E-mail sales@rarewineco.com
Web www.sonic.net/~rarewine/

Store size 6,000 sq. ft.
Ship? Yes
Deliver? Yes
Owner Mannie Berk
Employees 6
Year opened 1992
Brands stocked 18
Bottles in stock 3,000
Favorite Champagne Krug
Other brands carried
Cheval-Gatinois, Gosset,
Heidsieck Monopole, Jacquesson,
Philipponnnat, Pol Roger,
Bollinger
Comments Specializes in rare
Cuvées and old vintages.

California:
Wally's

2107 Westwood Blvd.
Los Angeles, CA 90025
Phone (310) 475-0606
Fax (310) 474-1450
E-mail mail@wallywine.com
Web www.wallywine.com

Store size 5,000 sq. ft.
Ship? Yes
Deliver? Yes
Owner Steve Wallace
Employees 50
Year opened 1967
Brands stocked 70
Best-selling Champagne
Clicquot, Billecart
Best-selling sparkling wine
Mumm, Domaine Carneros
Favorite Champagne
Billecart, Gosset
Favorite sparkling wine
Iron Horse, Roederer L'Hermitage
Other brands carried
Krug, Laurent Perrier, Piper
Sonoma, Salon
Comments
One of the premiere stores in L.A.

California:
Wine House

2311 Cotner Ave.
Los Angeles, CA 90064
Phone (310) 479-3731
Fax (310) 478-5609
E-mail wine@winehouse.com
Web www.winehouse.com

Store size 18,000 sq. ft.
Ship? Yes
Deliver? Yes
Owner Bill Knight
Employees 25
Year opened 1973
Brands stocked 65
Bottles in stock 2,000

Best-selling Champagne Clicquot
Best-selling sparkling wine
Roederer
Favorite Champagne
Joseph Perrier, H. Billiot
Favorite sparkling wine
Iron Horse, Roederer
Other brands carried Gimonnet,
Pommery, Seaview, J, Gruet,
Cartier, Jean Milan, Pierre Peters
Comments
Arguably, the largest wine selection
in California. One of the top in
the WeStreet User-friendly sales
people and an excellent cellar of
old and rare vintages.

California:
Wine Exchange

2368 North Orange Mall
Orange, CA 92865
Phone (800) 769-4639
Fax (714) 974-1792
E-mail wines@winex.com
Web www.winex.com

Store size 7,200 sq. ft.
Ship? Yes
Deliver? Yes
Owner Steve & Craig Zanotti
Employees 12
Year opened 1982
Brands stocked 70
Bottles in stock 3,000
Best-selling Champagne Clicquot
Best-selling sparkling wine
Veuve Ambal
Favorite Champagne Krug
Other brands carried
Billiot, Laetitia, Chartogne-Taillet,
Diebolt-Vallois, Lassalle, Pierre
Gimonnet, Drappier, Bruno
Paillard
Comments One of the top retailers
in the state with an amazing
selection of everything. Specializes
in hard-to-find items and offers
them at very competitive prices.

California:
Wine Expo

2933 Santa Monica Blvd
Santa Monica, CA 90404
Phone (310) 828-4428
Fax (310) 828-2969
E-mail wineexpo@earthlink.net

Ship? Yes
Deliver? Yes
Owner Ali Biglar
Employees 6
Year opened 1993
Brands stocked 250
Bottles in stock 20,000
Best-selling Champagne A Robert
Grand Cru Blanc de Blancs Les
Mesnil NV, Michel Labbe
Best-selling sparkling wine
Taltarni Brut Tache, Australia
Favorite Champagne
Gosset, Billiot, Egly-Ouriet,
Gaston Chiquet, Gimonnet
Favorite sparkling wine Fay Drei
Es Metodo Classico Nebbiolo Brut
Other brands carried Vilmart &
Cie, Legras, Larmandier-Bernier,
Pierre Peters, René Geoffroy, A.
Margaine, Gaston Chiquet,
Jacques Selosse, Bruno Giacosa
Comments House of Botafogo!
Clearly the most impressive
selection of small, artisan
producers in the WeStreet Never
shy, always interesting. We are
dedicated to providing the largest
selection of the best quality and
value Champagnes and Bubblies in
the Western Hemisphere. This
explains the absence of most of
the most Big 'Brands' and the
plentitude of small, grower
produced Grand Cru Champagnes.

Colorado:
Argonaut Wine & Liquor

700 E. Colfax
Denver, CO 80203
Phone (303) 831-7788
Fax (303) 839-8305
E-mail
argonaut@spiritsusa.com
Web www.argonautliquor.com

Store size 25,000 sq. ft.
Ship? Yes
Deliver? Yes
Owner Scott Robinson
Employees 45
Year opened 1940
Brands stocked 160
Bottles in stock 100
Best-selling Champagne Clicquot
Best-selling sparkling wine
Mumm Cuvée Napa
Favorite Champagne
Dom Pérignon. Bollinger NV
Favorite sparkling wine
Chandon Brut
Other brands carried Devaux,
Jepson, Marwood, Zardetto, Pierre
Peters, Rene Geoffroy, Gimonnet
Comments One of the top stores
in the nation with over 8,000
items, excellent service and
competitive prices. Family owned
and operated.

Delaware:
Kreston Liquor Mart

904 Concord Ave.
Wilmington, DE 19802
Phone (302) 652-3792
Fax (302) 652-3725
E-mail DonKreston@aol.com
Web www.krestonwine.com

Store size 8500 sq. ft.
Ship? No
Deliver? No
Owner Don Kreston

Employees 21
Year opened 1933
Brands stocked 200
Bottles in stock 5,000
Best-selling Champagne
Perrier Jouët
Best-selling sparkling wine Korbel
Favorite Champagne Pommery
Favorite sparkling wine
Domaine Chandon
Other brands carried
Bruno Paillard, De Venoge,
Drappier, Feuillatte, Tarlant,
Gruet, Gimonnet
Comments Largest wine selection
between New York and Florida

Illinois:
Sam's Wines & Spirits

1720 North Marcey Street
Chicago, IL 60614
Phone (800) 777-9137
Fax (312) 664-7037
E-mail sams@samswine.com
Web www.samswine.com

Store size 33,000 sq. ft.
Ship? Yes
Deliver? Yes
Owner Fred Rosen
Employees 70
Year opened 1949
Brands stocked 200
Bottles in stock 15,000
Best-selling Champagne Clicquot
Best-selling sparkling wine
Kriter, Roederer Estate
Favorite Champagne Krug
Favorite sparkling wine Bellavista
Other brands carried
Moscow Golden Crown,
Montsarra, Taltarni, Pierre
Jourdan, Drappier, Delamotte,
Audoin de Dampierre, Gimonnet,
Feuillatte, Heidsieck Monopole,
Vilmart, Gratien, Margaine
Comments An institution in
Chicago for 50 years. Easily one of
the top five stores in the country.

Indiana:
Kahn's Fine Wines

Keystone Store
5369 North Keystone Ave.
Indianapolis, IN 46220
Phone (800) 621-8466
Fax (317) 257-6092

Carmel Store
313 E. Carmel Dr
Carmel, IN 46032
Phone (317) 817-9463
Fax (317) 817-9470
E-mail
info@kahnsfinewines.com
Web www.kahnsfinewines.com

Store size 6,000 sq. ft.
Ship? Yes
Deliver?
Owner Jim Arnold
Employees 40
Year opened 1978
Brands stocked 70
Bottles in stock 3,800
Best-selling Champagne
Moët White Star
Best-selling sparkling wine Rotari
Favorite Champagne
Clicquot Gold
Favorite sparkling wine
Roederer Estates
Other brands carried Vranken,
Seaview, Heidsieck Monopole,
Feuillatte, Tribaut, Deutz, Argyle,
Kupferberg, Lanson, Schlumberger
Comments This two-unit
operation boasts a superb wine
selection at the Keystone location
and a fine wine and food selection
at their other site on Carmel.

Louisiana:
Sam's Wines & Spirits

Vieux Carre Wine & Spirits
422 Rue Charters
New Orleans, LA 70130
Phone (504) 568-9463
Fax (504) 529-3056

Store size 3,000 sq. ft.
Ship? Yes
Deliver? Yes
Owner Todabo Brothers
Employees 8
Year opened 1987
Brands stocked 110
Bottles in stock 5,000
Best-selling Champagne Clicquot
Best-selling sparkling wine Mumm
Favorite Champagne
Krug, Alfred Gratien
Favorite sparkling wine Mumm
Other brands carried Montaudon,
Ruinart, Charles Heidsieck,
Pommery, Nino Franco, Argyle,
Krug, Laurent Perrier, Etoile
Comments Largest selection in the
region. Tasting bar.

Massachusetts:
Berman's Wine & Spirits

55 Massachusetts Ave.
Lexington, MA 02420
Phone (781) 862-0515
Fax (781) 862-7088
E-mail
info@ bermansfinewines.com
Web
www.bermansfinewines.com

Ship? Yes
Deliver? Yes
Owner Joel Berman
Year opened 1909
Brands stocked 70
Bottles in stock 3,000
Best-selling Champagne Taillevent
Best-selling sparkling wine Antonin

Truffer
Favorite Champagne
J. M. Gobillard
Other brands carried
Taillevent, Truffet, Gobillard,
Haut Villers, Gruet, La
Morandina, Etoile, Schramsberg
Comments
Great selection. This direct
importer has quite a list of hard-
to-find items and a 90-year history.
Comments
Largest selection in Kansas City.

Missouri:
Gomer's Fine Wine

South Kansas City Store
9900 Holmes Street
Kansas City, MO 64131
Phone (816) 942-6200
Fax (816) 942-7753

Mid Town Store
388 Broadway
Kansas City, MO 64111
Phone (816) 931-4170
Fax (816) 756-2376

North Kansas City Store
8995 N.W. Highway 45
Parkville, MO 64152
Phone (816) 746-0400
Fax (816) 746-1875

Lee's Summit Store
Corner of 3rd Street & 291
Highway
Lee's Summit, MO 64063
Phone (816) 524 4045
Fax (816) 554 9269

Lenexa Store
12740 West 87th Street Parkway
Lenexa, KS 66214
Phone (913) 894-0600
Fax (913) 894-1146
E-mail via www.gomers.com/
contactus.html)
Web www.gomers.com

Store size 10,000 sq. ft.
Ship? Yes
Deliver? Yes
Owner Edward Moody
Employees 20
Year opened 1972
Brands stocked 58
Bottles in stock 1,500
Best-selling Champagne Clicquot
Best-selling sparkling wine
Roederer
Favorite Champagne Pol Roger
Favorite sparkling wine J
Other brands carried
Bollinger, Dom Ruinart, Deutz,
Salon, Bruno Paillard, J, Einhard,
Flynn, Handley, Argyle, Ferrari

Missouri:
The Wine Merchant, Ltd

Original Store
20 South Hanley
Saint Louis, MO 63105
Phone (314) 863-6282
Fax (314) 863-5670

West Country Store
355 Ozark Trail Drive
Ellisville MO 63011
Phone (636) 230-6750
Fax (636) 230-6737

Mid-county Store
12669 Olive Boulevard
Creve Coeur MO 63141
Phone (314) 469-4500
Fax (314) 469-0460
E-mail
winemerchantltd@aol.com
Web
www.winemerchantltd.com

Store size 4,800 sq. ft.
Ship? Yes
Deliver? Yes
Owner Charles Prince
Employees 7
Year opened 1992
Brands stocked 100
Bottles in stock 5,000

Best-selling Champagne
Ayala, Ployez-Jacquemart
Best-selling sparkling wine
Lucien Albrecht
Favorite Champagne
La Salle, Selosse
Favorite sparkling wine
Lucien Albrecht
Other brands carried
Bellavista, Gratien, Jepson, Peter Rumball, Trouillard, Yalumba, Biltmore, Blue Point, Gruet, J
Comments
Lots of accolades for this three-location operation. Very friendly staff and first-class selection.

North Carolina: Fowler's

112 South Duke Street
Durham, NC 27701
Phone (919) 683.2555
Fax (919) 956-8403
E-mail
customerservice@fowlersfoodandwine.com
Web
www.fowlersfoodandwine.com

Store size 17,000sq. ft.
Ship? Yes
Deliver? Yes
Owner
Mimi Jardine and Dan Fairris
Employees 40
Year opened 1925
Brands stocked 85
Bottles in stock 1,400
Best-selling Champagne
Jacquesson & Fils Brut Perfection NV
Best-selling sparkling wine
Marwood Brut
Favorite Champagne Krug
Favorite sparkling wine
Highfield Elstree Brut
Other brands carried
Drappier, Deutz, Egly-Ouriet, Lassalle, Oudinot, Gatinois,

Ferrari, Tarlant, Jacquesson, Alain Robert, Henriot, Baumard
Comments
Founded in 1925, Fowler's is a fine food and wine store renowned for it's extensive and complete selection of wines (one of the largest on the east coast!). Most of the selections being handcrafted, artisanal wines made in small quantities. Every vintage of every (non-allocated) wine is tasted to assure the highest quality.

North Carolina: Wine Merchant's Warehouse

1901-B Mooney Street
Winston-Salem, NC 27103
Phone (336) 765-8175
Fax (336) 765-8178
E-mail Budzky@aol.com

Store size 2,000 sq. ft.
Ship? Yes
Deliver? Yes
Owner Chris Gallos
Employees 6
Year opened 1991
Brands stocked 220
Bottles in stock 12,000
Best-selling Champagne
Domaine Reinhart
Best-selling sparkling wine
Iron Horse
Favorite Champagne
Perrier Jouët Rose
Favorite sparkling wine J
Other brands carried
Avinyo, Billecart, Feuillatte, Pol Roger, Yalumba
Comments If it's available in North Carolina, they'll get it.

New Jersey:
Gary's Wine & Marketplace

Madison Store
121 Main Street
Madison, NJ 07940
Phone (973) 822-0200
Fax (973) 822-3556

Livingston Store
277 Eisenhower Pkwy
Livingston, NJ 07039
(973) 992-4441
Bernardsville Store
Morristown Rd (Route 202)
Bernardsville, NJ 07924
Phone (908) 766-6699
E-mail info@garyswine.com
Web www.garysmarket.com

Store size 10,000 sq. ft.
Ship? Yes
Deliver? Yes
Owner Gary Fisch
Employees 50
Year opened 1987
Brands stocked 70
Bottles in stock 3,000
Best-selling Champagne Clicquot
Best-selling sparkling wine Korbel
Favorite Champagne Bollinger
Favorite sparkling wine Gruet
Other brands carried
Trouillard, Deutz, Pol Roger,
Salon, J, Charbaut, Gruet,
Ruinart, Bollinger
Comments One of the top stores
in New Jersey, the Wine Spectator.
And, for good reason. Very
qualified staff.

Nevada:
The Wine Cellar at the Rio

3700 Flamingo Road
Rio Suite Hotel & Casino
Las Vegas, NV 89103
Phone (702) 252-7777
Fax (702) 252-7651

Ship? Yes
Deliver?
Owner Harrah's
Employees 35
Year opened 1997
Brands stocked 60
Bottles in stock 35,000
Best-selling Champagne
Roederer Cristal
Best-selling sparkling wine Bouvet
Favorite Champagne
Taittinger Millennium
Favorite sparkling wine
Schramsberg Rose
Other brands carried
Krug, Salon, Pol Roger,
Dampierre, Taittinger Collection
Comments Incredible selection of
large format, older vintages and
very rare items. Restaurants offer
tasting flights that are unheard of
elsewhere. Verticals of Krug and
Dom are their specialty.

New York:
Astor Wines & Spirits

12 Astor Pl.
New York, NY 10003
Phone (212) 674-7500
Fax (212) 673-1218
E-mail customer-service@
astrouncorked.com
Web www.astrouncorked.com

Store size 5,000 sq. ft.
Ship? Yes
Deliver? Yes
Manager: Bill Kenny
Year opened 1968

Brands stocked 180
Bottles in stock 18,000
Best-selling Champagne Clicquot
Best-selling sparkling wine
Mionetto Prosecco
Favorite Champagne Jacquesson,
Guy Larmandier, Krug
Favorite sparkling wine
Mountadam
Other brands carried
Paul Drouet, Gosset, Paul
Laurent, Pannier, Drappier,
Charbaut, Larmandier, Krug,
Orient Express
Comments Huge store with just
about everything. Great attitude.

Ohio:
Arrow Wines & Spirits

2950 Far Hills Ave.
Dayton, OH 45419
Phone (937) 298-1456
Fax (937) 298-8571

Store size 7,000 sq. ft.
Ship? Yes
Deliver? Yes
Owner Michael Frank
Year opened 1934
Brands stocked 75
Bottles in stock 2,300
Employees 41
Best-selling Champagne Clicquot
Best-selling sparkling wine Korbel
Favorite Champagne Egly-Ouriet
Favorite sparkling wine
Chandon Reserve
Other brands carried
Tarlant, Jean Milan,
Clavelin, Schramsberg, J,
Gruet, Egly-Ouriet, Gratien,
Robert Hunter
Comments
Largest independent store in
Ohio.

Oklahoma:
Ranch Acres Wines & Spirits

3324-A East 31st Street
Tulsa, OK 74135
Phone (918) 747-1171
Fax (918) 743-8476
E-mail Ranchacres@email.com

Store size 6,000 sq. ft.
Ship? No
Deliver? No
Owner Mary Stewart
Employees 18
Year opened 1959
Brands stocked 70
Bottles in stock 3,400
Best-selling Champagne Clicquot
Best-selling sparkling wine
Seaview
Favorite Champagne
La Grande Dame
Favorite sparkling wine
Domaine Carneros Le Rêve
Other brands carried Delamotte,
Pommery, Dampierre, J, Gruet,
Bruno Paillard, Green Point,
Henri Abele, Ruinart, Seaview
Comments Specializes in great
service and value.

Texas:
Wiggy's

1130 W. 6th St,
Austin, TX 78703
Phone (512) 474-9463
Fax (512) 474-5384
E-mail wiggys@texas.net
Web
www.wiggy.home.texas.net

Store size 3,100 sq. ft.
Ship? No
Deliver? Yes
Owner Tim Kutach
Employees 8
Year opened 1973
Brands stocked 90
Bottles in stock 4,000

Best-selling Champagne Clicquot
Best-selling sparkling wine
Cristalino
Favorite Champagne
Billecart, Delamotte
Favorite sparkling wine
Pacific Echo, Argyle
Other brands carried
Bruno Paillard, Jacquesson, Egly-Ouriet, Ferrari, Delamotte, Feuillatte, Gratien
Comments Voted best liquor store in Austin four years in a row. Great sales people.

Virginia:
J. Emerson, Inc.

5716 Grove Avenue
Richmond, VA 23226
Phone (804) 285-8011
E-mail
jemersn@richmond.infi.net

Store size 3,200 sq. ft.
Ship? N/A
Deliver? Yes
Owner J. Emerson Tashjian-Brown
Employees 5
Year opened 1985
Brands stocked 50
Bottles in stock 2,000
Best-selling Champagne
Delamotte Blanc de Blancs
Best-selling sparkling wine
Gruet Blanc de Noirs
Favorite Champagne
Bollinger Grande Année,
Billecart-Salmon Rose Cuvée Elizabeth
Favorite sparkling wine
Highfield Elstree Brut
Other brands carried
Chartogne-Taillet, Delamotte, Feuillatte, Trouillard, Adami, Elstree, Green Point, Sparr, Cruchet, Gruet, Billecart, Trouillard, Turgy
Comments The Champagne

selections are but one example of the great improvements made to this store in recent years.

Wisconsin:
Star Liquor

1209 Williamson Street
Madison, WI 53703
Phone (608) 255-8041
Fax (608) 255-8051
E-mail info@starliquor.com
Web www.starliquor.com

Store size 1,500 sq. ft.
Ship? No
Deliver? No
Owner Jerry Morgensen
Employees 6
Year opened 1973
Brands stocked 50
Bottles in stock 2,000
Best-selling Champagne Clicquot
Best-selling sparkling wine
Roederer Estate
Favorite Champagne Tarlant
Favorite sparkling wine Roederer
Other brands carried
Pol Roger, Jacquesson, Salon, Tarlant, Iron Horse, Domaine Carneros, Jacquesson
Comments Small, boutique store with temperature controlled fine wine cellar featuring rare and exotic offerings.

Wisconsin:
Otto's Wine Cask

4600 W. Brown Deer Road
Milwaukee, WI 53223
Phone (414) 354-5831
Fax (414) 354-5971

Store size 12,000 sq. ft.
Ship? No
Deliver? No

Owner David Kujus
Employees 10
Year opened 1945
Brands stocked 60
Bottles in stock 2,000
Best-selling Champagne Moët White Star
Best-selling sparkling wine Korbel
Favorite Champagne Clicquot
Other brands carried Jacquesson, Drappier, Heidsieck Monopole, Gloria Ferrer, Philipponnat, Mirabelle, Gruet, Etoile
Comments
This is their fourth and largest store. The chain was founded in 1955.

Wine name

Price	Available from	Score

Wine type Red White Rosé

Sweetness	Depth of colour	Body	Nose	Palate	Finish
Extremely dry	Watery	Very light	Below par	Below par	Below par
Dry	Light	Light	Average	Average	Average
Medium-dry	Light-medium	Light-medium	Fair	Fair	Fair
Medium	Medium	Medium	Good	Good	Good
Medium-sweet	Medium-full	Medium-full	Very good	Very good	Very good
Sweet	Full	Full	Excellent	Excellent	Excellent
Intensely sweet	Opaque	Massive	Great	Great	Great

Mousse	Acidity	Evolution	Status
Firm	Too much	Peak	Great classic or great gulping
Soft	Balanced	Can keep	
Bubbles	Not enough	Lay down	
Tiny			
Medium			
Coarse			

Ticking these boxes saves repetitive notes for every wine tasted and further comment is kept short, sharp and to the point.

Comments

Wine name

Price   **Available from**   **Score**

Wine type   Red   White   Rosé

Sweetness	Depth of colour	Body	Nose	Palate	Finish
Extremely dry	Watery	Very light	Below par	Below par	Below par
Dry	Light	Light	Average	Average	Average
Medium-dry	Light-medium	Light-medium	Fair	Fair	Fair
Medium	Medium	Medium	Good	Good	Good
Medium-sweet	Medium-full	Medium-full	Very good	Very good	Very good
Sweet	Full	Full	Excellent	Excellent	Excellent
Intensely sweet	Opaque	Massive	Great	Great	Great

Mousse	Acidity	Evolution	Status
Firm	Too much	Peak	Great classic or great gulping
Soft	Balanced	Can keep	
Bubbles	Not enough	Lay down	
Tiny			
Medium			
Coarse			

Ticking these boxes saves repetitive notes for every wine tasted and further comment is kept short, sharp and to the point.

Comments

Wine name

Price	Available from	Score

Wine type Red White Rosé

Sweetness	Depth of colour	Body	Nose	Palate	Finish
Extremely dry	Watery	Very light	Below par	Below par	Below par
Dry	Light	Light	Average	Average	Average
Medium-dry	Light-medium	Light-medium	Fair	Fair	Fair
Medium	Medium	Medium	Good	Good	Good
Medium-sweet	Medium-full	Medium-full	Very good	Very good	Very good
Sweet	Full	Full	Excellent	Excellent	Excellent
Intensely sweet	Opaque	Massive	Great	Great	Great

Mousse	Acidity	Evolution	Status
Firm	Too much	Peak	Great classic or great gulping
Soft	Balanced	Can keep	
Bubbles	Not enough	Lay down	
Tiny			
Medium			
Coarse			

Ticking these boxes saves repetitive notes for every wine tasted and further comment is kept short, sharp and to the point.

Comments

_____

_____

_____

Acknowledgments

First and foremost, I would like to thank Jon Croft and, particularly, Matt Inwood, at Absolute Press (which also publishes my *Christie's World Encyclopedia of Champagne & Sparkling Wine*) for putting this guide on the shelf in record time.

As ever, my gratitude cannot be properly expressed to the hundreds of producers who at great expense send me samples from all over the wine world, but I desperately hope they realise I remain appreciative of the trouble they take, especially those whose wines that fail to pass muster (because I have no preconceived ideas about what may or may not happen in future editions when a new vintage or a different cuvée might qualify). My thanks also go to all those who kindly received me during visits for this guide to Champagne, Alsace, Germany and California. My humble apologies to those I intended visiting in Portugal, Texas (yes Texas) and Argentina, but a flood – our second in less than two years – got in the way!

I am greatly obliged to the following, who either organised tastings in the wine areas indicated, set up large centralised tastings in London or orchestrated industry-wide shipments of samples to my tasting facility: Monique Denoune, Pierre-Etienne Dopff, Philippe Durst, Richard Kannemacher and Olivier Sohler (Alsace); Avril Abbott and Hazel Murphy (Australia); Madame Martinez (Bordeaux); Nelly Blau Picard (Burgundy); Bob Iantosca, Philippa Jones, Rob McNeill, Paige Poulos, Jenny Stewart and Paul Wagner (California);

Françoise Peretti (Champagne); Norman Cowderoy (England and Wales); Cathérine Manac'h (France); Riccardo Ricci Curbastro and Alessandra Zanchi (Franciacorta, Italy), Owen Bird (Franciacorta and Italy generally); Madame Aurousseau (Gaillac); Anne Whitehurst and Ulrike Bahm (Germany); Nicolas Visier (Jura); Christine Behey Molines (Limoux); Claire Duchêne (Loire: Crémant, Anjou and Saumur); Georgina McDermott (Loire: mostly Saumur); Claudine Izabelle (Loire: Crémant, Touraine, Montlouis and Vouvray); Katherine O'Callaghan and Georgina Duval (New Zealand); Thierry Mellenotte and Jean Gaber (Rhône: Die and St-Péray); Monsieur Bouche (Savoie); Jeff Grier and Lynn Sheriff MW, CWM (South Africa) and Robert Burgess and Graham Hines (Wines from Spain).

Special thanks to Elliott Mackey, Dona Bottrel and Freddy of The Wine Appreciation Guild, San Francisco. Immeasurable gratitude to my friend Jeff Porter of Evenlode Press for taking in and forwarding all the wines submitted, not forgetting his invaluable services in supply organic vegetables and recycling pulp fiction. A hearty slap on the back to my wife Pat for logging the wines onto the database and setting up all the blind tastings. I must also thank Nathalie Wilsker for last-minute database assistance. Once again my sincere apologies for any omissions.